Toward Cherokee Removal

Early American Places is a collaborative project of the University of Georgia Press, New York University Press, Northern Illinois University Press, and the University of Nebraska Press. The series is supported by the Andrew W. Mellon Foundation. For more information, please visit www.earlyamericanplaces.com.

ADVISORY BOARD
Vincent Brown, *Duke University*
Cornelia Hughes Dayton, *University of Connecticut*
Nicole Eustace, *New York University*
Amy S. Greenberg, *Pennsylvania State University*
Ramón A. Gutiérrez, *University of Chicago*
Peter Charles Hoffer, *University of Georgia*
Karen Ordahl Kupperman, *New York University*
Mark M. Smith, *University of South Carolina*
Rosemarie Zagarri, *George Mason University*

Toward Cherokee Removal

Land, Violence, and the White Man's Chance

Adam J. Pratt

The University of Georgia Press
Athens

Paperback edition, 2022
© 2020 by the University of Georgia Press
Athens, Georgia 30602
www.ugapress.org
All rights reserved

Portions of chapters 3, 4, and 5 appeared previously as "Violence and the Competition for Sovereignty in Cherokee Country, 1829–1835," in American Nineteenth Century History 17, no. 2 (2016): 181–97, and are reprinted here by permission of Taylor & Francis Ltd.

Most University of Georgia Press titles are available from popular e-book vendors.

Printed digitally

Library of Congress Control Number: 2020937240
ISBN: 9780820358253 (hardcover : alk. paper)
ISBN: 9780820358260 (ebook)

Paperback ISBN 978-0-8203-6264-9

Contents

	Acknowledgments	ix
	Introduction	1
1	Order and Sovereignty	11
2	Disorder in the Disputed Territory	26
3	The Slicks and the Pony Club	49
4	The Convergence of State and Federal Policy	72
5	The Georgia Guard and the Politics of Order, 1830–1832	92
6	The Georgia Guard and the White Man's Chance, 1832–1836	121
7	The Militia and the Coming of Order	150
	Conclusion	171
	Notes	179
	Bibliography	201
	Index	215

Acknowledgments

Although I did not realize it at the time, the seeds for this project were planted when my family, like so many others, moved to metro Atlanta in the mid-1990s. My new home felt different and mysterious, in part because it kept the names of an older, but also more present, past. I fished for trout in the Chattahoochee River, while a local hardware store and the youth baseball league, both called Ocee, all kept place-names that predated American settlement.

When I left for college, the first upper-level history courses I took covered Andrew Jackson and Indian Removal. One in-class debate became so heated so quickly that a student began to cry (I still point out to Paul Anderson, the professor of that class and my undergraduate mentor, that I was not the reason those tears were shed). When I went off to graduate school, it was that single day in that single course that stuck with me. It demonstrated to me the power that the past holds over our current lived experience—and our emotions. It was not a surprise to me, then, when I went to my adviser and told him I wanted to study Indian Removal and not the politics of Civil War memory.

As he did on countless occasions, Gaines Foster leaned back in his chair, bemused look on his face, and asked me to explain myself. My inarticulate rambling obviously worked. Gaines shepherded me through the program at LSU, helped me network with other scholars, gave me encouraging feedback, and at the end of it all, more importantly, insisted that I call him his friend. It's a friendship that I cherish to this day. My graduate studies were also supported and enriched by other mentors. Paul Paskoff plied me with enough diner food to last me a lifetime. As his longtime TA, I learned more about how to teach well from him, though Paul will inevitably be disappointed in this manuscript because of its dearth of quantitative evidence. William Cooper intimidated me to no end, though he has also been one of my kindest supporters. Gibril Cole always had a funny story to tell me and reminded me that I was doing good work. Victor Stater and Suzanne Marchand were the most humble and gracious supporters one could ask for. They also paid me to do work for them in the summer when graduate assistantships ran out. It's a kindness I'll never fully be able to repay.

My fellow graduate students at LSU were also a continued source of strength and support, and it's a joy to see them succeeding in so many ways. Michael Robinson's and Kat Sawyer-Robinson's generosity is incomparable. Michael and Melissa Frawley are generous beyond belief. Spencer McBride, who came to my office every day of our last summer in Baton Rouge, is the consummate professional. Andrew Wegmann is a treasure; his love for France and cats is unsurpassed. Matt Hernando is the most careful and tireless researcher I have met. Katie Eskridge and I shared an office for what was doubtless the longest year of her life. David Lilly patiently educated me on the finer points of the English Premier League. Nate Buman and Lauren Haugh are the best Iowa State fair guides. Vanessa Varin, Kristi Whitfield Johnson, Jason Wolfe, Alan Forrester, Greg Beaman, and Clara Howell all deserve special mention for making the graduate program at LSU an incredible experience. As always, Patrick McKinney, Zack Vernon, and Tommy Huycke demonstrate limitless friendship. Chris Childers and his wife, Leah, are the truest of friends. We bonded in Louisiana during Hurricane Katrina and since then Chris has been the best man at my wedding and a constant source of support and encouragement. He has read every word of this book all while writing two books of his own, raising three daughters, and calling me incessantly to complain about politics. His example of professional engagement, scholarship, and teaching are standards to which I can only hope to aspire.

Most of the research for this book was conducted at the Georgia Archives in Morrow. The staff there were incredibly helpful at a time when the General Assembly had cut funding to many public institutions. These cuts forced the archives to close its doors during much of the week, making research difficult. The staff, however, bore these artificially imposed burdens in a professional manner that made working

ACKNOWLEDGMENTS / xi

there (when I could) a delight. The staff at the UGA Hargrett Library expressed great interest in my project from the start and offered a tremendous amount of aid. I spent a long day at Emory, which, due to a freak snowstorm, closed campus early. Luckily, Bob Elder took me in, so I didn't have to sit in traffic. The Interlibrary Loan staffs at both LSU and the University of Scranton have been most diligent in helping me find sources.

The community of historians that I have come to know and admire have also had a hand in shaping this book. Jeff Bremer, Mark Cheatham, Andrew Denson, Andrew Frank, Jeff Forret, Chase Hagood, Andrew Hartman, Reeve Huston, Whitney Martinko, Lydia Plath, Alaina Roberts, Rachel Shelden, Katy Shively, Greg Smithers, David Thomson, Jeff Washburne, and Jonathan Wilson have all offered camaraderie, encouragement, and reminded me that though doing the work of a historian can be isolating, being part of this profession means one can never be lonesome.

When I arrived in Scranton, I never imagined that it would become home. My colleagues in the Department of History, Susan Poulson, Larry Kennedy, Bob Shaffern, Shuhua Fan, Aiala Levy, Sean Brennan, Christopher Gillett, Jeff Welsh, Jennifer Kretsch, and Michael DeMichele, are all dear colleagues who have supported my work and teaching. Roy Domenico is a model colleague and a fine scholar whom I see every day plugging away on his own work. I always know where he is, whether in our building or while leading travel courses, by listening for opera. David Dzurec has read drafts of the first two chapters and offered invaluable commentary. Moreover, he is a tremendous example of leadership in our department whose friendship and guidance have helped me develop into a better historian. I have also been lucky to meet colleagues whose friendship is irreplaceable. Hank Willenbrink and Yamile Silva, Andrew LaZella and Melissa Wollmering, and Matthew and Renata Meyer are constant sources of laughter, conversation, and good company (even when Matt talks about Nietzsche). Sharing the experience of becoming a parent with them has been one of the unexpected joys of my life.

One of my first days on campus, I went to the library to find a few books. I happened to run into one of the librarians who gave me a tour of the building. In the whirlwind of moving and preparing for classes, it was impossible for me to imagine that just a few years later we would be married. Since then, Sheli McHugh has been a constant and unfailing source of laughter, encouragement, and love. She never fails to remind me that there is more to life than work, all while maintaining a level of engagement, leadership, and professional recognition that bewilders me. More importantly, she keeps me from spending all my time in the past. This is especially true now that our daughter, Penelope, has joined our family. Sheli tells me frequently that she is a strong and independent woman of the 1990s, and her ability to juggle the everyday tasks of raising a child while taking on new responsibilities professionally has proven her right. I am beyond proud and happy to be her husband.

From a young age, my parents, Linda and Randy Freel and Kevin and Jane Pratt, nurtured (perhaps tolerated is more accurate) my love of history. Whether it was visiting used bookstores or taking me to historical sites on family vacations, they rarely complained. They also demonstrated what hard work looks like. I doubt they imagined their son would heed their example to become a historian and move to Pennsylvania. They certainly never imagined how long it would take me to finish school, or a book, for that matter. The rest of my family, Jessi and Jason Englert, and Andrew and Madison Freel have been avid supporters since we were young. Although I do not make it home as much as I should, their unwavering encouragement is invaluable.

At the University of Georgia Press, my manuscript was guided through the editing and peer-review process by Walter Biggins. Walter's unfailing guidance did much to improve the quality of my work, and his editorial suggestions were most welcome. The anonymous peer reviewers also saved me from many a mistake. Their suggestions made this book much better. In spite of all the help I have received on this project, the work is my own. And I accept responsibility for it.

Toward Cherokee Removal

Introduction

As federal forces worked their way through the Cherokee Nation in 1838, they went house to house ordering Cherokee families to leave their land. Little had been done in terms of preparation because of a widespread rumor that negotiations between John Ross, the Principal Chief of the Cherokee Nation, and Martin Van Buren, the New York Democrat occupying the Oval Office, would come to an arrangement that would delay the process. In March, Ross departed his home near present-day Chattanooga and made his way to the capital to deliver a petition to U.S. lawmakers and, he hoped, to meet with the president. Throughout April and May, Ross worked dutifully to negotiate a better deal for the Cherokees. Those discussions met with little success. When Georgians read that Van Buren might consider delaying expulsion or that control of the process could be turned over to the Cherokees, rather than the U.S. Army, their unbridled anger became a potential issue for Governor George R. Gilmer. Gilmer had first been governor for a two-year term starting in 1829 but was trounced when he ran for reelection two years later. He put his name forward again in 1837 and, when he won, returned to Milledgeville to oversee the expulsion of the Cherokees.

The rumors swirling through the disputed territory—land claimed by both the Cherokee Nation and the State of Georgia—about the potential for a new treaty caused Gilmer a great deal of anxiety. What he feared was a widespread outbreak of violence that had the potential to slow or halt removal altogether. The same fears motivated him when he was first in office. Gilmer had spent much of his first term advancing the idea that the threat of violence emanated most strongly from poor whites who trespassed on Cherokee land, a notion that proved politically unpopular. In his mind, the white population that lived beyond the state boundary could do irreparable harm to the state's claim to sovereignty by acting in illegal and brutal ways. During a gold rush that began in 1829, an onslaught of whites trespassed on Cherokee land looking for gold and turned the disputed territory into a breeding ground of chaos and uncertainty. Gilmer turned to violence as an acceptable means of establishing the authority of the state. The spring of 1838 saw him employ the same strategy to exert influence and control over inhabitants in the disputed territory.

In his first term, Gilmer relied upon state power to stabilize the borderlands and to exercise state sovereignty. In his second stint as governor, however, Gilmer and the federal government worked together to expel Natives rather than troublesome white intruders. Indeed, for all of John Ross's protests, his bargaining could not halt the operation that General Winfield Scott had planned for months. The operation, in fact, was already in motion by the time Ross left his home for the American capital. When the military campaign commenced, Cherokee families were forced from their homes without belongings or food. Most were then sent to hastily constructed forts, which were little more than open-air stockades that had been built by members of the state militia, who were also stationed at these posts as guards to prevent escape. The prisoners suffered incredible hardship brought on by a lack of supplies and the outbreak of disease. Once the journey to Indian Territory began, their plight worsened. Sickness and disease weakened the displaced, and thousands died as a result.

Cherokee Removal and the Trail of Tears, although they were the direct results of federal policy articulated by Andrew Jackson, were hastened by the State of Georgia. Starting in the 1820s, Georgians flocked onto Cherokee land, stole or destroyed Cherokee property, and generally caused havoc. Although these individuals did not have official license to act in such ways, their actions were useful to the state. The lengthy campaign of violence and intimidation engaged in by white Georgians splintered Cherokee political opposition to removal and convinced many Cherokees that remaining in Georgia was a recipe for annihilation. The state, however, did not rely only on individual actors to force the issue. It also sanctioned violence directed at undesirable people living in the disputed territory, both white and Cherokee. Although the use of force proved politically controversial, the method worked. By expelling Cherokees and lawless whites, state politicians could declare that they had made the disputed territory safe for settlement and the enjoyment of the white man's chance.

This phrase, "the white man's chance," became prominent during the hotly contested gubernatorial election of 1831. It signified a commitment made by the state government to its citizens in which the state would create economic opportunities for some of its citizens by taking away or limiting the prospects of others. The state had long involved itself in supplying white settlers with land that had been taken from Native peoples. After the Revolution, the state claimed land stretching west to the Mississippi River and used land bounties as a way to entice soldiers into the patriot cause. After a series of fraudulent and corrupt land deals tarnished early efforts to sell land to prospective settlers, the state agreed to hand over its western lands to the federal government as long the government worked to expunge competing land claims made by Native nations. This so-called Compromise of 1802, predicated on the peaceful displacement of Native peoples, was the leverage used by the state to force the federal government's hand on the issue. Within its new constrained borders, state officials rolled out a radical program of land distribution that raffled off former Native ground to white farmers. The lottery program exemplifies the types of government actions that privileged whites in general, even if they did not win the lottery. Policy initiatives like land distribution worked to create a society that provided each white male with an equal chance of land ownership.[1]

The lottery scheme fit into the prevailing spirit of the times, best personified by the presidency of Andrew Jackson, white male equality. Usually any discussion of equality in this period is dominated by political equality that transformed voting away from a republican system that privileged property owners to a more democratic system that gave each male a vote. Land distribution took the idea of political equality in a different direction. It offered each male citizen a single chance to win land but then shied away from guaranteeing their economic success or advancement. Some won high-quality land that allowed for cotton cultivation; others won land that could not sustain subsistence agriculture. The chance, in other words, was a promise made to white citizens to create policies that would allow for their economic success, but it did not guarantee the success of individuals or take responsibility for their failures. The white man's chance, though, pointed to a way of thinking that saw rights and opportunities as a zero-sum game: in order to increase the opportunities for poor whites, someone had to have their rights and economic potential reduced. The commitment to maintain and expand the white man's chance promised nothing but dislocation and disruption for those who stood in the way.

In order to fulfill its vision, the state had to act in ways that often contradicted American federalism. Because the U.S. Constitution granted the U.S. government the sole power to treat with Natives, many state leaders felt constrained by their inability to provide more land to whites and needed a way to make federal officials proceed with treaty negotiations. During the 1820s and 1830s, the state became closely tied to the political ideology of states' rights as a way of ensuring that continued land cessions occurred. Historians generally locate the impetus for a virulent brand of states' rights as a southern mechanism to defend slavery. South Carolina led the way when it nullified a federal tariff in 1832.[2]

Aside from a commitment to protect and expand the institution of slavery, Georgia's politicians also relied on states' rights rhetoric and action when it came to competing sovereignty with Native nations. Starting in the 1820s, one vocal political faction, led by George M. Troup, used the logic of states' rights to declare that the state had sovereignty within its borders, even over Native nations with federal recognition. In 1825, some Creek leaders, led by William McIntosh—Troup's cousin—signed the Treaty of Indian Springs, which ceded all Creek land with the state's borders. When McIntosh was murdered by other Creeks, a Creek delegation traveled to Washington, D.C., to renegotiate the land cession. When the new Treaty of Washington revoked the older treaty and left some land for the Creeks inside the borders of Georgia, Troup balked. He threatened violence if the Creeks stayed.[3] President John Quincy Adams proved unwilling to start a conflict over the issue and acquiesced when a new treaty reached his desk in 1827 that essentially reaffirmed the terms of the Treaty of Indian Springs.[4]

Like Troup, Gilmer also desired to extend state power and the white man's chance but struggled to claim sovereignty in the disputed territory that both the Cherokee Nation and the state claimed. For starters, the federal government recognized the Cherokee Nation through a variety of treaties, the first of which dated to 1785. Federal recognition meant that the Cherokees also had a type of sovereignty that the United States was obligated to respect. However, it was not just federal recognition that created Cherokee sovereignty. In addition to treaties, the Cherokee Nation ratified a constitution of its own in 1827. Such a public declaration of power flew in the face of the state's claim to power and sovereignty. The contest over sovereignty was more than rhetorical for the Cherokees; it was existential. The new constitution obligated the newly formed government to enforce laws and to guard entry into the Nation. In short, it would function in the same way as any independent nation with claims to territorial sovereignty.[5] By doing so, the Cherokee Nation's constitution heightened the tension over the contest for sovereignty and caused it to take on new urgency.

Land-hungry Georgians cared little for legal pronouncements and forced the issue of control over the disputed territory. Rather than wait for official concessions, white Georgians trespassed in droves onto Cherokee land. Although politicians from Milledgeville to New Echota fretted over the likelihood of a violent outbreak between illegal white intruders and Cherokees, the state did little to prevent its citizens from crossing the permeable boundary, and the Cherokees struggled to maintain their borders. Prior to 1829, whites intruded on Native ground for a variety of reasons. Many engaged in criminal activity, especially theft of Cherokee property. Others wanted land that they figured they could take from Cherokees. Individuals taking land and causing an uptick in criminal activity were important weapons in the American arsenal to force concessions. Indeed, many Cherokees believed that the state had a vested interest in continued intrusion. Life became so unstable and unpredictable that Indian leaders accepted concessions in order to help make life better for their people and to appease the American thirst for land. Although federal forces and a newly created Cherokee police force had the power to expel intruders, their efforts to halt their flow did little to discourage more interlopers from crossing the border.

After 1829, thousands of whites made their way onto Cherokee land in search of gold.[6] If the authorities responsible for policing the Nation's borders prior to 1829 proved ineffectual at expelling intruders, the new influx of border crossers overwhelmed their meager resources. Large, roving bands of gold seekers flouted both Cherokee and U.S. authorities in their search for riches in the streams and rivers that flowed through Cherokee land. These intruders caused political problems for each of the three political entities that claimed to have some form of authority over the territory in question, but Gilmer recognized the fundamental problem the intruders caused his state's claim to sovereignty.

Underlying the state's argument for sovereignty was the claim that its extension of sovereignty would coincide with the creation of order. The concept of order was rooted in the type of society envisioned by state politicians when they talked about acquiring Cherokee land. Sober-minded pronouncements from politicians saw settlement as a beneficial process that would transform Cherokee country from a wilderness into a garden. Sturdy settlers would bring with them their commitment to democratic principles and institutions, their belief in equality, and their economic know-how. In this sense, order was an idealized vision of the benefits that white settlement entailed. In political discourse, especially after the gold rush, order contrasted with what did not currently exist within the Cherokee Nation: social stability and lack of crime, brought about by good governance, that would allow residents to prosper. In this sense, order denoted a stable and predictable social environment. The argument made by Gilmer and other state leaders about order rested on the acquisition of sovereignty. Only state sovereignty over the disputed territory could bring this well-ordered vision of society to fruition. The drive to create a well-ordered society played a significant role in the expulsion of the Cherokee Nation from much of their homeland in the American South.[7]

Georgia's politicians saw the lack of order in the disputed territory as a threat to their designs on the expansion of the white man's chance. Inherent in both ideas was a deeply ingrained view of race. State leaders' argument that white settlers provided order implied that Cherokees were incapable of doing so. Moreover, the idea of the white man's chance was predicated on a government providing opportunities to white settlers. The state's prospects for providing either or both of those ideas was stymied by the continued presence of the Cherokee Nation and the confusing social world of the disputed territory. Reports that came from the region pointed to the fact that whites and Cherokees intermarried, that most elite Cherokees had white parents, spoke English, and some had even adopted slavery. To Georgians, these individuals were threatening because they defied the strict prescriptions that white Americans expected of racialized others. Although Americans at the time calculated the ancestry of these individuals, it is important to note that these men and women were Cherokees no matter their complexion or ethnic makeup. Cherokee society was matrilineal; individuals traced their belonging in the Cherokee Nation through their mother's clan regardless of the parents' complexion. State leaders differentiated between the different communities in the backcountry by referring to skin color, though these descriptors came laden with innuendo and racist overtones. Their statements implied that elite Cherokees were not "real" Cherokees and that the state's actions were designed to protect "pure" Cherokees. Accounts at the time refer to "mixed-race" and include discussions of "blood." I avoid these constructions unless they are used in a direct quotation. I employ "multiracial" as a way of denoting the lived experiences of many Cherokees, who frequently found themselves being defined by Americans who were confused and intimidated by the intelligence and skill of the Cherokee political leadership.[8] Although not all multiracial Cherokees were members of the economic or political elite, both Gilmer and President Jackson scapegoated multiracial Cherokee leaders as the ones preventing the state's expansion. The only cure for this problem, as they saw it, and the surest method of preserving "authentic" Cherokee culture, was the implementation of strict racial separation.

The conjoined problems for American political leaders of racial mixing and social disorder had a single solution: Jackson's Indian Removal Bill, which passed Congress in May 1830. The state began its campaign of expulsion by ramping up its efforts to demonstrate legal sovereignty over the Cherokee Nation. In 1828, the state passed the "extension law," which literally extended the state's legal structure over that of the Cherokees.[9] This law relegated Cherokees to second-class status and demonstrated that there would be no political recognition of the Cherokee Nation as a sovereign entity. But to enforce this, the state relied upon violence and the threat of violence. Violence undergirded the entire enterprise of the state's exertion of sovereignty and the negation of Cherokee nationhood. To do so, the state created a paramilitary unit called the Georgia Guard that spent much of its time terrorizing Cherokee civilians and abusing trespassers and eventually ministers. The state adopted violence and short-term disorder as a way of hastening Native expulsion so it could expedite the creation of the white man's chance.

By placing the contest over Cherokee land at the center of state politics during the Jacksonian period, other controversies are seen in new lights. For example, historians have recently placed an increased emphasis on the ways in which states interacted with Native people. The vagaries of antebellum federalism allowed the states wide latitude when they interacted with and tried to control Indigenous peoples. Although the Intercourse Acts regulated economic relations, the states had a great deal of power at their disposal. This fit well with the state's conception of its own power in the 1830s. Gilmer wedded his faction to the idea of states' rights and even nullification. Their support for nullification, though usually it takes a back seat to the more famous controversy that embroiled South Carolina, ignores the fact that Georgians *did* nullify federal law when the state passed the extension law.[10]

The contest over sovereignty looked different for those Americans living near the national boundaries. For the white Georgians and Cherokees who called these places home, regardless of on which side of the border they lived, the constant uncertainty and threat of violence permeated their everyday existences. When a group of white horse thieves, the Pony Club, used the chaos of contested sovereignty to carve out a criminal empire, white farmers worked closely with their Cherokee neighbors to form a vigilante group called the Slicks, who put a stop to the criminal element.[11] It was near the borders of Cherokee national space where liminal actors crossed permeable national boundaries in a spirit of cooperation and community to solve problems that affected multiple towns and villages. U.S. history is littered with similar instances of cooperation between Americans and Indians. Although these episodes could point toward a more harmonious lived experience between two peoples, they instead punctuate the larger history of U.S. nation-building. Most encounters between whites and Cherokees were fraught with tension. Instead of forming relationships that mitigated the anxiety wrought by the contest over sovereignty and intrusion, Georgians expected to replace Cherokees on their land and worked to acquire access to Cherokee land and resources however they could.

The story of land claimed by both the Cherokees and Georgia was not unique in the United States, the American South, or even the state. The project of American expansion highlights the growing power and confidence of the American republic and the widespread acceptance of using state-sponsored violence against Indigenous Americans.[12] The implementation of Indian Removal in Georgia highlights the comfort that many Americans had with the nation-building project and the use of violence to bring it into being. That violence was usually not mindless or purposeless. Rather, it was calibrated to implement policy and to bring about the conditions necessary for the perpetuation of the white man's chance. Violence was necessary for the state to achieve the outcomes it desired and is therefore an important part of the story of the Cherokee's expulsion and the contest over sovereignty in the disputed territory.

The disputed territory was more than just a physical space where Georgia, the U.S. government, and the Cherokee Nation vied for political supremacy. For the Cherokees, it was their home, a place made for them by their gods and tended by their ancestors, who were buried there, which consecrated the land. For Georgians, it was a space where their vision for the future could be realized. Where the state's power could reach its full potential, where its citizens' economic interests could flourish, and where issues of race and power could be clarified. For both white Georgians and Cherokees, their hopes for the future hung in the balance.

* * *

The bulk of the discussion that follows focuses on the actions of white Georgians. I use the word "whites" when discussing this group, though I understand that it collapses ethnic social markers that were important at the time. However, in doing this, I follow the usage of people in this time and place. John Ross and other Cherokees frequently used the compound "whitemen" to describe the people causing them trouble. At times, this word filters its way into the reports being sent to the governors from people living in the disputed territory. In the same vein, I tend to refer to members of the Cherokee Nations as Cherokees. I also want to be clear about the distinction between "intruder" and "settler." In the minds of Georgia's politicians, settlers were intrepid pioneers, often land lottery winners, who paved the way for order. Intruders were criminals who trespassed on Cherokee land, and most of the time, the word was used derisively and to denote misconduct and illegal behavior. To be clear, however, Cherokees saw anyone residing on their land without permission, regardless of how long they stayed or their intent, as intruders. For both state leaders and Cherokees, it is important to note that intruder always meant white people, usually poor white people, though they rarely used "white" in conjunction with "intruder." Similarly, state political leaders rarely used the word "frontier" in a positive context. Individuals who resided beyond the state's border within the Cherokee Nation were suspect and frequently had their character and motives called into question. More recently, historians have shied away from the term because of its association with American triumphalism and a narrow view of territorial acquisition that erased Native dignity and self-determination.

In place of the narrow use of the word "frontier" to describe American westward expansion, scholarly discourse has replaced this approach with a comparative and global perspective. The process of European expansion and the planting of "settler societies" has allowed for comparative approaches to flourish. Instead of American exceptionalism, settler colonies across the globe relied upon what Patrick Wolfe has called the "logic of elimination" to erase Native peoples from land that settlers coveted.[13] Viewed through this lens, American settlement, expansion, and relations with Natives fits into a larger global project that emerged from Enlightenment thinking that categorized whites and Natives into distinct and unequal racial groups. The racial and subsequent legal distinctions imposed by settlers onto Native peoples frequently, though not

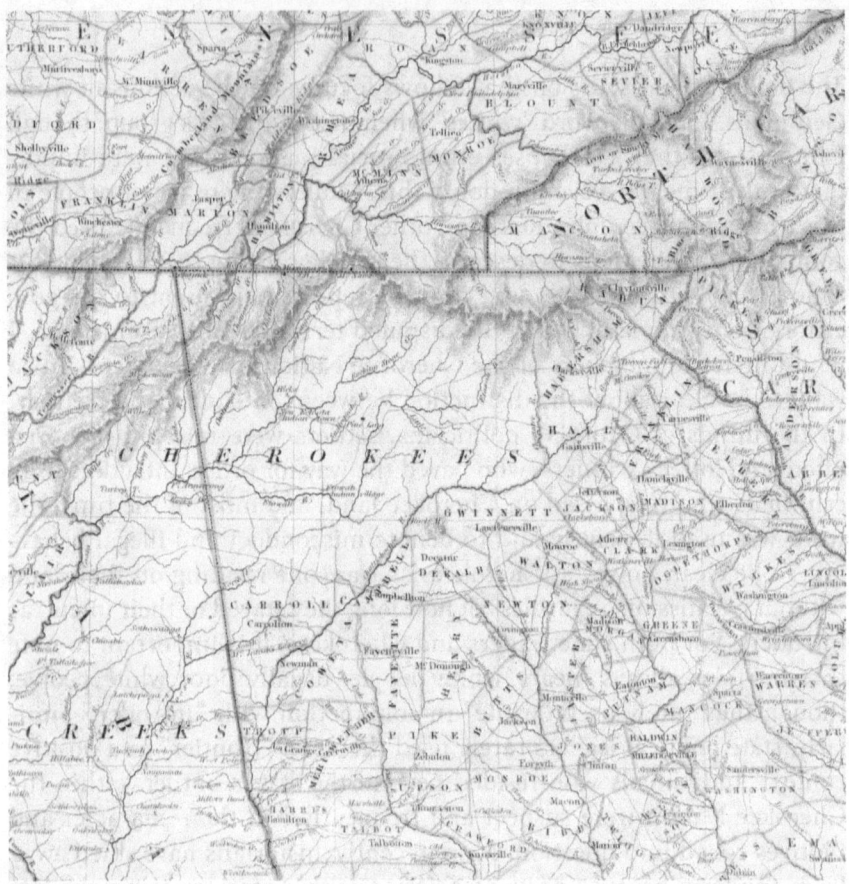

Detail of North America Sheet XII, "Georgia, with Parts of North and South Carolina, Tennessee, Alabama, and Florida," in *Maps of the Society for the Diffusion of Useful Knowledge* (London: Baldwin & Cradock, 1833). Original in possession of the author.

always, led to genocide. The historian Jeffrey Ostler, however, maintains that America's Indian policy was inherently genocidal, both before and after Andrew Jackson. Moreover, Adam Dahl shows that the growth of democracy has gone hand in hand with Native dispossession.[14] The story of the Cherokee Nation and the burgeoning democratic spirit in Georgia confirms these scholarly trends. For the white man's chance to flourish, the Cherokee Nation had to cease to exist. State leaders used violence to make both of those things happen.

1 /   Order and Sovereignty

In 1787, William Wofford and twenty-one of his neighbors from Turkey Creek Cove in North Carolina moved south and west and eventually settled on land at the base of Currahee Mountain, near the present-day town of Toccoa, Georgia. It is unclear if Wofford and the other settlers knew they had settled on Cherokee land, but they had. Part of the confusion sprang from the imprecise ways that surveyors "ran lines," or marked boundaries, though possibly Wofford knew he had settled on Native ground and decided to take his chances. If the actions of the settlers were legally dubious, so too was their behavior once they arrived. Reports about the neighborliness of the Wofford settlers varied. Return J. Meigs, the federal agent assigned to the Cherokees, reported to Benjamin Hawkins, the superintendent of Indian Affairs, that the Cherokees resented the conduct of their new neighbors. Hawkins himself, though, reported that the settlers "have conducted themselves well and appeared to be a poor, decent, orderly and industrious set of people." The governor of Georgia agreed. "It appears . . . [they] have conducted themselves very orderly and have preserved harmony with the Indian tribes," wrote Josiah Tattnall to President Thomas Jefferson.[1]

It was no accident that both the man responsible for Indian Affairs and the governor resorted to descriptions of orderliness when discussing the Wofford settlers. Order was the overriding concern of political leaders who fretted over the replicability of self-government beyond the state's boundaries. Tattnall needed the Wofford settlers to behave in such a way to impress upon federal officials the lawfulness of the settlers and therefore the legitimacy of their claim to the land. State and federal authorities paid little attention to the settlement until 1798, when Benjamin Hawkins surveyed the area and determined that the Wofford settlement fell on the wrong side of the boundary line. When Jefferson entered the White House, the nature of the Wofford settlement remained undetermined, so the new president set out to solve the problem while also seeking to make it clear that the federal government, rather than the states, controlled Indian policy. Although state officials wanted their citizens to move onto Native ground eventually, they wanted it to happen after the land had been annexed by federal negotiators, at least in theory. Still, from the perspective of the federal officials, there was no denying the usefulness of the Wofford settlers as a way of expediting the process.

To strengthen the federal government's hand in Indian affairs, Jefferson needed Congress to solve several problems that had long plagued border communities. For starters, the exact location of the national boundary proved elusive. In a March 1802 law, Congress set out to rectify that problem and by doing so took a firm lead in land and Indian policy when it passed the Trade and Intercourse Act of 1802, which spelled out the official boundaries of the United States. At times, the law seems to forgive the Wofford community's transgressions. The imprecise methods used to mark the nation's boundaries created not a small amount of confusion. Even with the new language that clarified the nation's borders, many areas claimed by the United States were delineated by transitory natural phenomena. Near what was called the Hawkins line, a white oak marked the boundary; at another point, a "large ash tree" served as the only demarcating feature.[2] In addition to clarifying national boundaries, the law laid out penalties for crossing those borders (fifty dollars or imprisonment for three months) or hunting game on the wrong side (one hundred dollars or six months in prison). Other crimes like horse theft, larceny, and murder also had punishments ascribed. The law stipulated that merchants required federal permits to cross the U.S. border and trade with Indian nations. Finally, the act prevented individuals from purchasing land from Natives and reserved that power for the federal government. Individuals who broke this rule risked a fine of one thousand dollars and up to a year in prison.[3]

It made sense that Wofford and his neighbors did not want to risk the steep punishments meted out in the Intercourse Act when they claimed ignorance as to the provenance of their deeds. However, because they had settled on the land prior to the law's passage, U.S. authorities were loath to punish them because they lacked a precise understanding of treaty boundaries. In July 1804, U.S. negotiators extracted concessions from the Cherokees, and the Wofford settlement, a strip nearly twenty-three miles long by four miles wide, was purchased from the Cherokees and became a part of the state of Georgia.[4] In exchange, the Cherokees received four thousand dollars and an annuity, though shoddy record-keeping on the part of the federal government prevented them from receiving those funds until 1825.[5]

Although the Wofford settlement typified borderlands interactions, at least when it came to acquiring land from Natives, the settlement's story skipped one major part of the land concession experience in Georgia: land disbursement. Once the Cherokees made the concession and the land became part of the state's territory, the state did not have to worry about disbursement because settlers already inhabited the land. Yet that was not the norm. Determining who would have access to conceded land acquired from Natives was inherently political. At stake was how to make access to Indian land equitable to state citizens who wanted land of their own.

Since the colonial period, rampant backcountry speculation by planters, merchants, and bankers inflated land values and made it difficult for poor whites and small farmers to acquire land legally, which led to frequent squatting by poor citizens who were otherwise denied access to land. Georgia's problem was more pronounced because of the vast amount of territory claimed by the state after the War of Independence, which stretched all the way to the Mississippi River. The sizeable western claim caused turmoil when legislators made a series of politically motivated and legally ambiguous land transactions. In 1794, the General Assembly sold off much of its western lands to four speculative companies for a fraction of their market value. These four companies in turn sold the land to settlers at exorbitant rates and gave kickbacks to state legislators and friendly newspaper editors who had supported the scheme. The fraudulent Yazoo sale quickly earned the ire of Georgia's Democratic-Republicans, led by James Jackson, who cried foul upon learning of the corrupt land deal. Gaining control of the state legislature, the Democratic-Republicans rescinded the sale and eventually transferred Georgia's western lands to the federal government in exchange for $1.25 million and a promise to "extinguish, for the use of Georgia, as early as the same can be peaceably obtained . . . the Indian title to all other lands within the State of Georgia."[6] This meant that the state gave up its claim to western lands for the certainty that the federal government would do away with land claims made by Native nations that overlapped land also claimed by the state.

With this so-called Compact of 1802, the federal government under Jefferson wanted to impose control and uniformity in the way that western lands were secured and distributed. Georgia's fraudulent sale went against the basic premise of fair and legal land deals that made western lands open, in theory, to all Americans. It is important to note the text of the Compact declares that the federal government would "peaceably" obtain the title to Cherokee land. By stating that the government's only method of land acquisition rested on peaceful negotiation was an important inclusion, for it prevented the use of force by government agents to secure title to Native land.

The Compact also mentions that only state and federal commissioners met to discuss the issues. From Georgia, James Jackson, Abraham Baldwin, and John Milledge convened with federal representatives James Madison, Albert Gallatin, and Levi Lincoln, and, after "a due examination of their respective powers," reached an understanding on how to deal with the state's western lands debacle. Negotiators "between the two Sovereignties" met in April 1802 to hammer out their agreement. That the Compact occurred between "two Sovereignties" who first had to discuss their "respective powers" shows how state and federal power worked in the Early Republic.[7] Because these two political entities exercised similar powers, it was important to clarify the relationship between state and nation. By recognizing only "two Sovereignties," the Compact of 1802 negated Native claims to either land, power, or sovereignty. The absence of Cherokee negotiators was both glaring and purposeful. Ignoring the Cherokees allowed both state and federal representatives to dispense land they did not yet own. This oversight is instructive, for it shows that state and federal authorities had designs on Native ground that had nothing to do with Native political recognition or cultural continuity.

For his part, President Jefferson got what he wanted out of the agreement: additional western lands that added to the national domain. His promise to extinguish Native land claims, peaceably, would take an inordinate amount of time and was something, therefore, that he did not have to worry about. The Intercourse Act of 1802 and the Compact of 1802 marked an important turning point in how federal and state leaders practiced Indian policy. The Compact cast a shadow over federal-state relations for the next three decades, as Georgians insisted the terms of the agreement be honored, though the federal government acted as though the agreement did not exist. If anything, the idea that Cherokee land would eventually belong to Georgians because of Jefferson's promise accelerated illegal settlement on Cherokee land and hastened the push to create an orderly society based on the principles of widespread landownership for state citizens, democratic institutions, and a concern for racial hierarchy.

The drive to acquire new lands had long compelled European expansion, not just in North America but across the globe. Europeans steeped in Enlightenment theory developed new ideas about land, specifically land as private property grounded in improvement, which came into sharper focus as they interacted with different societies whose models of land stewardship differed from their own. Central to the European mode of thinking about land was "improvement," which meant an incessant need to tame the wilderness, plow fields, plant orchards and crops, and build barns and farmhouses. Improvement was designed to master the landscape, to make nature more efficient at producing crops and therefore more profitable for industrious farmers. Improvement and land title went together. Without private property rights, improvements made to any land would always be in jeopardy. On the other side, Native societies, according to many Europeans, lacked property rights because they had not gone about improving their land. Instead, they were content to migrate over the land in search of game to hunt and other food to gather. The transitory nature of Indians in the European imagination meant that colonists saw Native title to land as tenuous at best. As we will see, this idea about the impermanence of Native southerners was wrong.[8] Therefore, when the first British colonists arrived in North America and saw the lack of improvements made to Native land, they invoked the "doctrine of discovery" and laid claim to land that was not theirs. The discovery doctrine, first articulated by Emer de Vattel, stated that European nations could lay a superior claim to land (in settler courts, of course) because unimproved land ran counter to the laws of civilized nations. Not improving their land meant that Natives could not claim it as private property.[9]

So strong was this belief in improvement that state political leaders used it as justification for Georgia's claims to sovereignty over Cherokee land well into the nineteenth century. According to John Marshall in the 1823 Supreme Court decision *Johnson v. M'Intosh*, the British "discovery" of North America gave them ownership over it, and this claim transferred to the Americans after the Revolution. The discovery doctrine as laid out in the *Johnson* decision converted Indigenous residents to tenants subject to eviction without notice.[10] For George Rockingham Gilmer, governor during part of the tumultuous decade prior to removal, the issue of land use was simple—industrious white farmers needed the land to extend a social and political regime that created order: "The millions of acres of land which are now of no value, except to add to the gratification of the idle ambition of the chiefs, must be placed in possession of actual cultivators of the soil, who may be made the instruments for the proper administration of the laws."[11]

In the wake of the American Revolution, Georgians looked covetously at land beyond their borders. Teeming with potential, "unsettled" lands held within them the promise of freedom and the perpetuation of self-government for the newly minted nation. That land, of course, was occupied by thousands of Natives, many of whom had allied themselves with the British during the War for Independence. The Cherokee Nation clung tenaciously to their land and a set of cultural traditions and beliefs that granted them stewardship over it. As members of those two groups encountered one another, the resulting interactions were complicated, unexpected, and laden with historical baggage. Benjamin Hawkins noted that the "old leven of Toryism" made the maintenance of peace on the border tenuous.[12] However, as more whites trespassed on Cherokee land, encounters between the two peoples grew tense.

Rather than delay land distribution, state politicians sought to mete out as much land to as many Georgians as possible. A repeat of the corrupt Yazoo sale that had embarrassed the state gave them pause about how they would do it. State leaders proposed, in 1803, a way of avoiding rampant speculation by disbursing land in the form of a lottery open to all white male citizens. Although this was not a new proposal—political divisions in the 1790s made the passage of the first lottery act untenable—the idea of a land lottery went against the current of the British colonial experience and offered a radical experiment in land distribution and state-directed economic development. In 1803, the son of a Revolutionary War general, John Clark, ushered through the General Assembly a lottery act over the opposition of William H. Crawford and George M. Troup.[13] The machinations involved with the passage of the lottery act instantly set Clark and Troup against one another, and political factions coalesced around the two men. A son of the bustling backcountry, Troup moved east at a young age and, after graduating from Princeton, began practicing law in Savannah. He derived most of his political support from Savannah's hinterlands. John Clark, meanwhile, earned his political support from backcountry settlers but enjoyed widespread appeal because of his service in the state militia during the Revolution. The two factions, Troupites and Clarkites, dominated state politics through the 1820s. Though each faction did have regional strengths, the power of personality drove state politics. Historians have sought to identify the policy differences between the two groups but have emerged rather empty-handed. One historian of the development of the Second Party System agrees: Georgians, argues Richard McCormick, engaged "in a hectic brand of politics that dealt not so much with issues as with personalities and which focused on the efforts of two competing personal cliques . . . to obtain space and power."[14]

Obtaining space—Indian land in this case—translated into assured political power. Each faction sought to outdo the other in rhetorical terms by urging federal negotiators to wring further concessions from Natives. That way, the individuals in power could claim success for the future distribution of land, which would hopefully then translate into success at the polls. It also created a sense of political loyalty between individuals and the faction who delivered on their promises. Under Clark's supervision in 1805, Georgia began raffling off Indian land. Even though state leaders wanted to take credit for dispensing so much land, it was the federal government that negotiated land concessions with Natives. Cherokee land concessions within the declared borders of the state of Georgia began with the conclusion of the Wofford settlement, and then hastened with the Treaty of Cherokee Agency in July 1817 and the Treaty of Washington in February 1819. Those three cessions saw much of what became northeastern Georgia change hands from the Cherokees to the state, which then raffled it off to settlers.[15]

After the first lottery in 1805, whites clamored for more opportunities to receive land. The number of opportunities to win, or "draws" available to each resident, depended on the residents' age, marital status, previous military service, and length of residency. Before the lottery, the governor dispatched surveyors to plat the land into sections, districts, and lots. On the day of the lottery, two large drums were filled with slips of paper. In one barrel, each piece of paper had a lot number; in the other, the names of the lottery contestants. The lottery organizers turned each drum, and one by one a lot and a name were drawn until all the land had been disbursed. The "fortunate drawers" paid a small fee for title to their land, usually around forty cents per acre.[16] Granting thousands of acres to the state's citizens was supposed to create the Jeffersonian ideal of a yeoman's republic and lead to an equality of condition among the state's landowners. Numerous scenarios existed that prevented many "fortunate drawers" from claiming their land. Some could not afford the nominal fee to lay a claim; others enjoyed the land they already owned;

some gave the land to family. Many winners sold their claim, hoping to make a tidy profit. Whatever the case, speculation returned even though the system had been designed to perpetuate a steadfast yeomanry. Some suspected that was the intent all along. Just before the 1832 lotteries, at least one editor objected to them as inherently corrupting because they engendered a "spirit of speculation" that the lotteries were supposed to bypass. Instead, they excited the passions of land-hungry Georgians and ratcheted up the pressure on the state to acquire more land.[17]

As recently acquired land filled up, whites moved beyond the state's boundaries to begin anew the process of intrusion, concession, and settlement. Once a concession had been negotiated, Indians relocated behind their new borders and watched as their former homes were occupied by the lottery winners. This pattern recurred until 1819, when the Cherokees refused further deals. After that date, migration onto Cherokee land continued, but because the Cherokees put a halt to more land giveaways, Georgian's rhetoric reached fever pitch as it became apparent that they would not have access to more land. The idea that the state was cut off from further land deals was an affront to many. As the tensions mounted for another two decades, state leaders warned of dire consequences if the Cherokees did not meet their insatiable demands. "The perplexing evils with which we are embarrassed can only be removed, by the entire *removal* or *extermination* of the Indian race," Governor Wilson Lumpkin warned.[18]

Lumpkin's threat of Cherokee eradication fit into a larger debate about how best to get Native land. At stake was not just space and power for political leaders but a more basic and all-encompassing mind-set and way of life that Georgians called order. As a cluster of interrelated ideas, order had as its guiding principle the establishment of a legal and political regime that could make and enforce laws that contributed to society's stability and progress. On the surface, an ordered society was defined by a lack of crime and violence that encouraged and safeguarded the development of agricultural improvements to private property as a way of creating a society of small farmers who would engender self-government and independence. Not only would farmers and shopkeepers look after their land and businesses, but they would also tend to the common good.

Race complicated the implementation and maintenance of order. For white southerners, the social aspects of order depended upon and perpetuated a strict racial hierarchy. Ascriptive inequalities ingrained in southern life and thought also determined the ways in which southerners organized their communities. Government leaders anticipated that white settlers would exert power over Cherokees when they moved into disputed territory the same way they did within the state's sovereign territory where Natives and blacks experienced legal subjugation that placed them at the bottom of southern life and outside of the political community. Though visible, these communities had few legal rights and little respect in the white republic. Georgians used a variety of tactics to induce white superiority, though none proved more effective than legal measures undertaken by the state legislature that regulated the lives of other racial groups. In 1817, legislators amended the state penal code rendering punishments for every manner of a crime, from insurrection to assault to arson, many of which were punishable by death if committed by blacks, but by jail time if committed by whites. The law also barred testimony in courts by blacks, rendering them powerless.[19] However, life in the disputed territory was not so simple. Clearly demarcated racial hierarchies did not exist; white supremacy did not have legal backing.

Racial overtones permeated political rhetoric about the Cherokees and their failure to bring order. Lumpkin wanted the current residents of the Cherokee country, whom he dismissed as "mixed breeds and white bloods," to halt their continued defiance of state sovereignty. He hoped that "the Indian peoples might become an interesting and worthy member of our great confederacy of states" by accepting American values that promoted social order and racial hierarchy. Even though it seemed as if he hoped the Cherokees might acculturate, he did not want that to occur where they currently resided. That land, he believed, should be reserved for whites. Only the settlement of the northern reaches of the state by white landowners could create social order. "Until this portion of the state was settled," he declared, "by an industrious, enlightened, free-hold population—entitled to, and meriting, all the privileges of citizenship," it would remain "altogether impracticable to enforce the Laws of the United States." Lumpkin's assertion that only a hardworking yeomanry could practice self-government, including the implementation of the laws, demonstrates the connection between social order, landownership, and improvement.[20] The need to replicate a society that perpetuated these ideas veered toward compulsion, so his threat to do violence to the Cherokees was not an idle one.

Because of the fluid nature of the political system, neither faction had an ideological monopoly on how to achieve the well-ordered society. When the state's political class discussed how order could be created, they talked in more organic, less forceful terms. Most politicians wanted to introduce law and order through civil authorities, meaning sheriffs and justices of the peace would bring suspected criminals to justice, while courts, judges, and juries would hear cases and render verdicts. As settlers moved into the freshly acquired territories ceded by the Treaty of 1819 and carved out new counties, local officials needed a guide to their duties and the laws they had to uphold. To meet their needs, a Georgia jurist, Augustin Smith Clayton, compiled the legal duties of the civil officers that comprised the bulk of local government, which covered all manner of legal classifications from apprentices to counterfeiters to smallpox sufferers. Clayton's volume of state laws made it easy for civil authorities to learn their duties and ensure a peaceful settlement of the state's newest counties. Of particular importance to officials, crimes that caused a "great disturbance of the public tranquility," called affrays, were particularly frowned upon. The state legal code delineated the responsibilities of various classes of citizens to deal with such occurrences. Private citizens, for example, could "lawfully part" combatants "till the heat be over," whereas constables and justices of the peace could use more force to part those engaged in fights. Clayton's book of responsibilities for civil officers also showed the emphasis placed on civil law as a means of preserving order.[21]

The legislature understood that the law was a key component in the creation of a settler society. In order to enforce those laws, the state needed agents and infrastructure that could respond to disorder and protect settlers, their property, and their racial privileges. This was done at the county level. After the Treaties of 1817 and 1819 had been ratified and land had been distributed to settlers in 1820, the state created new counties. Courthouses and jails, often some of the first public structures built in new settlements, created a legal edifice for the enforcement of local, state, and national statutes and provided a way to extend state and national laws into Native ground. After the Treaty of Cherokee Agency in 1817, three new counties appeared the following year: Gwinnett, Habersham, and Hall. In the following eight years, the legislature incorporated four more border counties, Rabun, Campbell, Carroll, and DeKalb, the latter three having been carved out of Creek land gained from negotiations at Indian Springs. The rush to create institutions that could provide order in those new counties occurred almost without pause. In Hall County, for example, construction on the inferior court began in 1822, a scant four years after incorporation, and the first jail appeared later that year. In Carroll County, the log home of William Wagnon served as the site of county business until the county levied a tax to build a more permanent structure.

From 1826, these seven counties bounded the Cherokee Nation. The settlers there acted as a bulwark against the perceived threat to order.[22] Even with these new counties, it seemed as though the civil agents were not up to the task of creating order. In early 1830, Gilmer requested that one of his superior court judges act more forcefully, demanding "the interposition of the civil authority in suppressing further violence on the part of our citizens."[23]

However much politicians expected settlers to act as the vanguard of order, those settlers saw themselves as the potential victims of an uncivilized, rapacious people who threatened the superiority of whites and who rejected self-government. "Are we as the people of a Sovereign State to be thus treated, is our property to be destroyed and the law afford us no security?" wondered the Carrol County lawyer Allen G. Fambrough. "Are we as free citizens to have our rights Jeopardized our persons attacked assaulted and abused and will the State say we are remedeless [sic], if so we who reside in frontier counties must retreat from the vindictive wrath of savage vengeance." Settlers arrived in the border counties expecting state protection but instead found themselves exposed to uncertainty and potential violence. Therein lay the central paradox of expansionism: as more settlers moved into the region, the threat of violence increased proportionally, but at the same time, state leaders wanted more settlers as a way of imposing order. The anxiety created by settlement, order, and sovereignty hampered efforts by state leaders to create an idealized society based on widespread land ownership and white superiority.[24]

When safety and security did not materialize as quickly as settlers living near the Cherokee boundary hoped, many argued for the use of military force to protect the state's citizens living there. As early as 1792, violence had necessitated some form of state-level military response. After the murder of eights whites in Franklin County had whipped the residents into a panic, Governor Edward Telfair dispatched three companies of mounted militia to the border "to give protection and confidence to the settlers."[25] The assumption made by most politicians, though, was that Georgians needed protection from Cherokee instigators. As chapter 2 demonstrates, white intruders and criminals were the primary culprits who undermined the implementation of order. The actions of these scofflaws raised problems from the state that boiled down to which government had the power to use force in the disputed territory. By 1830, one editor in Milledgeville, tired of the dithering, sought to convince his readers of the state's power. The "unfortunate condition of the country"

caused him to wonder which authority had "the right and the ability
. . . to restore and preserve peace and harmony within its disordered
borders?" As he saw it, three options existed. First, the Cherokees could
attempt to stabilize the backcountry, though he doubted they could:
"The Indians are utterly incapable of preserving the internal quietude
even were the right conceded to them." Such a concession meant the
state recognized Cherokee sovereignty, something it had no intention
of doing. The editor felt similarly about the second option: "It is totally
impracticable if not impossible for the General Government to do so is
equally certain." Here the editor drew on the growing resentment toward
the power of the federal government, and, with the next possibility, demonstrated his leanings toward the use of state authority. Only one answer
satisfied the editor: "It is confidently answered that the State of Georgia
is that power."[26]

A growing chorus of voices echoed the idea that the state had the right
to use military force to create order. "Nothing but a strong military force
can arrest the evil while the county remains in its present condition," an
editor in Macon wrote. Using language that mimicked the Nullifiers, the
editor concluded that the "repeated and increasing atrocities call loudly
for the interposition of the strong arm of the government." A military
response meant mustering county militias and having them dispense
justice, violently if need be. During backcountry chaos, Georgians called
loudly on the state government to interpose itself between what they saw
as defenseless citizens and the violent ravages of Cherokees.[27]

Although a tension existed between those who wished expansion to
be a process of the law and those who called for more militant measures,
a consensus had emerged regarding the power of the state. Emboldened
by the new political philosophy of states' rights and its efficacy in dealing
with the federal government regarding Indian policy, state leaders began
undertaking bold action to demonstrate what states' rights looked like.
Starting with the land lottery, the state had increased economic opportunity for many poor whites and helped usher in the spirit of equality
that grew during the Age of Jackson. By 1824, a fundamental political
shift worked to alter how the state practiced politics and electioneering.
In that year, in response to growing egalitarianism and a cry of underrepresentation in smaller counties, the legislature relinquished its role
as presidential elector and turned that responsibility over to the people
beginning with the next presidential election. This effort built on legislation passed in 1824 that opened gubernatorial contests to all white
male citizens, regardless of property ownership. As the expansion of

the electorate occurred in Georgia, the South, and the rest of the United States, politics changed accordingly.[28]

The first gubernatorial election to be held in Georgia decided by an expanded electorate occurred in 1825 when the incumbent, George M. Troup, ran against his longtime rival John Clark. Drawing on frustration over the situation with the Creeks and Cherokees—and the expressed desire for land by voters—Troup promised to expel the Indians from within the bounds of the state. By tapping into this populist vein, he borrowed much of the inflammatory rhetoric practiced by the Clark faction. By doing so he incorporated the most popular elements of the Clark faction, united the interests of coastal planters and backcountry farmers, and won by a narrow margin. When the votes were tallied, Troup collected 20,545, while Clark mustered 19,862. Troup had won the state's first democratically contested elections by 683 votes.[29]

Troup's stance on Indian affairs differed from that of previous governors because he successfully transformed it into a states' rights issue. Troup focused his early efforts on the Creeks. In 1821, the Treaty of Indian Springs saw federal treaty-makers negotiate with Troup's cousin, the Creek leader William McIntosh, into conceding their remaining land in the state for a paltry sum, though McIntosh himself profited financially and secured a permanent reservation in Georgia. Invoking the sovereignty of his state, Troup balked when President John Quincy Adams rescinded the treaty upon learning of its fraudulent nature. Adams negotiated a new treaty with different Creek leaders—McIntosh having been assassinated as a conspirator by Creek warriors—and the Senate easily ratified it. Troup, however, refused to observe the new treaty and dispatched surveyors into the Creek Nation to ready the region for a lottery. Adams announced he would send in the army to enforce federal law; Troup mustered the militia and dared Adams to do so. Eventually, Adams backed down, and, as historian Sean Wilentz phrased it, "permitted the nation to surrender to a state." When Troup declared that the federal government held no sway over Indian affairs within the state of Georgia, he sparked the growth of a racially potent brand of states' rights rhetoric that flowered in the controversy over Cherokee Removal.[30]

The imbroglio over the Indian Springs treaty, especially the breakdown between federal and state leaders, played into the growing sense that the state had to act on its own and reassert its sovereignty. To do so, it adopted many of the stances of the growing states' rights movement, whose supporters in South Carolina and the rest of the South were called Ultras. At the end of 1827 the General Assembly announced: "The lands in question belong to Georgia—She must and she will have them." The whole impulse of Cherokee sovereignty flew in the face of Georgia's claims to Cherokee lands promised to the state by the Compact of 1802. Drawing on this agreement, the legislature argued that Georgia, prior to the accord, could have resorted to force in order to expel the Cherokees and that it did not surrender that right when it signed the Compact. Thus, Georgia could still resort to violence if Congress continued to tarry on the issue: "There is nothing in this provision which prevents the United States or Georgia from resorting to force; on the contrary, this right seems to be admitted." Though the fiery rhetoric threatened violence, the legislature toned down its threatening message by insisting that the state would "not attempt to improve her rights by violence until all other means of redress fail." The Assembly insisted that the United State government fulfill its end of the Compact and remove the Cherokees for good. If they failed to act, then legislators during the next session had the authority to extend state law over the "lands in controversy."[31] If this occurred, then the Cherokees would be granted private property rights but could retain only, at most, one-sixth of their current holdings.[32]

In 1828, when it became clear that Andrew Jackson would run against the incumbent John Quincy Adams, a perfect confluence of federal and state politics occurred. Georgians flocked to Old Hickory's banner. Voters knew Jackson's reputation as an Indian fighter and a man who would uphold promises to resolve the Cherokee problem in favor of the state. In fact, both the Clark and Troup factions supported Jackson to such a degree that John Quincy Adams did not even appear on the state's election ballot.[33] Adams's dithering during treaty negotiations to remove the Creek Indians from the state had, according to Representative Wilson Lumpkin, "rendered Mr. Adams peculiarly obnoxious to the people of Georgia." No "true hearted Georgian, not blinded by prejudice," could fail to support Jackson.[34] Lumpkin's statement proved prescient; of the more than twenty thousand votes cast during the presidential election, upward of nineteen thousand went to Old Hickory.[35] The near unanimity of Georgia's voters in the Election of 1828 demonstrated the level of support within the state for Indian policy that favored white landowners and not Indian sovereignty. Georgians wanted Cherokee land, and they saw Jackson as the best way to get to it.

When writing to Secretary of War John C. Calhoun in 1824 to confirm the legitimacy of the agreement with the Cherokees regarding the Wofford settlement, Thomas Jefferson recalled the controversy "because no case of intruders ever occurred which excited more anxiety."[36] At the time, this may have been the case, but within five years, an intrusion far exceeding that of the Wofford settlers would occur and plunge the region and the nation into a crisis. As the state's insistence on order and sovereignty heightened, the crisis tested the will of Georgia's politicians to adhere to its nascent democratic practices that demanded the addition of new lands for settlement. Although Andrew Jackson's election emboldened the white electorate, no guarantee yet existed that the president, a nationalist, would tolerate the Ultras' rhetoric and allow the state to take the lead in Indian affairs. The Cherokees looked hopefully toward the newly elected president as a potential partner in their project to establish their own sovereignty despite his reputation as an Indian fighter. Wherever one stood at the borders between the United States and the Cherokee Nation, trepidation dominated and uncertainty ruled.

2 / Disorder in the Disputed Territory

Although Andrew Jackson entered the White House promising to rewrite the laws governing the United States' relationship with Native nations, Congress had long sought greater clarity in its dealings with those nations and the conditions of the people living within them. In 1820, Jedidiah Morse petitioned Secretary of War John C. Calhoun to perform such a task with the aim of "devis[ing] the most suitable plan to advance their civilization and happiness."[1] When Morse issued his findings for Indians residing in Georgia—meaning he already ascribed to that state's formulation of its sovereignty—he called for the continuation of Washington's civilization plan: the Cherokees, he believed, should be "educated where they are, raised to the rank and privileges of citizens, and merged in the mass of the nation." In other words, Morse called for the abolition of the Cherokee Nation and for the eradication of Cherokee customs and folkways. Indeed, he argued, the agents of the civilization policy, in this case the American Board of Commissioners for Foreign Missions, favored the approach.[2] However, one of the ministers residing on Cherokee land at the Moravian mission at Springplace, Johann Renatus Schmidt, balked at Morse's assessment. Morse could "not have set out a sillier plan for the civilizing of the Indians," he wrote to a colleague in North Carolina. Most objectionable to Schmidt was the fact that Morse's plan called for troops to be stationed at missions, thereby giving the impression that the government wished to convert Indians at bayonet point. "Is this not a Jesuit plan?" Schmidt asked in horror.[3]

In the same way that some Georgians argued about the use of force in creating order, the federal government also concerned itself with force as a useful tool for regulating life in Indian Territory. Because, as it turned out, life in Cherokee country was indeed disordered. Crime, violence, and a healthy disdain for the rights of Cherokees encouraged "intrusion," or white people's trespass on Cherokee land, to increase in frequency. From the vantage point of the Moravians housed at the Springplace mission, their experiences offered them a unique perspective on the precarious nature of life in Cherokee country, though they did not fear violence from federal forces. That threat emanated from the state. "Georgia would not hesitate to use . . . armed force," warned John Gambold, the lead missionary at Springplace. "There can really be no doubt that Georgia is prepared and willing to help itself to possession of this country by driving our or destroying the Cherokees," he concluded in an 1824 letter.[4]

If peaceful Moravian missionaries worried about the state's threat of force, they were also eyewitnesses to the ways that the Cherokees sought to assert their own sovereignty. To do this, the Cherokees had to show that they had the will and capability to create a version of order that did not necessarily mesh with their own cultural traditions. Though this trend began after the War of 1812, its most forceful expression came after members of the Cherokee National Council signed the Treaty of 1819 and refused to sign over more land. Other elements of the nation-building project were concerned with intrusion and upholding justice. These efforts posed a threat to the state's version of sovereignty, where the rhetoric emanating from Milledgeville would make it seem as if Cherokee incursions onto state soil were the sole factors that led to disorder. Nothing could be further from the truth.

The most noticeable means of limiting crime or punishing criminals at the disposal of the Cherokee government was the Cherokee Lighthorse, a small group of mounted police. Its members fulfilled their obligations, though the scope of the problem was enormous. In October 1823, for example, the Lighthorse visited the Springplace mission while trying "to catch a notorious horse thief." The patrol stayed the evening, and the missionaries prepared them breakfast in the morning. Before they departed, Little Broom, the captain of the patrol, encouraged the "scholars," the young Cherokee students at the mission, to "diligence and obedience." Seeming emboldened by the address, the Lighthorse went on to Coosawattee and captured the thief, who was then delivered to the

National Council gathered at Newtown. Initially sentenced to death, the thief was spared the firing squad and was instead whipped, though the Council threatened that if the man was ever captured again, he would face immediate execution.[5]

The Lighthorse Patrol had been created to stymie the workings of thieves and doled out punishments when they apprehended the culprits. Moreover, the Patrol acted as evidence of Cherokee sovereignty. The fact that it enforced laws meant that the Cherokees had the authority to create laws, that Cherokees abided by those laws, and a consensus existed regarding the fate of those who broke the law. In spite of that, many Georgians resented the supposition on the part of the Cherokees and rejected the idea of Native sovereignty altogether. To counter those assertions, the Cherokees met in 1827 to codify both their government and their sovereignty. At stake was not just the larger question about sovereignty and the place of the Cherokees in the growing United States but more basic questions about how to protect their borders from intruders.

In the writings of Americans living near the Cherokee Nation, though, the Lighthorse Patrol is seldom mentioned. Instead, the actions of individual Cherokees who went out searching for their livestock or that of their neighbors seemed to be an almost constant occurrence. The historian Julie Reed has demonstrated how vital the ethic of *osdv iyunvnehi* was to the perseverance of Cherokee communities in the period after removal. This practice of kinship, egalitarianism, and communalism also permeated Cherokee life during the 1820s and 1830s.[6] Although John Ross and the rest of the National Council demanded sovereignty and territorial integrity, they lacked the resources to impose this desire. This made the Cherokees appear weak and engendered a mind-set among intruders that they could do what they wanted without repercussions. What the new Cherokee Nation may have lacked in governmental institutions, it more than made up for with cooperation among its citizens. That spirit of cooperation, called *gadugi*, or a type of communal labor, encouraged Cherokee communities to form partnerships that sought out lost property as a way of stabilizing their own neighborhoods. In other words, Cherokees worked together to solve problems within an established cultural tradition as a way of easing the dislocations caused by property theft, white settlement, and the encroaching market economy. Although they had varying degrees of success, these actions demonstrated the agency and solidarity of Cherokee communities in the face of constant encroachment.

***

Just as Georgians sought a form of order to direct the changes wrought by the Revolution, Cherokees grappled with a world in which their societal values underwent rapid flux. Prior to the Revolution, the Cherokees entered a precipitous cultural dislocation, as much of their land was parceled off to grasping colonists and as the traditional concept of harmony evolved to meet new circumstances. As pressure for their land increased, the Cherokees hardened their position on acculturation and land concessions. As a result, in the 1810s, nationalism blossomed. This renascence sought to unite the Cherokee people into an immovable political nation that refused any further concessions. Instead, as some Cherokees adopted aspects of republican values at the expense of traditional values, they also experienced political and economic divisions that undermined those nationalistic impulses.[7]

For the Cherokee people, the repeated land concessions that occurred not just in Georgia but also in Tennessee, Alabama, and the Carolinas capped more than a century of disruptive social change that had fundamentally altered Cherokee folkways and customs. The most defining aspect of the Cherokee worldview was the ethic of harmony, which rested on a balance of opposing forces. In the natural world, men and women, war and peace, and animals and plants all helped balance Cherokee society. The balance dictated by harmony prescribed acceptable patterns of behavior and deportment and delineated the proper way to live. Harmony instructed Cherokees on the proper way to live in tune with the natural and spirit worlds and also dictated how the various clans and towns could live in concert with one another as and other nations. The idea of harmony necessitated some degree of reciprocity in the dispensation of justice. A murder committed by one Cherokee against another, for example, required a similar action against the perpetrator to "still the crying blood" of the victim's family. Such a method of preserving harmony ensured balance between the towns and clans so that one could not gain power or influence over the other.[8]

Harmony not only dictated a balance between clans and towns, but it also asserted a type of equality between the sexes when it came to the maintenance of social order. Most aspects of Cherokee life were strictly gendered: women took responsibility for agriculture and child-rearing; men for hunting and war. The seven Cherokee clans were all matrilineal, meaning that a child's membership in a clan was determined by the mother. Clan ties dominated most aspects of Cherokee life, including connections to the land. According to Cherokee lore, the spirits created the land specifically for the use of the Cherokee people. By burying their dead in it, they had sanctified it and claimed it as their own. Lacking a system of land ownership, the Cherokees held the land in common, though individuals could be granted tenure for certain parcels.

Settlers had difficulty parsing the nuance of everyday Cherokee life. The clan-based system of kinship, especially the importance of maternity in determining clan membership, and the autonomous nature of villages, posed problems for some white settlers who expected to deal with nation-states led by white males.[9] Others found ways to benefit from this practice. As more whites encroached onto Cherokee land and turned Native ground into contested ground, some Scots-Irish had moved into the Georgia backcountry seeking profits and new trading partners. Because of Cherokee stipulations that only a Cherokee could trade within the Nation, many white men found Cherokee wives and by doing so became adopted members of Cherokee society. Following the matrilineal Cherokee tradition, their bicultural children enjoyed all the rights and protections offered by their mothers' clans. Their offspring, though considered Cherokees in the eyes of their people, were "mixed-race" by American standards. Some of these individuals readily adopted plantation agriculture and the practice of racial slavery that brought them into the world of American commercialism and the benefits and problems of the market economy, though they abided by the rules of Cherokee society. These men and women became the cultural and political elites of the Cherokee Nation.

Surrounded by cotton-planting southerners, bicultural Cherokees most readily copied the agricultural practices of their neighbors to gain acceptance in the white South. Plantation agriculture disrupted traditional Cherokee tribal patterns of land use that had stressed communal stewardship and care rather than individual ownership. Along with landownership and plantation agriculture, another disruptive element to normative patterns of Cherokee life involved the introduction of chattel slavery. For centuries, the Cherokees had used slaves as a labor force but had never considered them property. With increased acculturation came distinctly American views on race, slavery, and property that undermined and contradicted those of the Cherokees. Traditional slavery went together with the notion of harmony because most slaves had been captured in warfare. In the harmonious Cherokee worldview, wars were retaliatory in nature and usually waged as a corrective to a past wrong. As colonial powers, and especially the U.S. federal government, clamped down on warfare between Native peoples, the nature of slavery itself changed from a temporary condition based on captivity to a permanent system predicated on racial subjugation. By adopting a race-based system of slavery, Cherokee men and women began to embrace ideas of racial hierarchy, which further undermined harmonious social relationships. Matrilineal relations dictated that property belonged to the wife, but the American plan of "civilization" promoted male property ownership and agricultural labor. The accumulation of slaves and private property became goals unto themselves. Once these changes solidified, Cherokee women lost much of their influence in day-to-day activities, as first Cherokee men and then African slaves replaced them as the primary agricultural laborers and providers.[10]

Slavery was not the only way the market economy made incursions into Cherokee land. In 1804, Congress requisitioned funds to construct a federal road through the middle of the Cherokee Nation. Designed to increase interstate trade and secure the timely delivery of the public mail, the federal road also allowed whites unfettered access to Cherokee lands. Carved out of wilderness by government workers, it made travel over previously unassailable terrain—dense forests, dismal swamps, and steep hills—not only possible but downright accessible to those with the desire to do so. Cutting from Augusta, Georgia, through the heart of the Nation, passing near the council grounds at Red Clay, crossing the Tennessee River at Ross's Landing and on to Nashville. The Augusta-Nashville road was but one in a series of roads constructed by the federal government that crisscrossed the American South, and it made a greater number of white-Native encounters inevitable.[11] The federal road, however, made controlling their territory increasingly difficult. Although the Cherokees did control a toll booth where the road crossed from Georgia onto their land, it did little to hinder determined intruders. Such a permeable boundary allowed for whites to access the Nation unimpeded, and once there, removing these unwanted intruders became an arduous task. The ease of slipping past federal or Cherokee patrols convinced many who never received permits to trade or reside within the Nation to try their luck squatting on farms and fields belonging to the Cherokees.

To solidify their sovereignty, the Cherokees slowly went about installing republican legal forms closely mirroring those of the United States. The full expression of self-government that the Cherokees adopted did not become law until 1827, though a series of legislative efforts prior to that date moved the Cherokees away from clan-based consensus building and toward a government based on written constitutional law. Not all Cherokees agreed on the best way to implement this new government, or even where that should happen. During the 1820s, leaders in the lower towns split with those from the upper towns on the merits of moving their people to Arkansas Territory. The sentiment for removal, however, waned as the Cherokees developed a romantic conception of nationalism, which they felt entitled them to their land. Nationalism, in turn, begat efforts to ensure territorial sovereignty.[12]

Beginning with a series of treaties signed with the United States government, first with the Treaty of Hopewell in 1785, the Cherokees asserted legal title to their land, though in exchange, they allowed Congress to have the power of regulating commerce with them. This freed Cherokees from having to negotiate with delegations from each bordering state, and in turn allowed a U.S. Indian agent to reside within Cherokee country. They also agreed to stop the violent retaliation against murderers that clan law dictated. Though a small concession, it undermined the Cherokee notion of harmony. Unable to perform retributive acts of justice, Cherokees had to take their grievances to federal officials who would determine the appropriate resolution. The nationalists, however, stressed the need for a strengthened, unified central government. Though it went against Cherokee tradition of decentralized authority, several towns in 1809 joined together to form a National Committee to oversee administrative duties and to treat with the U.S. Indian agent.[13]

Less than a decade later, in an effort at greater centralization, the Cherokees eschewed their reliance on traditional law and turned to written laws with the Political Reform Act of 1817. Often called the first written Cherokee constitution, the reform solidified the importance of acculturated Cherokees. The result was an Indian nation whose institutions began to resemble those of the United States. It created a General Council that met to create legislation and established the Lighthorse Patrol to police their borders, prevent intrusion, and arrest Cherokee men and women who had broken the law. In essence, the Cherokees had formed a nation, complete with a system of courts and a police force designed as an expression of Cherokee national sovereignty, which contradicted the claims of both the United States and the State of Georgia.[14]

In December 1827, the Cherokees went even further when they ratified their first written constitution. Closely resembling the U.S. Constitution, the Cherokee version crafted by twenty-one elected delegates to a convention adopted patriarchal republican institutions and ideals and adapted them to suit "civilized" Cherokee cultural forms. For instance, it created a three-pronged national government consisting of executive, legislative, and judicial branches but never mentioned the clan system and forbade the traditionally important role women had played in the dispensation of justice. In writing their constitution, the delegates had three primary objectives.

First, the constitution formalized the Nation's boundaries to establish its sovereignty. Cherokee national sovereignty lay not in a mythic past, according to the new constitution, but from "treaties concluded with the United States." This argument meant that national self-determination depended upon the relationship with the United States. Moreover, land and sovereignty, in this formulation, went hand in hand. To retain both their sovereignty and land, the Cherokees reaffirmed their determination that their borders "shall forever hereafter remain unalterably the same." The preservation of national boundaries, of course, proved most vexing to whites in Georgia, as did the whole notion of Cherokee sovereignty.[15]

If the Cherokee vow to maintain their homeland upset prospective white settlers, additional statements in the constitution did even more to cement Cherokee permanence. The second goal of the new constitution promoted a form of Cherokee cultural nationalism. In strident terms it rejected one of the prongs of the civilizing program of the United States by affirming that Cherokee citizens held property in common, though it recognized that individual citizens had the right to make "improvements" to the land. By emphasizing common over private landownership, the Cherokees asserted that their own cultural practices would persist. The emphasis on improvements, however, is important, for it shows the centrality of land stewardship in Cherokee thought. It also underscores how they had adopted Euro-American agricultural practices, as discussed in chapter 1. However, the newly nationalized land policy prevented individuals from "dispos[ing] of their improvements in any manner whatever to the United States, individual states, nor to individual citizens." This clause reaffirmed the Cherokee commitment to communal stewardship and preserving their territorial integrity by preventing private land sales.

Third, the Cherokee Constitution of 1827 sought to prove to American officials that the Cherokee people had fully adopted "civilized" ways. Hoping to show that their republican constitution amply demonstrated just how successful acculturation had been—even if it inherently rejected much of that program—they submitted their plan of government to President John Quincy Adams for approval.[16]

For many Cherokees, the new constitution proved problematic because it disrupted timeless cultural ways, according to historian Theda Perdue:

"By reordering inheritance and depriving clans of coercive authority, the council seriously undermined the matrilineal kinship system on which women's traditional status partly rested."[17] Cherokees who rejected contact with whites saw the constitution as a tool of empowerment for the elites—a document legitimizing a small, influential, and well-connected segment of the community—that marginalized the many. The signers did not represent a majority of the Cherokee people, and, in fact, their lives differed greatly from those of their constituents. By 1838, twelve of the signers owned more than 20 percent of the slaves present in the Nation and farmed a plot four times the size of an average Cherokee farmer. The signers also differed from the rest of the Nation economically not only because they represented the values of a growing market-based middle class but also because of their elite economic status. Only four delegates were "full bloods," and they could do little to prevent the bicultural signers from privileging their adopted cultural forms in the new constitution. Nothing proved more central than slavery and race to the "civilized" faction of the increasingly powerful multiracial elites.[18]

The constitution adopted a strict blood quantum and defined anyone as a "negro" who had black parentage. Those defined as "negro" could not vote, "hold any office of profit, honor or trust, under this Government," and were denied other rights reserved for Cherokees who passed the test of racial purity. A law passed by the General Council in April 1828 went even further, stipulating that no free blacks were allowed into the Nation and were deemed "intruders" unless they had a permit for residency. The growing centralization of power into the hands of the planter elite coincided with the Cherokee acceptance of slavery. Many of the laws created by the new republican government, designed expressly to secure private property, further fastened slavery onto the Nation. For those Cherokees trying to mimic the hegemonic racial system of their white planter neighbors, it made sense to legally discriminate against blacks to show that they had fully embraced white cultural and legal forms. Their discriminatory policy provided, they thought, all the proof needed. In this way, the Constitution of 1827 looked like other state constitutions in the South, even Georgia's.[19]

On the boundaries of the Cherokee Nation, order and harmony met, overlapped, and intertwined much as the two societies harboring those assumptions did. White Georgians advanced their values into the backcountry while Cherokee men and women sought a way of preserving the old and adapting to the new. With the Constitution of 1827, the Cherokee signaled their ability to reach an agreement between the two worldviews.

Georgia's politicians were much less willing to accommodate those currently possessing the land. The U.S Indian Agent Hugh Montgomery, himself a Georgian, understood that the political climate within the state prevented any real chance for an accord between the Georgians and the Cherokees: "The prevailing idea in Georgia, especially among the lower class, is that they are the Rightful owners of the soil. . . . [I]ndeed, sir, there is only one point on which all Parties, high and low, in Georgia agree, and that is that they all want the Indian Lands!"[20] Having ratified their constitution, the Cherokees felt emboldened when it came to the preservation of their land. Developments in Georgia, though, would upset their newly acquired confidence.

When the Cherokee Constitution reached the public in Georgia, the reaction was fierce. The editor of the *Milledgeville Southron* could not hide his incredulity: "The Cherokees have come to a *decisive* and *unalterable* conclusion *never to cede away* any more lands." As the editor saw it, the federal government had the ability to force the Cherokees to sell their land, but its refusal to exercise that power equated a breach of the Compact of 1802. The state had to act. The strengthening Cherokee Nation and federal dalliance require "nothing but energy to bring to a final and successful issue, the controversy existing between the State on the one part, and the General Government with the Indians on the other."[21]

The idea that the federal government was in league with the Cherokees was a prominent concern in Georgia. In particular, some pointed to the success of federal acculturation policy as the main threat to the state taking possession of the disputed territory. In Congress, one of Georgia's representatives, Richard Henry Wilde, wanted the federal government "to ascertain how far white persons had been concerned in forming this constitution for the Cherokees, and to what extent they had been engaged, in inciting those Indians to acts which are at war with settled policy of the United States." Wilde was hinting at his fear that whites and elite Cherokees were manipulating unacculturated Cherokees for their own political gain. The idea would form more fully in later years, but one can see the beginnings of a racialized view of the Cherokees: elite leaders were unscrupulous and political charlatans; unacculturated farmers needed protection. Georgians believed themselves to be acting in the best interests of unacculturated Cherokees who had been beguiled by political leaders and other whites who encouraged them to resist further land concessions.[22]

Other politicians agreed with Wilde's assessment. According to Gilmer, an enervated Cherokee people had become subservient to a politically active class of Cherokee planters. Rather than a government that mirrored that of the United States, Gilmer saw in the Cherokee Nation not popular sovereignty but "the rule of that most oppressive of governments, an oligarchy."[23] The "oligarchy" of elite Cherokee politicians spoke English, practiced Christianity, and, most troubling to Gilmer, utilized the American legal system to forestall removal. These Cherokees undermined American notions of white supremacy because they had adopted important aspects of southern life and thereby threatened the expansion of a social order that necessitated a strict racial hierarchy.[24] State leaders thought the cultural and institutional similarities with Cherokee elites had gone far enough. Many worried that the more American forms the Cherokees adopted, the more difficult expelling them would become. For Georgians, federal acculturation policy ensured that the Cherokees could secure allies in Congress—especially a growing northern cadre of congressmen who connected Christian morality and antislavery rhetoric to their plight. Georgia's congressmen argued that their state sovereignty was threatened because the Cherokees' defenders claimed the supremacy of the federal government in matters relating to Indian policy. Thus, much of Georgia's reaction to the Cherokee Constitution of 1827 stemmed from its fears over congressional inaction on the Compact of 1802 and growing public sympathy that put the state in the wrong.

The threat to order was tangible. Not only were Native leaders rejecting ideas about whiteness, but near the Cherokee border, settlers felt threatened. On the floor of the House of Representatives, Wilde recounted stories he had received in letters from Georgians living near the border. White settlers, he reported, had been "greatly annoyed by the intrusion of the Indians in their neighborhood." So contentious had these encounters become that an "affray" erupted that left one settler and one Indian dead. Wilde wanted some way to require Cherokees to remain on their own land. He assured his audience that "we prevent our own citizens from intruding on their ground," and he sought some way to impose those controls on the Cherokees. "The effect might be to save many lives," he closed.[25] Although he was correct that making each group stay on their own land would probably preserve peace, he was wrong when he identified the Cherokees as the primary intruders. Nothing could be further from the truth.

Emboldened by the election of Andrew Jackson and worried about the prospects of the Cherokee Constitution, members of the General Assembly passed momentous legislation in the winter of 1828 that solidified the state's position on sovereignty. The law extended the state's jurisdiction over the territory and people living on the land claimed by both the state and the Cherokee Nation. The extension law, as it became known, not only pushed state law beyond its recognized boundaries but abolished all "laws, usages, and customs" of the Cherokee Nation. Taking effect on June 1, 1830, the extension law not only subjected Cherokee residents to state law, but it also prevented the Cherokees from testifying in state court against whites. Borrowing methods and concepts the state had used to subjugate blacks, the extension law announced the inferiority of Cherokees and prevented them from seeking legal redress in state courts. It also required all whites living in the disputed territory, except for federal agents, to apply for license to continue residing there. The law expressed the state's formulation of sovereignty and white superiority and sent thinly veiled threats to Native residents: Georgia was a white man's country, and there would be no physical space or legal recognition for anyone else. The legislature gave the Cherokees two options: leave, endure hardship, and persist; or stay, endure hardship, but vanish.[26]

Politicians who envisioned an orderly people settling on Cherokee land soon had their hopes dashed when it became apparent that the practice did not mirror their convictions. Instead, white people took advantage of the relative lawlessness brought on by the contest over sovereignty. The lack of authority, in fact, seemed to attract certain types of settlers. George Featherstonhaugh, an English traveler, observed the social world of the Cherokee borderlands as he traversed the rivers and roads of the Cherokee Nation. Featherstonhaugh noted that most of the white population looked "as melancholy and lazy as boiled cod-fish," owing to their poor diet and voracious drinking habits. What the "parsnip-looking country fellows" enjoyed the most, however, was "political disputation in the bar-room of their filthy taverns, exhibiting much bitterness against each other in supporting the respective candidates of the Union and States-rights parties." When he arrived at Springplace, Featherstonhaugh noted that "almost every store in the place was a dram shop," and the amusement of the townsfolk consisted of visiting each shop in turn and getting "red-hot drunk with whiskey."[27]

Making his way to the National Council meeting at Red Clay, Featherstonhaugh also encountered dozens of Cherokee men and women on similar journeys. At one inn, a "halfbreed youth" and his wife, a "pretty Cherokee creature," stopped for medical attention. The man had tumbled from his horse after becoming "beastly drunk" and had been struck by the horse's hoof. It was not the wounded youth that drew

Featherstonhaugh's attention but his wife, who took her husband's injury as mundane, because she "was probably accustomed to see him drunk every day." At a tavern between Springplace and Red Clay kept by a man named Bell, Featherstonhaugh could only procure "filthy pieces of bad cake" to eat. When he asked a Cherokee woman, presumably Bell's wife, who could speak some English, why the tavern keeper did not keep cows to make milk and cheese, she only replied that "it was too much trouble."[28] The Englishman's encounters obviously revolted his delicate sensibilities.

Others agreed with Featherstonhaugh's assessments of the whites who lived in the disputed territory. As early as 1825, the federal Indian agent stationed in the Cherokee Nation, Hugh Montgomery, commented on the makeup of the whites who inhabited the area: "I need not tell you, that there are in this as in every frontier country, a great number of disorderly people, who hang on between the white and red people, and act as a kind of pioneers to civil society." On "the Georgia frontier in a few years past" the undesirable population had increased "owing to the noise about treaties" and the potential for free land. Montgomery's observations about the "disorderly people" implied that they did not belong to polite society. He also noted that many of these disorderly residents functioned as the first wave of white residents and moved between two different societies. Two years later the state sent surveyors into Carroll County to plat the land gained from the Creeks for a lottery, and one citizen complained to the governor, "You may rely upon this fact; that it is the *vilinous* white men in this part of the country, who instigate the Indians to be troublesome."[29]

Steamboats also provided easy mobility into and out of the Cherokee Nation. After the extension law went into effect and more Georgians moved into the backcountry, especially after 1832, steamboats began plying the waterways. The town of Rome, Georgia, founded in 1834 at the confluence of the Etowah, Oostanaula, and Coosa Rivers, became the region's primary cotton market because of its prime riverine location. On board the steamships, travelers encountered a microcosm of the disorderly white community found on the edges of civil society. What they found disgusted not a few observers. Most notable to one English traveler, Thomas Hamilton, was the brazenness with which passengers displayed weaponry. A collection of walking sticks in the corner of the main cabin aboard one steamer all concealed daggers, which struck Hamilton as the most "unmanly and assassin-like weapon," something he probably did not mention to the men carrying them. Men armed to the teeth, guilty of conversation "interlarded with the vilest blasphemy," engaged in habitual drinking and gambling that continued unabated day and night. On Hamilton's first voyage, not even the captain was immune to such practices. In fact, the captain, "one of the most flagrant offenders," became "decidedly drunk" and could not even pilot the boat. The few ladies on board, quite sensibly, remained in their cabins. Hamilton noticed a wide assortment of the white men who inhabited the backcountry but speculated that "many have fled for crimes, to a region where the arm of the law cannot reach them." In short, just like life aboard a steamship, the community on the state's border was violent, with alcohol use and gambling prevalent, and with women occupying specific roles.[30]

Americans tend to romanticize the initial wave of pioneers who "conquered" the wilderness and made it safe for further expansion. In antebellum Georgia, the initial wave of settlers caused consternation rather than admiration. Although there are overtones of class derision in the statements made by elites about the backcountry population, especially the "disorderly" whites, other concerns bothered them as well. Racial mixing vexed many a politician. Instead of demonstrating mastery as they anticipated, whites saw racial mixing as a sure sign of degeneracy and the loss of vitality. On the border between the Cherokee Nation and the state, white settlers and Natives interacted in ways that put the superiority of whites in question. Deeply rooted beliefs that savagery corrupted civilization were not easily dispelled. Illustrating the fears of Georgia's leaders, a traveler, "Eugenio," published an account of his journey through the Cherokee Nation in the *Macon Telegraph*. Having passed through western Tennessee on his way to Georgia, and "fatigued with a long and toilsome day[']s ride over the mountains," he anxiously awaited the first sight of "one of those small hamlets which indicate a white settlement." He instead happened upon a "cluster of cabins" and inquired of the owner, a "deeply intoxicated . . . man of gigantic stature in the Indian costume," if he could stay the night. The man denied him permission to enter his home and, to add emphasis to his refusal, passed out in the threshold. At that point "a little dark eyed Indian girl" admitted him into the house. Inside, he expressed surprise at the comforts that awaited him: tea service, a well-cooked supper, and a drawing room stocked with the latest books and a piano. The eldest daughter, only seventeen, played the instrument for her guest and excelled at her rendition of "Home Sweet Home," which she played with "pathos and feeling." That night he learned the family's history. The father, not an Indian at all but a white man, had once been "a man of considerable talent and literary acquirements." However, his prolonged "intercourse with the savages" had taught him "brutal habits" and encouraged his "indulging in drunkenness." In spite of the daughter's refinement, the message was clear: racial mixing on the edges of American space degraded whites and caused them to lose essential characteristics that made them superior. By focusing on the corrupting presence of "savages" and the fragility of "civilization" at the edges of American power, the *Telegraph*'s story of the traveler fed into the growing unease about the border community.[31]

In spite of the story's warning, bicultural individuals accounted for only a fraction of the Cherokee population. A census conducted by the *Cherokee Phoenix* in 1828 listed 144 men and 61 women who had married into the Nation; a War Department census in 1835 listed 201 whites who had a Cherokee partner. By 1835, the number of white-Cherokee marriages accounted for fewer than 10 percent of the total number of Cherokee households, while the number of mixed-race individuals accounted for roughly 18 percent of the Cherokee population.[32] Although relatively small, the mixed Cherokee population proved worrisome for Georgia's leaders.

The idealized social order envisioned by state leaders faced a difficult implementation on the edges of state power. Proximity to a different racial group put American assumptions of order up against borderland realities. As white and Cherokee people interacted on Native ground, the pragmatic need for economic exchange and social interactions trumped preconceived notions about a racialized other. However, what state leaders learned was that the presence of the Cherokees attracted a type of white person who had no interest in order. Instead, they exploited the lack of legal authority in the liminal spaces claimed by both the state and the Cherokee Nation.

At the heart of the disruption directed at Cherokees was property theft and destruction. In 1842, the U.S. Claims Commission catalogued the litany of complaints levied by Cherokees against American citizens. The most common type of restitution sought by claimants was payment for the theft of horses, livestock, and hogs.[33] Hetty Vance wanted compensation for a mare stolen from her pasture "supposed to be done by a notorious horse thief by the name of Mosley." When some of Vance's friends tracked Mosley, they found the thief and the horse "at the house of John Willows about 75 miles" away from Vance's farm. Unable to recover the animal, Vance's friends confirmed Mosley's connection to a ring of bold horse thieves. This type of encounter became altogether common in the border region. Cherokee men and women continually had to track down horses, hogs, and cows that had been taken from their farms and fields. These communal activities—efforts to trace property that had been stolen—demonstrate the importance of *gadugi* in Cherokee life.³⁴

The communal work involved with returning stolen property, at times, became all-encompassing. In 1821, Tahlegalooraytee had a horse stolen from him along the Cherokee-Alabama border, and the next year Young Bird claimed that five white men came to his farm and "drove off twenty head of hogs, some of them pork hogs, into the white settlements." In another case, Peggy Helms charged that "she had her horse stolen by white men in the limits of Georgia." Some of her friends attempted to recover the horse when they saw it in the possession of a Georgian, but, she lamented, "there was no chance for a Cherokee to recover property at the time." Other Cherokee men and women tried to recover their property, and most met with failure. Goose Langley pursued a missing steer to the Georgia state line but never recovered it. Langley "tract my cows . . . to where they crossed the [Chattahoochee] River," but had to return home empty-handed because he lost their trail. Four Killer encountered the same problem.³⁵ For thieves, livestock served as an easy target because of the porous nature of the boundary and the ease with which they could sell the stolen goods. Cherokee farming methods did little to alleviate the problem. Cherokee farmers usually left their livestock unattended to wander the hills and forests in search of their own forage. Though national law stipulated the height and build of fences and commissioned rangers to track down stray cattle, these efforts met with little success. Horse and cattle thieves, therefore, had no difficulty taking whatever they desired. Unattended horses and cattle also proved popular marks because thieves could unload them quickly, and the distances they could cover made it difficult for the rightful owners to reclaim their property. Even if the Cherokees did find their stolen animals, claiming them within state bounds and in state courts proved impossible because of the legal restrictions imposed on Cherokees by the extension law.³⁶

The constant disruption destabilized Cherokee life, and the closer to the border one was, the more uncertain life became. At least twice in the span of five years, a Cherokee, Lacy Christy, had livestock stolen from his property. First, in 1830, when John Holcomb took a chestnut sorrel "with no cause." Five years later, Christy lost a mare to Hest Walker, a "U.S. citizen travelling thro that part of the country," which he later sold for about forty dollars. Atawluny, a resident near Raccoon Town, had a new fur hat, four horses, and sixty hogs appropriated from his land, "each taken from him by citizens of the U. States." Peacheater claimed that whites had stolen three yokes of oxen, eleven head of cattle, six yearlings and a few hogs from his property. Knowing the name, or at least the nationality, of the thieves, and in Christy's case, the amount that his mare had fetched on the black market, meant that at some point the Cherokee had tracked his property but could not recover it. George Blackwood had fifty hogs stolen from his land by Buck Herrod, "a notorious thief who served his two duties in the Georgia state Prison for theft," but Blackwood never recovered them. Two years later, Filo, another white man, pilfered two of his remaining hogs. Charlatehe had horses stolen from him in 1832, 1834, and 1835 by a white man the Cherokee knew only as Rattlesnake. When he encountered Rattlesnake, the thief would not give up the horse. Whortleberry had a brown horse and eleven head of cattle taken from him in 1829. When he tracked them to the "white settlements," he and his friends could not "overtake" the thieves. Two years later, he lost thirty-five hogs to a white settler named Stark. Some Cherokees had the aid of federal authorities to help them reclaim their property, but even that rarely helped. Wassassee, who had his horse stolen from him in 1829, was perhaps the unluckiest when it came to reclaiming his lost property. Not only did he lose his horse, but in the botched attempt to reclaim it, he lost a fifteen-dollar saddle and a twenty-dollar rifle, and was injured to boot.[37]

In spite of the growing number of settlers moving into the borderlands, whites and Indians knew one another intimately. That Cherokee residents knew the names of the thieves, could discuss their reputations, and even knew the amount of time some Georgians had served in prison, spoke to the great degree of contact between the two groups. Furthermore, those Cherokees who hunted down stolen property had awareness of, if not familiarity with, the locations of fences who fueled the illicit borderland economy. When every type of moveable property was for sale, from hogs to humans, at least some people in the backcountry thrived on the chaos sown by the intruders. Moreover, the sources available only demonstrate the property that Cherokees lost; they say nothing about property that Cherokees regained. This means that instances of stolen property could have been even more rampant than what was reported, but if Cherokees recovered property by themselves or with their neighbors, then they did not report it as lost or stolen.

The complaints reaching federal officials about the amount of property being taken out of the Cherokee Nation prompted the federal government into action. In December 1825, to appease frustrated Cherokees and to clamp down on the illicit economic activity not permitted by the

Intercourse Acts, Hugh Montgomery alerted his subagent J. G. Williams to the increasing amount of crime near the border. "As you will probably meet with complaints from Indians, while on the different Frontiers, about property Stolen from them," he instructed Williams "to attend to their complaints." That meant that not only could the subagent authorize the Cherokees to pursue their lost property, it also meant the agent should use his authority to assist them "as far as is convenient . . . in searching out their property." However, the aid Montgomery promised did not always make amends for lost property. When Thigh Walker lost a horse near the Hightower River, he went looking for it. He located it sometime later in Kingston, Tennessee. When a white witness swore on oath that the horse belonged to the Indian, Walker could still not claim it. Finally, Williams ordered the thief to surrender the horse, but the command went unheeded. Even federal directives mattered little to the unruly frontiersman.[38]

Other forms of moveable property, especially slaves, were also popular targets for backcountry criminals. In February 1837, William Mosely "took sick and died" just as he and his family were preparing to emigrate to Arkansas. However, before he became ill, he allowed one of his slaves to travel to Walker County, Georgia, to visit his mother before he, too, was forced west. Once the slave had left and Mosely died, the heirs never again saw the slave because he had been taken from his mother's owner "by citizens of the U. States [from] Rayburn County, Georgia so that the heirs has lost the slave and his services." The heirs, upset not so much by the loss of their slave as by the loss of the value of the services he rendered, asked the federal government for $1,500 in recompense for the loss of their chattel, and $100 per year from the labor that he would have otherwise rendered.[39] The presence of black slaves owned by Cherokee families complicated the usually stark dichotomy drawn regarding race in the antebellum South. That whites stole them from Cherokee slave owners reinforced the complexity of backcountry life. No doubt Cherokee slave owners served to remind poor whites of their place in society. Stealing slaves and then owning their labor became a quick path to acceptability and mastery.

Violent crimes also plagued Cherokee families. Hetty Vance had numerous run-ins with intruders. In 1823, Vance found herself boarding five whites from Georgia when her home mysteriously burned to the ground along with $2,300 worth of hidden bank notes. Though no one saw the five men set fire to the house, neighbors caught and "examined" them on the matter: "From all that could be ascertained in the answers it was firmly believed that they were guilty of the charges."[40] Elizabeth Ware and her husband lived on Shoemaker Creek within Georgia's claimed territory and encountered trouble with the extension law. "Owing to the oppressive character of the laws of the state towards citizens of the Cherokee Nation," Ware declared, her "husband was compelled to absent himself from home which left her in a defenceless condition." Why he had to leave state boundaries is mysterious—unless he was a fugitive from state justice—but when he did, he left his family exposed. With her husband gone, whites burned her house to the ground as a way of forcing off the Native inhabitants, so they could move onto that particular swath of land.[41] House burnings proved so pernicious because they destabilized Cherokee families and made them fearful for their safety in their own country. The fact that Cherokee families had their homes burned underscored the uncertain and chaotic nature of life in the borderlands and the ease with which encounters with frontier whites turned dangerous.

Other women likewise had their livelihoods jeopardized by the destruction of property. Three sisters, Nancy, Alecy, and Sinny, had much of their livelihood taken from them in 1820 when white intruders burned three hundred bushels of their wheat crop. To compound their problems, the white marauders then set fire to their house and destroyed an additional fifteen acres of unharvested corn. The three sisters speculated that such a malicious crime was an act of revenge undertaken by intruders after federal troops cut down their corn to compel them to leave.[42] Like Vance and Ware, the three sisters had to cope with seemingly random, yet purposeful violence that was often directed at women. The gendered component to border crime highlighted the subordinate position women occupied in the mind of the white "disorderly" population. Cherokee men rarely were firsthand victims of crime. Their livestock disappeared in the night or when the owner was out of sight. Perhaps this was a way for thieves to avoid detection, but more than likely it was a way for them to avoid conflict. Women, on the other hand, experienced crime and violence firsthand, often in broad daylight. The gendered component to backcountry crime allowed whites to intimidate women who had no recourse or means to protect themselves from the ravages of the intruders.

Other Cherokee women faced victimization from men whom they should have been able to trust. The beleaguered Hetty Vance ran into trouble with whites from Georgia in 1830 when her husband, Henry Vickery, died. A few years later she married John Vance, a white Georgian. Hetty had few property rights because state law denied Indian women the right to own property. Therefore, when she remarried, property left to her by her first husband transferred to her new spouse. The estate's administrator, Oliver Stricklen, a lawyer from Georgia, demanded payment from Hetty when he learned that she had sold some of the property before signing away control of the estate to her new husband. When Hetty refused to give him the money, Stricklen "forced her negroes off," whom he later sold, taking the proceeds as her payment. Soon thereafter, Stricklen had Hetty "carried to the white man's jail." When her husband notified the court of what had occurred, the court ordered her freed by a writ of habeas corpus, but she handed over her bank notes to Stricklen "in order to keep undisturbed her liberty." Stricklen also terrorized Margaret Baumgarter, who lost eight horses and two dozen cattle when Stricklen stole the livestock "for the benefit of another." To white men, even to a man like Oliver Stricklen who was supposed to uphold the law, exploiting Cherokee women and their property proved easy enough in the chaotic borderlands.[43]

White men professing love and devotion exploited other Cherokee women. Americans too poor to buy land of their own, or too luckless to win it in a land lottery, could improve their prospects through marriage. Once he had married a Cherokee woman, a white man had certain privileges, including land to farm or trading rights within the Nation. Some Cherokee farmers even took on white sharecroppers. For Robert Rodgers, it brought monetary rewards to which he had no right. When federal agents in 1832 began enrolling Cherokees for removal to Arkansas, Robert applied "as the head of his family for a numeration from the agent." Once the enrolling agent began disbursing payments that compensated enrollees for their improvements, Robert took the money and left Betsey, his wife of nearly twenty years. Betsey became distraught, not just because her husband had left but also because the payment was possible because she belonged to the Nation. Without his marriage to Betsey, Robert "had no such right without a lawful connection with a Cherokee woman, he being a white man." In 1833, Jesse Townsend, a member of the Georgia Guard, married the niece of a prominent Cherokee named Captain Oldfields. On the eve of his wedding, he consulted a judge to see if he could have Oldfield's abandoned property transferred to him as a condition of the marriage. He showed his fiancé a false bill of sale, and she agreed to the purchase, never knowing that Townsend had never spoken with her uncle and saw her as a way to get at the land. Cherokee women faced vulnerability to violence and crime not only from intruders but also from men they had taken into their homes. As the political pressure increased to expel the Cherokees, women in particular faced a continual stream of problems that weakened Cherokee resistance to removal.[44]

Some even tried to take their grievances to state courts but met with little success. If a Cherokee stole a horse or pig from a settler and crossed the boundary, few legal options existed for the settler to retrieve the property. A Cherokee who had livestock taken by a white person had even less chance of legal redress. For example, in the April 1829 term of the Carroll County Superior Court, a Cherokee man named Soft Shell Turtle sued a Georgian named Grief Felton for the theft of a "certain sorrel mare about six years of age of the value of eighty dollars as of his own right & property." Felton seemed to admit to the crime when he confessed he had no defense other than stating that he was white and the plaintiff an Indian. The judge agreed with this reasoning and ordered Soft Shell Turtle to pay Felton more than ten dollars in court costs. When Bill Silk, a Cherokee, was accused of an "alleged crime that would not have hurt him in the courts of his own country," he had to leave the state because of the legal abuse heaped on him. In another case, Jacob Harnage could not recover the horses stolen from him by "Young John and Old John Stansel" because he did not have "the power to get redress from them as they were white men of Halbersham [sic] County." Though the state legislature probably never imagined that the extension law would allow for backcountry crime to flourish, it did precisely that. With impunity from legal redress, white Georgians used the extension law as a way of legalizing property theft from Cherokees.[45]

The cases of Soft Shell Turtle, Bill Silk, and Jacob Harnage exemplified the ways in which Georgia's legal system exerted power over Cherokee residents living near the state line. By June 1830, new counties had not been created in Cherokee territory, but the extension law had gone into effect. The ease with which Felton could claim that the Cherokee had no case because he could not claim citizenship, along with the lack of the deliberation and the steep fine imposed by the judge, demonstrated that he agreed with Felton's rudimentary argumentation. Although it appeared that the state had acquired all the power it needed with the extension law, the growing menace posed by dangerous white men seemed to undermine the state's arguments about order. Cherokee residents and sympathetic whites residing in the border counties tolerated the loss of property; reports of violent retaliation seldom cropped up.

In these instances, the Cherokees in search of restitution appear hapless and naïve. Why go to state courts for legal redress after the extension law had gone into effect? Why did the judges even hear the cases when it was clear that state law forbade that from happening? Perhaps the judges wanted to make a point about the power of the state over those individual Cherokees, or perhaps they wanted to demonstrate the disdain in which they held the Cherokees and therefore slapped them with harsh fines. For the Cherokees to go to such lengths to recover their property speaks to the frustration that had been mounting for years. Moreover, it shows that they demanded dignity and respect, even though the state law afforded them none.

Throughout the Cherokee Nation, fear and consternation were constant companions. Although the Cherokee Nation had made a bold assertion of sovereignty in 1827 and had begun a trend of centralization that went against traditional practices of communalism, these moves did not prevent more intruders from stepping onto Cherokee land helping themselves to moveable property. Instead, it became apparent to the Cherokees that their newly formed government could not stem the loss of those goods. Even the initiative taken by individuals to recover stolen property in the spirit of *gadugi* amounted to little more than symbolic efforts to keep communalism alive. As Georgia asserted its power, Cherokees suffered at the hands of emboldened white settlers. Although John Gambold at the Springplace mission worried about an overt use of force by the government, the real threat to Cherokee stability and persistence was not the overwhelming power of the state but, rather, how that power encouraged thousands of individual white intruders to disregard Cherokee law, borders, and property. Such brazen disregard for Native legal forms only grew worse. Although the state could declare that it had taken the lead when the General Assembly passed the extension law, it was unprepared for its ramifications.

In the autumn of 1828, a hunter ranging through land owned by his pastor stumbled upon gold on the banks of the Chestatee River. Throughout the remainder of 1828 and well into the spring of the following year, few outside the region knew of the find. Then, in August 1829, the *Georgia Journal* caught wind of the story and published the first account of the state's two working, profitable gold mines: "So it appears that what we long anticipated has come to pass at last, namely, that the gold region of North and South Carolina would be found to extend into Georgia." Predicting the chaos and uncertainty that the mines would breed, the *Journal*'s editor urged the legislature to "prohibit, under severe penalties, the working of any gold or silver mines in the State."[46] By the fall of that year thousands of gold seekers and fortune hunters had descended upon the north Georgia hills. Although the first find did not occur on Cherokee land, miners discovered that the deposits extended northward, and they soon made their way onto Cherokee land. Anxiety, chaos, and violence followed in their wake.

The first national gold rush had dramatic consequences for those living on the Georgia-Cherokee border and dampened their prospects of enjoying a peaceful existence. As thousands of unwanted prospectors poured into the backcountry, state leaders and Cherokee councilmen sought ways of preventing bloodshed and of asserting control of the disputed territory. For Georgia, the chaos in the backcountry allowed it to extend its authority at the expense of the Cherokee sovereignty. The Cherokees fully understood that their way of life and their tenuous grip on their homeland could soon come to an end and would use the opportunity to seek federal assistance in maintaining their boundaries. Though the contest between Georgia's order and Cherokee harmony had raged for nearly three decades, the discovery of gold brought it to a fever pitch.

3 / The Slicks and the Pony Club

In August 1829, a Cherokee hunter on the north bank of the Chattahoochee River—the boundary separating the Cherokee Nation from the state of Georgia—came under fire by a group of whites after a boy had seen the hunter and mischievously warned his neighbors that a score of Cherokees "with hostile intentions" would soon cross the river. Residents in that neighborhood organized a posse and fired on the lone hunter they spied across the river. The hunter, busying himself with securing his quarry onto the horse, did not even know he had been fired upon until he arrived home and noticed his mount's bloody wound. By morning, saddled with a dead horse, the owner sought to retaliate against those who had killed his mount, though the *Cherokee Phoenix* did not record his actions. The bloodletting feared by political leaders on both sides of the river began with the shooting of a horse.[1]

As news of the gold find in the northern reaches of the state and in Cherokee country spread, state, federal, and Cherokee Nation leaders feared the outbreak of violence. What they got, instead, was banditry, lawlessness, and personal violence, but few killings. As more whites rushed across the Chattahoochee and on to Cherokee land, the idea that the intruders would not spark violence was naive. Such an overwhelming rush of humanity into the backcountry created confusion and chaos that left white and Indian residents reeling. Though they had grown accustomed to dealing with property theft, the sheer magnitude of the "Great Intrusion" disrupted community ties and threatened to drown Cherokee society and its tenuous position.

As the lawlessness mounted, the Cherokees pointed out the obvious disparities between their own comportment and that of the intruders. As the intruders continued their flagrant disregard for Cherokee laws, the Cherokees used the language of "savagery" to disavow the actions of the intruders. As physical attacks on Cherokee residents increased, they found it easier to lay claim to more civility and decorum than could Georgia's ravenous miners. Elias Boudinot, the editor of the *Phoenix*, reprimanded "these savage whites" for their brutal attacks on peaceful Cherokee men and women. Having "outstripped the Indians in deeds of blood," he hoped they would receive swift and sufficient punishment for their crimes. When the intruders showed no signs of relenting, the Cherokees decried those who "have acted more like savages towards the Cherokees, than the Cherokees towards them," but were still "permitted to continue in their unlawful proceedings, notwithstanding the frequent complaints made to the agent."[2]

As winter set in, the intruders' search for gold became increasingly desperate, and they settled for anything that could turn a profit. According to the *Phoenix*'s editor, "white men eight in number, well armed with guns, in the dead of the night . . . came into Hightower, and forcibly enter[ed] a house, kidnapped three negroes, two of whom were *free*, and made their escape into Georgia." Whites also entered Cherokee land for other purposes. One posse from Habersham County rode into the disputed territory "with hostile intentions" and attempted to arrest more than a dozen Cherokees who had "punished a notorious thief" from Georgia. The posse was intercepted by Cherokees who demanded that the "savage invaders" make restitution for slaughtering a hog. When the Georgians refused, the Cherokees confronted the armed men and took a gun as payment. These encounters illustrate the ease with which Georgians could cross the border but also the ways in which Cherokees acted to prevent their disruptive and violent acts.[3]

The sense many had was that the gold find was close to tipping the disputed territory into unmitigated violence that would permanently destabilize the area. What began with the killing of a horse in August escalated with the kidnapping of black Cherokees the following month, and, in December, had reached a boiling point when a posse of armed Georgians entered the Cherokee Nation seeking a group of Cherokees who had violently reprimanded a white horse thief. The last episode is worth exploring. As chapter 2 demonstrated, crime and disorder had long been a part of Cherokee life near the state's border, and although individual Cherokees had sought out their own stolen property or that of their neighbors, only small episodes of violent retaliation had occurred. At the end of the decade, that was no longer the case. The Cherokees and some of their white neighbors were fighting back.

Prior to the gold rush, most of the crime and violence had affected Cherokee property. Although this made life uncertain and unpredictable, community efforts to return that property strengthened community ties and traditional cultural practices. As more whites flooded into the backcountry, life on both sides of the border became disrupted. In Carroll County, a newly created border county, residents proceeded to intimidate county authorities and hoard power for themselves. Called the Pony Club, this group of "disorderly" whites sought to concentrate the efforts of backcountry thieves into one profitable and powerful organization. Local residents—both white and Cherokee—who wanted to put a stop to horse thieves' intimidation, turned to vigilantism to rid the area of the club's pernicious influence. In doing so, the Slicks, the residents who opposed the Pony Club, adopted a version of order that embraced violence as a legitimate tool of creating it. However, their version of order was named after a Native punishment. This hybrid community and its desire for order were unacceptable to the state leaders, who frowned upon interracial cooperation. In the end, the Slicks imposed order in Carroll County and laid the groundwork for other efforts that utilized violence as a tool to create social control. The complicated legacy left by the Slicks had important consequences and demonstrated the usefulness of violence to create a well-ordered society.

Most reports regarding the Pony Club did not mention it by name until 1829, the same year the gold rush began. A Cherokee man, Thompson Tucker, noted its rise as early as 1822, when he told Claims Commission investigators in 1842 that a bay horse he owned worth eighty dollars had been stolen from him "by a company of persons at this time known as the Pony Club," who were all "citizens of the United States of the State of Georgia." Tucker hired a man to retrieve his property but to no avail. Known for their "acts of theft on the property of Cherokee citizens," the Pony Club started small but soon became a serious threat. Although no other documentation exists that dates the Pony Club prior to 1829, Tucker's attribution of his horse's theft to the Club seven years before its probable formation emphasized the influence that it exerted on his memory.[4]

The Pony Club began as a group of loosely allied thieves who made use of backcountry conditions to prosper. The explosive population growth and contest for sovereignty all converged in Carroll County, the locus of the Club's power. Carroll County also provided a promising haven for the band of thieves because of specific conditions. Proximity to the state line only increased the ease of transporting stolen goods across jurisdictional boundaries. Pony Club thieves traveled into the Cherokee Nation to steal horses, cows, pigs, and other moveable property, and then sold the expropriations to farmers in Carroll County and Alabama, to passing traders, or to prospectors. Rival authorities had little success tracking down stolen property as it passed from Cherokee country, Georgia, and Alabama. Two additional factors contributed to the growth of the Pony Club in Carroll County. First, a large tract of land lying north of Carroll County called the Creek Strip offered refuge for the Club. Second, because of the disputed boundaries, several hundred Cherokees lived within Carroll County. Their status as legal nonentities made them desirable targets for thieves. Last, the fragile condition of civil government within the nascent county allowed the Club to muscle its way into the county government as a means of consolidating its power.

Much of the Pony Club's early success came from it first base of operations, called the Creek Strip or Vann's Valley. What became the Pony Club by 1829 had its beginnings four years earlier when Governor Troup urged the ratification of the Treaty of Indian Springs despite its obvious fraudulence. When the Treaty of Washington abrogated and replaced the previous one in 1826, it did nothing to solve a key ambiguity over a parcel of land, which lies north of Carroll County's northern boundary but south of the Coosa River, and extended east to Buzzard's Roost Island. Georgians cried foul over the new treaty, claiming it had infringed upon the state's sovereignty. Part of the negotiations designed to placate irate Georgians allowed them to survey the new border between Georgia and the remaining Creek land under the supervision of a group of Creek commissioners. This part of the negotiation was brokered by two Cherokee leaders, John Ridge and Richard Vann, who intervened when treaty negotiations almost broke down—and received fifteen thousand dollars apiece for their services. The border that the treaty charged Georgia to survey became a serious problem over the next three years. Troup selected a colonel in the state militia, Samuel A. Wales, to conduct the survey. Wales reported that Georgia had been shorted one hundred thousand acres promised to it in the treaty negotiations because of a misunderstanding over a particular parcel of land.[5]

The treaty become problematic because it did not explicitly state whether a piece of land claimed by the Cherokees that had previously belonged to the Creeks had been extracted as a concession. The state maintained that the Creeks had signed away the Strip when they ratified the new Treaty of Washington, which commanded them to "cede to the United States all the land belonging to the said Nation in the state of Georgia." The Creeks argued that they had ceded the Strip to the Cherokees two decades prior to any treaty with the United States and could not give it away again. The Strip now belonged to the Cherokee Nation. State leaders claimed that no such transaction occurred and that the Creeks ceded the land to the United States, and thus eager farmers from Georgia, when they signed the new treaty.

Georgians clamored for the land. When Wales ran his first line, a "Statesman & Patriot" lamented to the *Augusta Chronicle* that the northern boundary was not "run off as high up the Chattahoochee as . . . it should have been," meaning the state had been deprived of acreage. To the chagrin of the self-described Patriot, the Creek residents who had feared that they would soon face removal could now remain snugly in their homes "*far within the Cherokee Nation.*" By the end of June 1829 Wales and his assistant, Thomas Lloyd, had finished their investigation of the "true boundary line." Wales surveyed the land south of the Etowah River and placed the boundary up to the river's southern bank, which moved the state boundary line north nearly twenty-four miles.[6]

As early as 1825, settlers from Georgia began moving into the Creek Strip and quickly developed a poor reputation. John Ross issued the first complaint to Hugh Montgomery, the U.S. Indian agent and the man responsible for enforcing the Intercourse Acts, that year. A group of "Counterfitters & horse thieves infest Nickajack Creek and Lowrey's Ferry," Ross cautioned, intimating that Montgomery should do something to remedy the situation. Other reports filtered in to Montgomery, noting that the "Border interest" had drawn in "Intruders" who had "burned & destroyed . . . improvements and crops." He promised to patrol a large portion of the "Georgia Fraction"—another name for the Creek Strip—in search of "those depreidators [sic] and try to bring them to justice," but he did not sound optimistic about his prospects. In 1826, Montgomery and a small squad, including an interpreter, a Cherokee named George Sanders, and four other Cherokees, entered the area. When they arrived in the Strip, they "Labour[ed]" with "Burning houses & fences & cutting down corn." Because of the "extreme heat, hard labor, & bad accomodations," Montgomery took ill and had to call off the whole operation. All told, the federal force found eleven families residing in the Creek Strip, which included nine plantations "under cultivation."

Montgomery reported to the secretary of war that he burned every house occupied by white intruders that he came across.[7]

The following spring, Montgomery again traversed the Strip to engage in the "extremely odious" work of removing intruders. His second venture apparently met with little success because two years later, in early 1829, more problems occurred in the area as Americans continued to move into it. When the Cherokee subagent traveled to the border he found Georgians "rapidly settling," while a group of at least seventy men from Alabama had moved east into the Strip and had "chosen places for settlement." One backcountry resident, Jack Leathers, himself an intruder in the Strip and charter member of the Pony Club, boasted to Montgomery that the subagent had not been within thirty miles of his property because other intruders had "frightened him off." Leathers reported that more than four hundred white families lived in the Strip, while Montgomery believed that at least one hundred families had taken up residence there. He issued a stern warning to the intruders in the Creek Strip, urging them to "remove immediately" and "save themselves as well as the government trouble & expense." Other than that, Montgomery was at a loss. Understanding that his meager force stationed at New Echota could do little to uphold the boundaries of the Cherokee Nation, Montgomery minced no words in his recommendation to the secretary of war: "I have no expectation that they can be kept off, without the aid of a military force."[8]

For settlers living close to the Creek Strip, the problem was not so much the number of intruders but their deportment. One resident from neighboring DeKalb County and owner of sixteen slaves, Alston H. Greene, complained that the occupants of the Creek Strip used their homes as "Harbers for stolen property." Greene wanted upstanding neighbors, "good men who would rent those places & would pay for them." He proposed to act as Gilmer's agent (for no compensation) "in order to get rid of the Poney Club & others of suspicious character."[9] Greene reiterated many of the problems found in the other border counties regarding the character of those who bred disorder and the need for good citizens to counteract their abuses. Further, his complaints also connected the maintenance of order to a landholding, virtuous population. Greene's account of the criminal activities in the Creek Strip accounted for the origins of the Pony Club. Though it began in 1829 as an extension of the criminal activity that had plagued the borderlands for a decade, its members used the absence of legal authority in the area to ply their wares and consolidate their operation.

The Pony Club, however, became much more proficient in its theft of Cherokee property than the unorganized frontier criminals who acted individually or in small groups. They posed a more dangerous threat to Cherokee sovereignty, for if the Natives could not halt a band of thieves, their claim to territorial sovereignty rang hollow. As the rightful owners of the Creek Strip, Cherokee leaders had a difficult time dealing with the influx of white intruders residing there. Many of the settlers who had moved into the Creek Strip, even those with honest intentions, ran afoul of federal law and should not have had access to land. Several families of Georgians thought they had legally purchased their land and improvements from Creek families who had left after the last treaty had been finalized. Though the white buyers felt that they held legal title to the land because money had changed hands, the Intercourse Acts and treaties concluded between the United States and the Creeks prevented individual American citizens from purchasing land or improvements from Indians. Federal law specified that only treaty negotiators could legally dispossess Indians of their land and only after they had made payment to the National Council.[10]

Without any clear indication of sovereignty, the Creek Strip attracted intruders who caused numerous problems, threatened order, and created conditions favorable to the success of the Pony Club. Within the contested limits of the Creek Strip, Cherokee leaders found gold seekers, white farmers, as well as horse thieves. Discerning between the three groups proved nearly impossible. Indeed, a white intruder could take up all three of those professions to make ends meet. The influx of transient gold seekers and thieves allowed men to congregate and coalesce into the Pony Club. Early in the gold rush, some of them decided that making money by taking Cherokee property looked more appealing than scouring frigid mountain streams for gold.

The Pony Club had its beginnings not only in the chaos that spawned border violence and the confusion wrought by the controversy regarding the Creek Strip but also in the peculiar demographic conditions of Carroll County. Formed in December 1826 from the last remnants of the Creek Nation, Carroll County quickly emerged as a refuge for criminals and land speculators, as well as those who sought to make something of themselves in a more honest fashion. Called the state's "last frontier" by one historian, Carroll County saw its share of violence and turmoil as it slowly transitioned from an area with Creek and Cherokee residents to a county inhabited primarily by whites and their slaves.[11] Carroll County's location on recently ceded Creek lands at the confluence of Alabama,

Georgia, and the Cherokee Nation made it a particularly desirable location because much of its soil had never cultivated cotton. Carroll also had peculiar demographic features, namely a significant number of Cherokee families who legally resided within the county because of the uncertainty regarding boundaries. Census-takers who enumerated the Cherokees residing in Carroll County listed them as free persons of color, which corresponded to the way the extension law classified them. Of the 3,419 people living in Carroll in 1830, the Census denominated 208 as free people of color and 487 as slaves. Carroll County, therefore, had a more complicated social system than the stereotypical white-black southern dichotomy. Though only about two hundred Cherokees resided within Carroll, their presence upset the notion of the state's desired racial order. Their presence also allowed for cooperative opportunities between Cherokee families and their new white neighbors.[12]

Cherokee leaders, though, had other ideas about the Pony Club's origins. Framing the growth of the Club not as the result of border country lawlessness but as a conspiracy by power-hungry Georgians, the Cherokees saw the Club as an extension of state authority and symptomatic of the depths to which the state would go to acquire Native land. With their recent declaration of sovereignty, the Cherokees had the most at stake in claiming jurisdiction over the Strip. According to Elias Boudinot, the editor of the *Cherokee Phoenix*, white citizens from Carroll "are still flocking in and possessing the land. Many of the most notorious members of the 'Poney club' are no doubt foremost in this business." For Boudinot and other Cherokees, the lawlessness wrought by the horse thieves was all part of an "expeditious" method of expelling the rightful landowners. By setting "loose such a community upon us," Boudinot declared, the "honorable" state of Georgia complicitly approved of their methods and saw the Pony Club as a means of intimidating the Cherokees into leaving. Conversely, Georgians saw a conspiracy afoot when they argued that the "chiefs, headmen, and warriors" of the Cherokee Nation comprised the rank-and-file of the Pony Club. Leaders on both sides of the border blamed the other for the problems plaguing the Creek Strip.[13]

Carroll County's location at the confluence of state and national borders, its proximity to the Creek Strip, and a domestic Cherokee population provided an ideal opportunity for a band of thieves to coalesce. With plenty of Cherokee property available, the ability to cross permeable boundaries, and a history of prolific crime as its backdrop, Carroll County proved fertile ground for a more powerful organization to evolve from its rather loose beginnings. The transformation began in February 1830, when a Cherokee squadron burned down the homes of white intruders in the Creek Strip and expelled them. The new direction the Pony Club took stemmed from this incident, and most of their activities after that date involved beatings, shootings, and intimidation not just against the Cherokees but also against members of the white community who opposed them.

Prompted by threats to their sovereignty in the form of intruders in the Creek Strip and with little aid forthcoming from the federal government, the Cherokees decided to act on their own. Though Hugh Montgomery had attempted to rid the Strip of intruders in 1826, 1827, and 1829, his efforts proved unsuccessful. Moreover, as demonstrated in chapter 2, individuals had some success recovering stolen property by working with their neighbors in a traditional context. Their actions did not reflect the sovereignty of the Cherokee Nation. The actions being proposed by Ross did. The National Council wanted to demonstrate its sovereignty by acting in a forceful manner against intruders.

It authorized John Ross to remove a group of intruders who had taken up residence in homes vacated by Cherokees who had voluntarily removed to Arkansas Territory. In February 1830, a squad of Cherokees, "with all possible lenity and humanity," expelled eighteen white families from their homes in the Strip. Convinced "that if the houses were not destroyed, the intruders would not go away," the Cherokees "determined on the expediency of setting fire" to the homes, but not before they let the families remove their bedding, cookware, and other movable property.[14]

When federal officials burned down the homes of intruders, state leaders did not put up resistance. When the Cherokees acted in a similar fashion, however, angered whites responded with fury. News of the Cherokee action spread into neighboring Carroll County, and the next night, February 4, a posse of at least twenty armed men led by the sheriff of Carroll County entered Cherokee land and arrested four Cherokees who had taken part in the house-burnings and expulsion. The four Natives had gotten drunk on whiskey before the posse caught them, and their condition prevented them from escaping. One, The Waggon, was beaten with the butt of a musket, while another, Chuwoyee, too drunk to stand, suffered a severe beating and was lashed to a horse so his captors could bring him to Carrollton. After he fell from the horse several times, the Georgians beat Chuwoyee "most barbarously" until he died. The posse continued on to Carrollton, but not before they unceremoniously dumped the "shockingly mangled" body on the road. The remaining

John Ross, the Principal Chief of the Cherokee Nation, opposed removal and the violent actions of the State of Georgia. He was a strong proponent of Cherokee sovereignty and insisted the federal government uphold its treaty obligations to the Cherokees. Thomas L. McKenny and John T. Bowen, *John Ross, a Cherokee Chief* (Philadelphia: Daniel Rice & James G. Clark, 1843), Library of Congress, Washington, DC. LC-DIG-pga-07513.

three Natives taken to Carrollton soon eluded their captors, but in the scuffle a roughened outlaw known as Old Philpot stabbed The Waggon in the chest. The retaliatory raid by the men from Carroll County came in the wake of the Cherokee's attempt to exert sovereignty.[15]

Allen G. Fambrough, Gilmer's appointed adviser in the county and the foremost prosecutor in Carrollton, informed the governor of what had transpired: "The sheriff of our county will set out today with a company of twenty men to take the company of house-burners or so many as we have been able to designate, which is nine." Upon the sheriff's return, Fambrough offered a glowing account of the foray into the Nation, claiming that "the Indians were much affrightened" when the sheriff's posse approached. The posse, according to Fambrough, made a hasty retreat when it came under fire: "One white man though a native of the nation whirled and fired his riffle [sic] at the crowd and some one of the company shot at him but no Injury done." When he learned that Carroll's sheriff had sought out the Cherokee squadron, the governor regretted "that any of the citizens of the state should have placed themselves out of the full protection of its laws by going" into the Creek Strip, "until its possession was peaceably obtained." Though he maintained that the state's "sovereign character" would soon extend over the Strip and its inhabitants, by February 1830 it had not. The extension law did not go into effect until June, so the sheriff and his posse had no legal authority on which to stand. Besides, the state legislature has given its "silent assent" to a War Department note reiterating that the Cherokees, and not the state, had sovereignty over the Strip.[16]

After the Cherokees expelled the intruders, the Pony Club altered its tactics. Beginning in 1830, the Club moved out of the Creek Strip and into Carroll County, where it began to exert undue influence over civil authorities in Carrollton for two reasons. First, by controlling members of the local county, the Pony Club could expand its activities unmolested by state and local authorities. Second, by appropriating the authority vested in the county by the extension law, the Club could use violence and intimidation against the Cherokees to subject them to the Club's actions. In this regard, the Cherokees who saw a conspiracy in the Pony Club's growing power were partially correct. Although the Club never had a mandate from the state authorizing it to pillage the backcountry, its members could count on state law to provide them immunity from legal recourse.

How the courtship between hardened criminals and supposedly upright county officials occurred is not recorded. Whether through intimidation or bribery, though, the Club, by 1832, counted, for starters, the sheriff's deputy, several constables and justices of the peace, at least two high-ranking prosecutors, and not a few militiamen in its ranks. Allen Fambrough served as the best example of a high-ranking official who had been coopted by the Pony Club. In July 1830, he breathlessly wrote the governor of a scheme undertaken by several whites in

Carrollton who passed fraudulent bank notes and bills of sale to Cherokee residents. One of Fambrough's informants, a white citizen of Carroll, planned on testifying against a justice of the peace, Ramson P. Boswell, and four or five of his coconspirators. Fambrough had also planned on using Cherokee informants, but the extension law prevented Cherokees from testifying against whites in court. Boswell and his confederates never stood trial for their crimes because the witness never testified against the Club. Despite Fambrough's efforts to seek out criminals, he did not prove immune to the growing power of the Pony Club. His seduction by the Club occurred rapidly, and it stands to reason that Fambrough, like the witness who would not testify, was threatened with bodily harm if he did not cooperate.[17]

Every good criminal organization needs a better lawyer to prevent its members from serving time, and it seems that the Pony Club found that lawyer in Fambrough. In the same way that the state couched its land grab in legal terms, the Club sought to use state law to its benefit. As early as 1828, Fambrough defended noted criminals and future Pony Club members in Carroll's Superior Court. In September 1828, Fambrough defended Richard Philpot from a suit filed by Jonathan Davis. The jury foreman, Samuel Leathers, another noted horse thief and Pony Club member, and the rest of the jury found for Philpot. The date of this trial is crucial, for it occurred before the Club's formation. It did, in any case, showcase strategies Fambrough later perfected, namely the intimidation of juries by placing vociferous thieves as jury foremen. Such a strategy, in theory, allowed Fambrough to secure nearly any verdict he desired. The Club's infiltration of the county's legal system helped explain why it proved so successful.[18]

By 1832, the system worked well enough to propel the Pony Club into a position of power. In a report to the governor, one state agent noted the impossibility of fully understanding "the outrages and injuries which the association called the Poney Club" had inflicted upon the local community: "Property stolen, honest men abused, and the civil authorities resisted were matters of no unusual occurrence." Indeed, so powerful had they become that when other residents filed charges, the Pony Club could assert its influence to ensure that securing a conviction was difficult: "Resort has been had to legal process, but all in vain; for out of the numberless prosecutions which have been instituted against the confederates of the Poney Club, not one has been successful. They are always present in sufficient numbers to swear each other clear of any offence with which they may be accused."[19] The *Macon Telegraph* reported that the Club, because it had "settled so numerously in neighborhoods," could elect "constables and justices of the peace from their own body." If any member "was seen marauding," due process against him was impossible to achieve because his comrades would ensure his discharge from any "exculpatory affidavits." Anyone who sued Club members, moreover, instead faced "fictitious charges" leveled "by the officers of the peace."[20]

Carroll's residents in 1832 had the impression that the Pony Club controlled the juries and verdicts of both the inferior and superior courts, though the Club's control was never as extensive as believed. For four years, Fambrough defended members of the noted gang of horse thieves. But even a lawyer with such prodigious talent for perverting justice could not guarantee every verdict. His most problematical client, Calaway Burke, had a violent reputation and was sued at least four separate times by other residents of Carroll County in the span of two years. In February 1831, Burke lost a suit and had to pay a creditor thirty-one dollars; in April he was sued three times and lost two of those cases and had to pay almost two hundred dollars' worth of debts and court fees.[21] In the same April session of the Carroll County Superior Court in which he was sued in three separate cases, Calaway Burke also served as the jury foreman in an important case involving two notorious criminals, Philip Bosworth and Reuben Philpot, one of the men who had beaten Chuwoyee. According to the suit, Philpot "Injured and damaged" Bosworth in March 1830 on the public road where he accosted Bosworth "with force & arms." Philpot pulled Bosworth from his horse and "did then and there with fists sticks stone and knives. .. bruise & wound" the victim and commenced "striking him on his head face heart shoulders & other parts of his body & by biteing and gouging with teeth thumbs and fingers," which eventually "crippled and disabled" Bosworth. The jury awarded Bosworth fifty-five dollars, though he had sought ten times that sum.[22]

In some instances, especially when particularly odious residents with poor reputations behaved in egregious ways, juries counteracted the Pony Club. In April 1831, when Calaway Burke was sued four times, it appeared that the center of the Club's power—Carroll County's courthouse—was no longer the refuge it once had been. Though the Club did not enjoy a perfect success record in court, its ability to put noted Club members like Burke into the jury box gave the impression that the Pony Club controlled the county's judicial system. The fact that Philpot had received only a fine and not a jail sentence emphasized the Club's power.

The judicial system's corruption dimmed the prospect of solidifying order in Carroll County. As fall gave way to winter in 1830, a rash of shootings and murders occurred on the Cherokee side of the border. In November, Carroll residents John A. Craddock, his two sons, and William Young traveled from within the Cherokee Nation to their homes in Carroll when another group of men, Johnston Lee, Jim Lee, and Sam Scott, ambushed them. Young "fell desperately wounded." The others left their fallen friend to fend for himself and fled for their lives. Once their targets fled, Sam Scott "Stamp'd" the injured man in the face and chest until he "Expir'd." According to the author of the report, Jacob R. Brooks, the perpetrators hailed from the Cherokee Nation, though he did not speculate the reason why the Craddocks and William Young had ventured there. Brooks also reported on "a most Horrid Murder" that had recently taken place within the Nation. He knew few of the facts, only that a white man's body had been found burned along with most of his personal papers. The grisly discovery stoked the fears of white residents in Carroll County, who fretted over the outbreak of more killings. Brooks confirmed the mood to Governor Gilmer: "Your excellency will perceive that a Crisis has arrive[d]," a time, he felt, when "Georgia must act efficiently or Submit. The excitement on this frontier is very Great."[23]

After the discovery of the burned corpse in mid-November, the Carroll County deputy sheriff, Henry Curtis, led a small group into the Cherokee Nation "on lawful business" to "levy an execution on some property": horses that Thomas York claimed had been stolen from him. Major Giles Boggess, one of the leading citizens of Carroll County and officer of the county militia, and definitely not a member of the Pony Club, accompanied the two men. The three men stopped for the night at an abandoned cabin but awoke to find themselves surrounded by a party of nearly twenty Cherokees. According to Boggess, the Cherokee arrested the three Georgians, "securely tied & forced [us] to put off to the [Etowah] Mission immediately without being allowed the privilege of our horses." When they arrived at the mission, the missionaries released the men from their "strings," but having no authority over them, they sent the Georgians, along with their escort, to a nearby detachment of U.S. artillery under the command of Lieutenant Fowler at the Sixes mine.[24]

Fowler informed the sheriff that "for some years" the people of the Cherokee Nation near Carroll County had been "mutch harased by a people cauled the poney Club," so Fowler had authorized any Cherokee living along the Etowah River to arrest "all *whites* who are intruders or those who atampt to Commit depradations on the parsons or property of Indians with in the Nation." Such a directive was authorized under the Intercourse Acts, though usually federal troops and not individual

Cherokees carried it out. So when Curtis, Boggess, and York entered the Nation with a warrant to seize two horses that had gone missing, the Cherokees had simply followed Fowler's command. The Cherokees did not recognize Curtis or Boggess, "but recognizing yorke and nowing that avast quontitey of thare property had passed thru his hands," they arrested all three "as a parte of the poney Club."[25] At this point, accounts of what followed diverge. Boggess stated that Fowler eventually sent the sheriff and his gang to a major at Camp Eaton, who released them and did nothing to prevent them from taking the horses by force—aside from treating the men from Carroll "verry scornfully." The *Phoenix* claimed that Fowler sent the men to his superior, who ruled in their favor and allowed them to take the two horses, but then jailed York for a night.[26]

In December, a party of twenty-five mounted men, a "Considerable number of the acnolleged poney Club," entered the Nation seeking to capture the Cherokees who had arrested the white men from Carrollton. Led by Giles Boggess, the mounted company came upon a group of Cherokee children and kidnapped "a lad of a boute sixteen tyed him and took him and the baste horse belonging to the family and maid thare escape." They returned a second time, chased and shot at two young Cherokee boys, and proceeded to kidnap another one, whom they kept for more than five days.[27] Underscoring the connections between the Pony Club and the civil authorities in Carroll, the sixteen-year-old boy they kidnapped, Joseph Beanstick, who, according the *Cherokee Phoenix*, "had no agency in the arrest of Curtis, Bogus, and York," was jailed for "four weeks during the coldest time of this winter, with no other covering than a cloak and an old saddle blanket."[28]

The interesting aspect of the posse's ride into Cherokee country concerned the group's makeup. Not all of the men in Boggess's posse were part of the Pony Club. It appeared that their mutual animosity could be set aside in certain instances, which included terrorizing Cherokee youths. One commenter on the posse's ride into the Nation noted, "all parteys Can unite in the opraising of an Indian," suggesting that by December 1830 two separate camps existed in Carroll County—the Pony Club and another group opposed to its actions—and that joint ventures into the backcountry could halt their rivalry.[29] Their shared desire to rid the backcountry of its Native inhabitants shone through in displays of "martial exploit . . . on their return march." With Beanstick in tow, Boggess and his companions "would occasionally form themselves on the road and discharge their fire-arms as a signal over the Cherokee youth in captivity." In spite of their mutual animosity, then, in December 1830 the two sides united to kidnap a Cherokee boy.[30]

The confusing tangle of relationships between the Pony Club, the citizens of Carroll, and the Cherokees made regulating the social world of the border increasingly difficult. That Boggess, the representative of law, would willingly work with the Pony Club in an effort to oppress the Cherokees demonstrates just how confusing these relationships and the motivations had become. In 1830, the threat of Cherokee reprisals weighed on their minds. However, it was the Pony Club and not the Cherokees who were working to destabilize the area. In December Boggess and twenty-four Carroll County militiamen sent a petition to the governor asking for "the liberty of forming a company & to furnish arms for the Equipment of Sixty horsemen." The men would all "still continue to doe military duty in their respective districts & hold themselves in constant readiness" to aid the sheriff in implementing the law. Because the "distance being so great & the progress of the malitia so tardy that offenders can scarsely ever be apprehended," the petitioners argued that a special mounted company would make more sense than cumbersome infantry. Boggess's intent to capture horse thieves partly explains why he entered the Nation with less than desirable company. Many of the militia's responsibilities in Georgia rested on its duty of aiding the sheriff to round up criminals or serve warrants. So it would not have been out of the ordinary for Boggess to assist Curtis with his duties. Boggess, then, had not joined the Pony Club, but he did want to enforce the law—even if that meant helping Thomas York, a noted thief, recover some of his property.[31]

With a respectable militia officer pushing for more forceful measures to quell border crime, state leaders refused to act, perhaps because Gilmer did not believe the reports coming from Carrollton. After all, his adviser, Allen Fambrough, was defending Club members in court. Content to wait for local efforts, namely civil authority, to establish order, Gilmer saw no need to resort to more forceful measures. Others saw the Pony Club as a pressing issue that demanded state attention. The *Macon Telegraph* argued that only "a strong military force can arrest the evil while the county remains in its present condition." The paper urged the legislature "to rid the country of this horde of thieves and counterfeiters." Indeed, the Pony Club's actions had only become emboldened because of a lack of enforcement. During the election of 1829, "a number of the *Ponyites* presented themselves at the polls in Carroll county, and offered to *vote!*" For the *Macon Telegraph*'s correspondent, the connection between expectations and rights of the citizenry was clear. Because the Ponyites "plunder and pillage where and whomever they please," they posed a threat to self-government and order. When the county magistrate tendered them to swear to the state constitution, the Club members assaulted the magistrate and "upset the ballot box" not because "they had any objection at all to *swearing*, but because their *honor* was offended." A few days later, the Ponyites rode into Campbellton in pursuit of a magistrate who had reclaimed a stolen horse from one of their members. The Club caught up with him, "violently assaulted and beat the officer, insulted the inhabitants, and galloped off again in triumph." The editor from Macon put it bluntly: "The extermination of this nest of pirates is of more importance to the State than the preservation of the gold mines."[32]

The citizens of Carroll County agreed. Though Gilmer was willing to wait for the border counties to implement order, those living in the county did not evince such magnanimity. Beginning in 1831, when citizens convicted Pony Club men in county court, the people of Carroll County began to push back against crime themselves. In the wake of his experiences in the backcountry, it had become apparent to Major Boggess that Curtis and his successor, Benjamin Merrill, had sold out to the Pony Club, that no real order existed in the county, and that someone had to stand up to the abusive gang. In early 1832 Boggess ran for county sheriff, and his candidacy gained widespread support from "honest" citizens. Carroll's residents, concurrent to the more formalized actions involving elections and juries, began a visible campaign of retaliation against the Pony Club. The fight for control over Carrollton's politics became so contentious that an actual street brawl broke out between the Pony Club and the supporters of the new sheriff. In the end, Boggess won, and according to one historian "this band of early outlaws diminished after 1832."[33]

Not sensing how much the power dynamic had shifted after the election, the Club resorted to their old tricks and tried to intimidate a jury to defame the sheriff. After the election Pony Club members charged Boggess with assault and attempted murder for his role in the street fight that occurred on election day. However, when the jury received the charges, they refused to accuse Boggess of any crime and applauded his efforts to clean up the town. The jury, instead, accused two lawyers, including Allen G. Fambrough—the governor's representative in the county—of conspiring with the Pony Club. The lawyer resented the charge. When the *Macon Telegraph*'s editor connected him to the Pony Club, Fambrough dared the "FLAGICIOUS LIAR AND POLTROON" to attack him in a manner befitting a man of honor. Furthermore, Fambrough, a noted member of Gilmer's Troup faction, noted that the *Telegraph* offered its support to the Clark party and no doubt speculated on his connections to the Club to "throw contempt upon that party, in state politics, in whose ranks I am proud to be found."[34]

The pro-Clark *Macon Telegraph*, though it certainly was out to score a political points, claimed the connection between Fambrough and the Pony Club not for overt political motives but because a jury had named him as the Club's benefactor. Much of the jury's resentment toward Fambrough came from a case in which citizens of the county connected him to the Club. In June 1832, Fambrough was present when his erstwhile client and member of the Pony Club, Calaway Burke, was shot and killed by one of the county's "honest citizens," John Goodwin. Fambrough, according to one witness, "was present when Burke was shot *armed* as his friend." Accompanied by Major John A. Jones of the county militia, the two had caused "most of the excitement" then plaguing the county, and "together with some of their friends, were the only persons who appear constantly armed in public."[35] By implying that only dangerous men appeared armed in public, the author of the report sought to discount the character of Jones and Fambrough, and, by extension, the rest of the Pony Club, further contributing to the swing in public opinion against the Club.

Though an emboldened jury had stood up to Fambrough, the rest of the Pony Club membership still excelled at concealing their identities. No one knew with any degree of certainty the extent of the Club or the rank in civil government to which its members had climbed. One report had their numbers ranging "from one hundred and fifty to two hundred members." At any one time, though, no more than "twenty-five or thirty" men were seen together, even at their primary rendezvous. When spotted by a traveler, "they dropped like turtles off a log" and vanished into the swamps near Hominy Creek.[36] Other than Fambrough, York, Burke, Curtis, Major Jones, and Old Philpot, determining the membership of the Pony Club proved difficult for several reasons. Few men walked around Carrollton announcing their allegiance; fewer still took legal recourse or had their names recorded; others employed aliases. Some Georgians speculated that much of the Club's membership was comprised of Cherokees. One account mentioned the ethnicity of the members, claiming their ranks "have been maid up parte of white and parte of red men"[37] While it would make sense that some form of multiracial cooperation existed between thieves, no other accounts confirmed this report.[38] Cherokee men, more than likely, worked within their communal traditions to work against rather than with the Pony Club.

Evidence suggests, though, that Cherokees and whites did work together to violently expel Pony Club members from the area. For Carroll's citizens, ridding the county of the Pony Club threat required more than a new sheriff in town. Beginning in 1831 and into 1832, when the "honest citizens" began to fight back against the outrages of the Pony Club, discerning its members became a much easier task. Members of both the white settler and Cherokee communities began to cooperate to expel the Pony Club. Those thieves who had the misfortune of crossing paths with the new group bore the telltale sign that they had been visited by their justice-seeking neighbors: flayed flesh. This group had two names, the Slicks or the Regulators. Each drew on a particular tradition, but both traditions revolved around the idea of community control through vigilantism. Cherokee men frequently whipped, or "slicked," the backs of horse thieves with hickory switches as many as fifty or even a hundred times. Thus, the Slicks practiced vigilantism within the Cherokee tradition of restorative communal work. Because these actions were sanctioned by the community, the Slicks delivered a form of extralegal justice. Whites also practiced slicking with their Cherokee neighbors but tended to call their group the Regulators. Drawing on the legacy of colonial social movements that sought to regulate backcountry life, Carroll County's Regulators shared similar methods, if not motives, with their namesake. The most successful regulations occurred between 1768 and 1771 in several North Carolina piedmont counties as an effort at establishing local control over an unfair legal system and a political structure dominated by lowcountry aristocrats.[39] The Slicks wanted to take control of a world quickly slipping from their grasp because of the lawlessness directed by the Pony Club and the ineffectiveness of both state and federal authorities in bringing ordered society into being. Rather than wait for an unresponsive state leadership to impose order, individuals in the backcountry banded together in a last-ditch effort at ending the Pony Club's reign. For the Regulators, "their [sic] seemed to be no other alternative left, but for the honest part of the community to subdue or expel the Poney Club, or themselves abandon the Country." Their regulation sought to impose the values of the community against those who made them a mockery; a charivari bent on restoring order.[40]

The most interesting facet of the Slicks, though, was not their namesake but their chosen form of punishment. Slicking had long been a method of punishment in Cherokee culture and very quickly became the telltale sign that a horse thief had been visited by the Slicks.[41] That a vigilante group on the border of the Cherokee Nation took up a Native form of punishment revealed much about the Slicks, their motives and methods, and about the syncretic, bicultural nature of life in the disputed territory. The permeability of the boundary between Georgia and the Nation facilitated cross-cultural communication between the Cherokees and their white neighbors, and it made sense for neighbors who had a stake in the region's stability to draw on a variety of cultural practices to protect their homes and families.[42] Both societies, though, interpreted the punishments meted out by the Slicks in different ways.

Many sectors of the polyglot backcountry population took part in controlling the behavior of their neighbors. All types of people, "Magistrates and Constables, Methodists, Baptists and men of no religion, old settlers and new comers, men of respectability and men of notorious character," joined in the regulation around Carroll County, where, by 1832, "A high degree of excitement prevailed every where, reason was drowned in clamour, and the laws gave place to the will of a furious multitude."[43] Even those across the state line in Alabama joined. By the summer of 1832, many of the Pony Club's efforts at acquiring new property had turned westward as white settlers flocked onto Creek lands opened up in Alabama by the Treaty of Indian Springs. The influx of settlers created new opportunities for the Pony Club to further enrich its members. "From the latter State," one reporter announced, "ponies, horses and cattle were taken in large numbers," and soon enough, the "spirited and sagacious" Alabamans "formed themselves into a society under the cognomen *Slickers or Sleeks*." Under the command of *"General Lynch*," the Slicks from Alabama "invaded our territory, observing however the greatest respect towards persons and property, except the members of the *Poney Club*."[44] When the Slicks did capture their quarry, their retribution was swift, "sometime whipping them soundly on the spot," or they would protract the anticipation by taking their captive into Cherokee country and "placing the lash in the hands of the aboriginals, who are said to leave seldom an inch of sound skin on the posterior part of the body between heels and the neck."[45] According to the reporter, the application of force had an altogether chaotic effect on the social world near the border.

The whippings inevitably brought the conflict between the Regulators and the Pony Club to a head, and eventually led to the murder of Calaway Burke. In April, Burke had been taken from his home and detained for several days. When released, he encountered one of his captors, Francis

Adams, in Carroll County and tried to drag him to the courthouse when a Slick from Alabama, John Goodwin, intervened. As the event intensified, more men arrived at the scene; some drew pistols and declared their intent to protect either Adams or Burke. Both sides agreed that a justice of the peace needed to sort out the mess, so a small party went looking for one. The Slicks, however, had sent off a messenger to gather more men, while one of the Pony Club went in search of Allen Fambrough. In the ensuing tumult, Burke managed to escape but reappeared with Fambrough, both of them armed with pistols. At this point, more Slicks arrived and shot Burke in the road.[46]

Soon after killing Burke, the Slicks commenced a well-coordinated and simultaneous series of raids targeting individuals in Carroll and Cherokee Counties, and Alabama. They beat a man named James Upton and another named Crawford Wright, who was taken from his family, tied to a tree, stripped, and whipped with "90 or 100 lashes." Further, the Regulators extorted a promise from Wright that he would not "law" his persecutors and that he would leave Georgia within twenty days. Nine more men were whipped within a short time span, including Old Philpot and Roberts, a state legislator from Hall County. After the outbreak of whippings, most of the Pony Club "made a sudden retreat" out of the county because of promises they had made under duress.[47]

In one respect, the Slicks represented the will of the community and its desire for order. To achieve that, they punished known criminals. Their methods shamed the victims because they inflicted the punishments in public spaces. The combination of horrific wounds and public beatings made identifying a horse thief possible. Once identified, Pony Club members received stern treatment, harassment, and vitriol from formerly agreeable (or terrified) neighbors. Slicking also signified mastery over an inferior in the American South. White southerners had long used the lash as a form of punishment and control. By employing it against whites, the Regulators completed the denigration of an accused Pony Club man: by slicking a white man, they had, in effect, named and shamed him.

If Regulators were imposing an honor-bound form of justice, they were also administering Cherokee law. Slicking a thief satisfied the harmonious values of the Cherokees because the punishment created balance. Not only was slicking part of traditional clan law, but it was also enshrined in the new constitution. For example, in December 1829, a Cherokee jury sentenced Jesse Stansell, a white horse thief from Georgia, to receive fifty lashes for stealing a horse, "which," declared the foreman of the jury, George Saunders, whose opprobrium of Stansell's toughness, if not his manhood, was glaringly obvious, "was fifty less than what is common in our country for such an offence." Despite the state's insistence that the Cherokees could no longer dole out legal punishments, Saunders and the rest of the jury had no qualms about executing Cherokee sovereignty: "We acted agreeably to the laws of our country in punishing the man." For Saunders, the matter proved a simple one. Stansell had broken the law within the Cherokee Nation and faced punishment according to its laws. Georgia's authorities did not see it that way. Stansell returned to Hall County, where he gave a deposition to the judge Augustin Clayton, declaring that the Cherokees had detained him upward of thirty hours "without any legal authority," stripped Stansell of his clothes, tied him to a tree, "and inflicted on the bare back . . . with large hickory switches fifty lashes, to the great effusion of his blood, the laceration of his back and sides, leaving deep wounds, gashes and bruises all the same."[48] The difference, of course, was that the Slicks acted outside the law, either state or Cherokee, but in a way their community supported.

Even though the Slicks enjoyed widespread backing, no consensus existed on their legitimacy. One editorialist, a self-described "Citizen of Carroll," attempted to defend the Pony Club but knew his efforts would prove foolhardy in the end: "No man can escape condemnation or the opprobrium of being friendly to the poney club who dares to disapprobate the lawless career of the regulators."[49] The "Citizen" understood the complexities of a vigilante movement. By using extralegal violence to masquerade as the true representatives of an orderly society along the border, the Slicks had created a version of an orderly community—one that relied upon cooperation across racial and national lines. Georgia's officials agreed with the assessment. In the summer of 1832, a general in the state militia, John Coffee, conducted a brief investigation but concluded that the Regulator furor had died down. The new governor, Wilson Lumpkin, could gaze upon the events that transpired in Carroll County and congratulate himself for not having unleashed the overbearing power of the state to control its own citizens. Even though he wanted order to take hold, Lumpkin saw no harm in "the late disturbances in Carroll and Cherokee counties." Lumpkin concluded "that whatever excesses may have been committed in the punishment of Bad men, the object of the party engaged in administering speedy correction, was founded in honest & upright motives." In an outright snub of Fambrough, the current governor labeled him as one of the real culprits, "who had become the advisors if not the aiders and abettors of a combination of bad men." Good citizens, however violent they became, had brought order to the borderlands and restored virtuous self-government to Carroll County.[50]

With a history of theft and violence, Carroll County's proximity to a multitude of borders and contested space, and its unique demographics allowed for the growth of a dangerous group of horse thieves, the Pony Club, to thrive along Georgia's boundary. The Club became adept at stealing Cherokee property and selling it to white farmers or intruders. Their organization also allowed them to control aspects of the county's civil authority. When the Club's actions reached a critical point, members of the backcountry community, both white and Cherokee, united briefly to rid themselves of the Pony Club. To do so, Slicks resorted to violent measures, which broke up the criminal ring and undermined the state's insistence on civil authority as the proper way to order the backcountry. The prospects of local control and of a lasting cross-cultural alliance waned as the immediate threat to stability subsided. Residents acted forcefully against the Pony Club because state and federal governments failed to act. Instead of targeting the Pony Club, though, both the state and federal authorities sought out larger threats to order, mainly the thousands of gold miners who had taken up residence within the Cherokee Nation. The Slicks, though, showed the practical applications of violence and how it could be used to create order.

4 / The Convergence of State and Federal Policy

As the gold rush intensified and society in the disputed territory destabilized, President Andrew Jackson ordered troops into the region to expel intruders and uphold the borders of the Cherokee Nation. Although conventional wisdom maintains that Jackson balked when the U.S. Supreme Court ordered his administration, in the 1832 case *Worcester v. Georgia*, to override the aggressive actions taken by the state, Jackson was in fact not averse to the exercise of military power in the borderlands to compel obedience to the law. However, he did not send troops at the behest of the Cherokee Nation or the Supreme Court. Members of the U.S. Army were dispatched into the Cherokee Nation at the request of Georgia's governor. Only a few months later, those troops were recalled, once again at the state's request.

Although the troops had some success when it came to the creation of a sense of order, they were not the first group to rely on violence to do so. The outbreak of violence in the Cherokee borderlands demonstrated the usefulness of violence as a tool to shape social norms and behaviors. The vigilantes known as the Slicks sought to create a type of order that saw them cooperate across racial lines to do away with the Pony Club, a group of horse thieves who had grown brazen in their own exertion of power that came at the expense of Cherokees living near the Georgia boundary. Force and violence, it seemed, could be used as a tonic for what ailed the borderlands. This lesson was not lost on George Gilmer, the governor of Georgia and ardent states' rights supporter. However, the breakdown of orderly society in the disputed territory caused by rampant crime, intrusion, and illegal settlement convinced Gilmer that the federal government needed to play some role in the maintenance of order.

For most of the nineteenth century, the government remained "out of sight" except at the nation's borders, where it played an important role.[1] The first intercourse law in 1790 tasked the United States with upholding the borders of Indian nations from incursion by American citizens. Although this certainly upset those citizens looking to profit from the tenuousness of Indian nations, the federal government nonetheless upheld the law as a matter of policy. The army was the force charged with this duty. Although the army's success at controlling entrance onto Native ground varied from place to place, in Andrew Jackson's American South, the spirit of white male egalitarianism that permeated society made the army's charge problematical. As more miners invaded Cherokee space, Natives expected the federal government to fulfill its obligation to the Cherokee people by helping maintain their territorial integrity. It became clear, however, that Jackson relied upon the state's actions as conducive to hastening the conclusion of his removal policy.

The contest for sovereignty between the state, the federal government, and the Cherokees intensified as waves of gold seekers made their way onto Native ground. Framing their struggle to retain possession of their remaining land as nothing short of an existential crisis, the Cherokees pled with the federal government to help maintain their national borders. As early as September 1829, John Ross urged Hugh Montgomery to immediately remove intruders. But a "difference of opinion" existed between the two men. Montgomery replied that because he did not have direct orders from the secretary of war, he was powerless to act. A month later those orders arrived from Secretary of War John H. Eaton, who gave Montgomery until the middle of December to expel the intruders.[2] Montgomery's actions were so ineffective that the Cherokees took it upon themselves to remove some intruders who had taken up residence in abandoned Cherokee property. For Ross, this was a way to ensure that any violent actions these people committed could not be "imputed to the Cherokees."[3]

Though the Cherokees had sent a powerful message when they expelled whites who had taken up residence in the Creek Strip in February 1830, their inability to contend with the overwhelming scope of the intrusion undermined their claim to nationhood. More importantly, the safety of their citizens was at stake because of the violent and lawless atmosphere created by the miners, whose gold-addled drive often collided violently with Cherokee residents attempting to go about their lives. Simply put, whites who made their way onto Cherokee land violated federal law, and the absence of a strong federal action to shore up Cherokee borders guaranteed, according to the *Cherokee Phoenix*, the continuance of "flagrant outrages committed upon our peaceable citizens and their property by intruders."[4]

The Cherokees, therefore, took a two-pronged approach when dealing with the intrusion. First, they advocated for the federal government to uphold the Intercourse Acts and expel white interlopers. Second, the National Council hired former attorney general William Wirt to bring their complaints to the federal judiciary. In July 1830, Ross reached out to the Cherokees' ally Jeremiah Evarts in the hope that he could persuade Daniel Webster to bring their case to the Supreme Court. When Webster declined, Evarts petitioned Wirt, who agreed to take up the case the following month. The legal strategy that Wirt would pursue was simple: he would petition Chief Justice John Marshall to issue an injunction against the state from enforcing the extension law.[5]

With the possibility that the Supreme Court could overrule the state's actions, Georgia's political leaders expressed a need for urgency and decisive action in dealing with the intrusion in the disputed territory, yet none was forthcoming from Washington. Likewise, the state government seemed paralyzed by the presence of so many miners. By May 1830, nearly a year after the gold rush had begun, Gilmer, anxious over the state's proper course, admitted to fellow Georgian and United States Attorney General John Berrien, "I am in doubt as to what ought to be done with the gold diggers." Perhaps not wanting the responsibility, Gilmer deferred to his counterparts in the General Assembly. "Our own Legislature must take the matter in hand," Gilmer urged. "They owe it to themselves and their constituents to rid the country of this horde of thieves and counterfeiters; and it is time something was done."[6]

Gilmer's initial hesitancy mirrored that of the General Assembly. Though the legislature had sought to solve the sovereignty issue when it passed the extension law, no one knew with any certainty if the law would survive a legal challenge. Underlying Georgia's claim to sovereignty was the desire of the state's citizens to possess the gold fields that littered the backcountry. Because the state considered itself supreme over the disputed territory, state leaders argued that intruders were trespassing upon state soil and stealing state resources. Even before the June 1 deadline for the implementation of the extension law, Gilmer declared time and again: "The state considers itself entitled to all the valuable minerals within the soil of the Cherokee territory." By not acting to prevent the miners from entering the gold region, the state "is now permitting itself to be plundered of its wealth from the strong desires of its authorities to avoid any collision with those of the general government."[7] Further, he issued a proclamation urging the intruders to depart because the state had extended its jurisdiction over Cherokee land and would not wait to "put an end to the lawless state of society which has hitherto existed among the gold diggers."[8]

However, when the Cherokee squadron ejected white Georgians from the Creek Strip in February 1830, it had the effect of not only empowering the Pony Club but also of steeling the governor's resolve and altering his course. Rightly understanding that a white backlash against the Cherokees could precipitate a crisis, Gilmer resorted to measures considered anathema to his states' rights platform: he asked for federal assistance. Writing to the commander of Fort Mitchell in Alabama, Gilmer informed the officer "that a party of white men headed by the sheriff of Carroll County is . . . entering the Indian Country for the purpose of arresting Ridge and his assistants." Gilmer cautioned the fort's commandant that such "conduct may excite the Indians & occasion unnecessary bloodshed." To stave off any violence, Gilmer informed the commander that he had already asked state civil authorities to "prevent any lawless attacks" upon the Cherokee living near Carrollton. To complement the civil authorities, Gilmer requested "a competent force" from Fort Mitchell "to prevent any further violence on the part of the Indians." In effect, Gilmer hoped the civil authorities in Carroll could restrain those Georgians looking to create mischief while federal troops acted as a restraint against potential Cherokee reprisals.[9] This was a lot to expect from the civilian officials in Carrollton, who were working closely with the Pony Club at this time, but it also demonstrates that he saw the actions of the Cherokee squadron that expelled white intruders from the Creek Strip to be a threat to the state's claim sovereignty.

As the leader of Georgia's states' rights party, Gilmer carefully tread the issue of federal intervention. Though he railed against federal interference as an assault on Georgia's rights in public, in private, the governor conceded their usefulness and succumbed to the reprieve their presence offered. Despite his certainty in the state's stance to the disputed territory, he admitted that the presence of federal troops "in the Cherokee country is very useful, in restraining the whites from trespassing upon public property, and committing violence upon the Indians. . . . The effect of their presence in restraining our citizens, ought not to be lost, if it can be helped." Gilmer was so hesitant over the use of federal troops that the day before he requested aid from Fort Mitchell, he reassured his adviser in Carroll County, Allen Fambrough, that circumstances did not require "the interposition of the military authorities."[10] Perhaps his hesitancy hid his hypocrisy, but Gilmer's vacillation over federal involvement showed the governor's conflicted feelings on the matter. Even though Georgia's leaders had, for a decade, staked out a policy asserting state sovereignty regarding Indian land that overlapped with the state's claims, Gilmer, at this uncertain hour, asked for federal aid.

Gilmer's approach divided the issue into two distinct problems. One was the state's problem, and the solution Gilmer posed had civil authorities attempting to prevent whites from crossing the border. However, once intruders crossed the border, they became a Cherokee and federal problem. Federal law stipulated that whites who crossed the frontier between the state and the Cherokee Nation had gone beyond the state's jurisdiction and therefore became subject to federal jurisdiction. At that point, expelling intruders became a Cherokee or U.S. Army responsibility. The approach Gilmer charted proved disingenuous: he argued that the state already had suzerainty over the disputed region because of the extension law, yet he wanted none of the responsibility associated with controlling the population therein. However fine a distinction Gilmer tried to draw, his proposed solution demonstrated an understanding of the political realities and underscored his desire to avoid a showdown with President Jackson over Indian policy. Instead, rather than competition, Gilmer's strategy marked the beginning of cooperation between state and federal authorities in their efforts to expunge Cherokee claims to their land.

Just as Gilmer wanted to avoid a confrontation with federal forces over the nature of the state-federal relationship regarding intrusion in the backcountry, he also desired order. So did federal officials. In February 1830, Secretary of War John H. Eaton wrote to the commander of Fort Mitchell to send troops into the Cherokee Nation. While the governor had tried to strictly limit the role of the army, it appeared that Eaton had other ideas. He dispatched the commander and his men to "advance forthwith" from their post in Alabama and prevent "any act of hostility that may be contemplated on either side." The orders implied that the military would ignore Gilmer's strategy for the time being and that the army would prevent any hostile acts that originated on either side of the border. In effect, that meant that soldiers could patrol land that unquestionably belonged to the state if they suspected violent assaults on the Cherokees were being launched from there.

Such an expansive and vague set of orders gave the commander, Brevet Major Philip Wager of the Fourth U.S. Infantry, wide latitude in dealing with the intrusion. In early March, Wager sent thirty-six men from Fort Mitchell to the gold region. Wager then issued an order to all whites living in the Creek Strip to leave but predicted trouble and feared that he and his men would have to compel them to depart. Wager's declaration required all persons digging for gold to leave the Cherokee Nation by March 25, 1830. One "gentleman recently from that section" informed a newspaper in Augusta that "the intruders have no such designs."[11]

With reports of hundreds and perhaps even thousands of intruders residing illegally within the Cherokee Nation, the small infantry detachment faced a difficult task. Fulfilling its orders became so arduous, in fact, that by December 1 nearly three hundred regular troops from both the Fourth Infantry and Second Artillery had been garrisoned at Camp Eaton (named after Secretary of War Eaton) adjacent to Scudder's Inn along the National Road near the Etowah River, to assist the initial detachment. By the following year, though, Camp Eaton had been abandoned by federal troops, and in their place resided troops from Georgia. Between March 1830 and December 1830 six companies of U.S. troops had been sent and then withdrawn into the Cherokee Nation. Though brief, their time along the Cherokee border ushered in a new period of violence in the disputed territory.

At the end of March 1830, the first federal troops made their way through Decatur in DeKalb County on their way to the gold mines to uphold Wager's commands.[12] Additional federal troops did not arrive until June. The initial detachment prepared a small encampment and patrolled the gold region. As more federal troops arrived, they scoured the countryside and expelled anyone suspected of mining for gold. In early June, they began conducting forays into the areas most densely populated with intruders. Their efforts proved somewhat effective, and by the second week of June, they had reportedly cleared out the mines in one small region. The miners, for their part, had not vacated the backcountry altogether. Many simply waited for the troops to leave the vicinity to continue their activities. Although the Cherokees remained confident that federal action would help alleviate some of the problems caused by intruders, they also knew the miners would return "unless the troops are stationed" permanently. Further irritating the Cherokees, other groups of "intruders snugly settled neatly on the whole extent of the frontier" avoided arrest and continued their work.[13]

Though Wager reported on a few early successes, efforts later that summer proved less effective: "The First of the attempts, to remove the Gold Diggers by U.S. Troops . . . has proved abortive. [The miners] are multiplying in number daily." With only thirty-six men at his disposal and a growing number of intruders, Wager's detachment of the Fourth Infantry stood little chance of making a thorough sweep through the mines or of preventing more miners from arriving. Having expelled some intruders who returned under cover of darkness, the infantry could do little more until they received reinforcements or took more forceful measures. The ineffectual efforts at clearing the mines worried some Georgia residents, who not only resented the federal presence but also wanted a chance to strike it rich. In August, a state agent reporting to the legislature affirmed the worst fears of the state's leaders: "I have no idea that either the resistance of Indians, the civil authority of this state, or the United States Troops, short of their shooting at [the intruders] and shedding blood, can or will remove the Gold diggers from the Cherokee Country, or even lessen the number, but for a few days." Without reinforcements and escalated force, Wager could do little more to prevent the intrusion.[14]

When Gilmer asked for Wager's intervention in the backcountry, he also made it clear that the state would do its part to prevent further intrusion. However, because of Gilmer's hesitancy to use force to prevent intruders from entering land claimed by the state, maintaining the integrity of the state's border proved difficult. Those in the area, however, did not express the same degree of uncertainty. In Hall County, an overzealous militia commander ordered his troops into the gold region and began arresting white and Cherokee miners. The militiamen soon found themselves in the custody of federal troops, who arrested the Georgians for violation of the Intercourse Acts. In a similar episode, Lieutenant Trenor of the U.S. Army observed a "party of armed men mounted on horses" passing his camp. When he inquired their reason for being on Cherokee land, he learned they were a local militia that was "about to make the Natives and other persons legally entitled to remain within the Indian boundaries and to enjoy the rights and privileges of a Native, desist from searching for Gold." Trenor saw this as contrary to his orders and an act of intrusion. When Colonel Hardin, the militia company's commander, declared that he was under direct orders from the deputy sheriff to uphold the extension law, they continued on their way. Trenor did not think the state troops had the authority to arrest Indians on Native ground, so he and his men chased after the Georgians. The state militiamen had already confined a few Indians when the federal troops overcame them at Pigeon Roost. The nineteen militiamen and deputy sheriff soon found themselves in the custody of U.S. troops.[15]

Trenor soon realized that he had potentially begun a problematic showdown with state forces and marched Colonel Hardin and the deputy sheriff to his superior. Even Gilmer was caught off guard when he read reports of Hall County's militia going into the gold region. His entire strategy had been predicated on using state forces to prevent more whites from intruding, not sending the militia beyond the boundary to expel intruders: "I have just received intelligence that the militia of Hall County are about to be marched into the country occupied by the Cherokees for the purpose of making prisoners of those who are engaged in digging." If that proved true, he ordered the release of any Cherokees that had been arrested. He instructed a colonel in the state militia to inform Hardin "that the governor alone," and not the deputy sheriff, "can call them into the service of the state, except in cases of sudden invasion or insurrection." When Gilmer learned that the militiamen had been released, he expressed relief: "It is desirable that the most cordial cooperation should exist between the U States and state government upon the subject of our Indian affairs."[16]

Even if the governor desired state and federal forces to work in conjunction with one another, Gilmer was in no position to dictate how federal troops interpreted orders. After June, the federal troops could more effectively stabilize the backcountry when they received reinforcements. The secretary of war dispatched a company of artillery from Charleston, one infantry company from Augusta, and another company from Fort Mitchell to assist the initial detachment in clearing the gold region of overzealous intruders. All told, this gave Wager 286 men to bring some semblance of control to the gold mines. Arriving at the beginning of September, the reinforcements allowed the previously overwhelmed command to pursue a more aggressive stance toward the intruders.[17]

In the middle of September, Wager boasted to his superiors about his success. With a larger force, the Fourth scoured the hills and hollows of the Cherokee Nation more effectively. He instructed his men "to arrest all persons suspected of being in any way engaged in the gold business," which he did not limit to mining. "Digers, buyers, pedlars, [and] shopkeepers" all faced expulsion for intruding upon Cherokee land. On his first foray with a larger force, Wager and his infantry managed to arrest more than two hundred intruders. After confining the prisoners for the evening, Wager sent two officers and fifty men to escort the intruders beyond the boundaries of the Cherokee Nation, "where they were dismissed." The remaining troops did not rest on their laurels congratulating themselves. Instead, Wager divided his forces and fanned them out across the gold region, urging them to "destroy the machinery, burn the huts & arrest all persons lurking in the neighbourhood." This action corralled another fifty intruders, who received similar treatment. Another report confirmed the actions of the troops: "The policy pursued is, to destroy the provisions, camp equipage, working utensils, or whatever else is found belonging to the diggers." Once apprehended by federal troops, the intruders "are conveyed to the nearest ferry, and put across the river free of charge."[18]

By the end of September, Wager confidently reported that the number of intruders arrested and expelled exceeded five hundred men, while those who fled before the troops could apprehend them "amount[ed] to thousands." Although the number of men expelled by federal troops could have concerned state authorities, more troubling was the makeup of intruders. At the Chestatee mines, Wager encountered a polyglot population that would have upset Georgia's order-obsessed leaders. Noting the "motley appearance" of the miners, he and his men encountered all sorts in the unorganized gold region, from "whites, Indians, halfbreeds, and negroes, boys of fourteen and old men of seventy" to more prestigious individuals like "two Colonels of Georgia Militia, two candidates for the legislature and two ministers of the Gospel, all no doubt attracted thither by the love of gold." Such a diverse lot also gave the troops difficulties. Wager warned Major General Alexander Macomb, the commander of the U.S. Army, that his men had to resort to more brutal measures to round up some of the trespassers. "It was impossible in every instance," Wager began, "to use the mildest measures" to detain the intruders, some of whom "were treated with more harshness than met my approbation," especially when the soldiers "were not under the eyes of their officers." This tended to happen when intruders ran away from the advancing soldiers, who then had to give chase. But Wager defended the harsher methods adopted by his men, especially as the intruders grew accustomed to the "gentle means hitherto employed." Once the intruders realized they faced no physical threat from the troops, they grew "so bold as to laugh at the idea of being driven off by the military and many of them became quite obstinate and impudent." The growing resistance of the intruders convinced Wager that his men needed to use more forceful measures to compel obedience. Once the troops became more physical, the intruders "commenced flying to the woods and mountains."[19]

Though perhaps some Georgians resented the presence of federal troops—especially politicians grandstanding on a states' right platform—others appeared ready to congratulate the efforts of the troops for achieving some control over the gold region. In Augusta, a traveler informed the staff of the *Chronicle* that he had seen "at least one hundred [intruders] on the road in one day who had been thus expelled from the territory, or taken the hint from this gentle specific administered to others." Hugh Montgomery was especially pleased with the results of the operation, informing Gilmer that the intruders fled the mines "Like Blackbirds before the Bayonet," when confronted by a detachment of determined soldiers. Others, however, still derided the efforts made by plodding government troops and championed the quick-footed miners: "Even if a body of troops should be sent against [the intruders], they would shelter themselves in the fastnesses of the country, and the moment the backs of the troops were turned, would be found pillaging in their rear."[20] The Cherokees complained when this occurred, claiming that the U.S. troops were more concerned with "the exercise of this *state right*" than with fulfilling their treaty obligations and protecting the Cherokees from the intruders. For the most part, the Cherokees were correct in assuming that state and federal forces had opted to cooperate. After U.S. forces had arrested the militia from Hall County, the hostility turned to cooperation. Federal troops, rather than dump intruders across the Chattahoochee River, now escorted them to county courts, where they were tried for trespassing.[21]

The gold rush that began in 1829 had picked up steam by 1830. The severe disruption it caused fundamentally altered life within Cherokee country. The intruders who lived there, however temporarily, altered the borderlands dynamic. As previously shown, borderlands violence had greatly upset Cherokee society, but it had also engendered some collaboration between legitimate white settlers and their Cherokee neighbors, who came together to punish members of the Pony Club. The vast number of intruders looking for gold rendered those community responses ineffective and necessitated a larger, better-coordinated pushback. A Cherokee delegation dispatched to Washington, D.C., at the behest of the National Council wrote to the president, confirming the salubrious effect the troops had on their country. "Besides the injury and perplexity our Citizens have to undergo," the delegates began, "we . . . respectfully solicit that orders for [the intruders'] removal may be issued, as early as practicable, and that measures be taken to guard against a future recurrence of this evil."[22]

However, the Cherokees were not keen on seeing every white person expelled from within their boundaries. Many lived on Cherokee land legally. Hugh Montgomery provided a list to federal forces that contained the names of those whites whom the Cherokees had authorized to live there. These individuals and their families were therefore immune from expulsion. The list included white men who had married into Cherokee society, licensed traders, and missionaries. The names on the list, more than fifty, demonstrate the different types of people connected to the Cherokees, and had brief comments describing the legal residents and their financial well-being. For example, Ambrose Harnage resided in Long Swamp and "has considerable property," while John Rogers, who resided in the Chattahoochee community, had "a few negroes & large stock." The list of white residents is interesting because it provides a glimpse into how this society was shaped. Of the fifty-two men listed, at least eighteen owned slaves. Others had their poverty noted, like George Freeman in the Chattahoochee neighborhood and John Rogers, who resided near Newtown. Two ministers lived in this area, and one man, John F. Wheeler, was a printer. Conspicuously absent in this list is any mention of women and children.[23]

These fifty-odd men and their families were at the heart of the intruders' complaints about the unequal treatment levied against them by the government. What is important to remember is that the state government based its claims to sovereignty on the concept of order, which rested on property ownership, land improvement, and white supremacy. The fact that whites were renting this property, which had been owned by Cherokee families who had emigrated to Arkansas Territory from the Cherokee Nation was not lost on state officials and their arguments about the superiority of their own way of life. The fact that so many Native improvements existed undermined arguments that underpinned the need for American control of Cherokee territory, namely that Native land stewardship practices were wasteful. Moreover, the state wanted in on the lucrative rental market. Gilmer was intrigued by the possibility of additional revenue streams and sent an agent, Archibald R. T. Hunter, to scour the backcountry for abandoned properties and evaluate their worth so they could be rented. Hunter understood the value of his work to the governor and knew that without his efforts "it *must* subject the State to great Loss."[24]

The increased amount of force used by the federal forces helped them clear the mines, but it also caused whites living in the borderlands to resent their presence. However successful U.S. forces may have been, their tenure in the backcountry proved fleeting for three reasons. First, even though some Georgians felt that the actions of the troops had a salubrious effect in the backcountry, others saw their actions as poisonous to the republic because it favored one group of whites over another. Because Wager only had orders to expel intruders from the backcountry, only intruders not on Montgomery's list faced the threat of expulsion. When troops came across whites legally entitled to live on Cherokee land, they took no effort to relocate them. In effect, what white Georgians complained about was that they were being punished by the federal government for breaking the law. Their criticism registered not as a cry against upholding laws but as an attack on a federal intervention that created distinctions between whites. Intruders charged the federal government with creating a false hierarchy that openly favored Cherokees and whites who had permission to reside on Cherokee land and discriminated against gold seekers from Georgia.

For Gilmer, such a show of favoritism by the federal government worried him to no end over the possibility of violent reprisal by whites living in the borderlands. His fears were not unwarranted. B. L. Goodman, a self-proclaimed "intruder on Indian land," reported to the governor the far-reaching "spirit of indignation" permeating the backcountry. As Georgia's intruders left the gold region they came across "white men of the [Cherokee] nation engaged in working the lots." Such a "hue and cry" arose from the intruders that he "feared that mobs may be got up that may cause blood shed." Goodman even reported that one militia captain had "gone so far as to call up his Company together preparatory to the removal of the Indians." An associate of Goodman's, Peter J. Williams, also wrote to Gilmer. Williams expressed considerable distress over the discrimination shown by the federal troops. After he had been ejected from Cherokee land, Williams met several miners making their way back into the gold region, convinced that they had "as much right to dig as the white men in the [Cherokee] Nation." Rather than an indiscriminate approach, Wager's men had selectively cleared the mines. Once the intruders had been driven off, the mines "were immediately taken possession of by the Indians and the whites connected with them, and . . . they were permitted to take the gold . . . without any resistance from the troops who had disposed the citizens of the state." Gilmer warned Jackson that bloodshed might soon follow because of the way Wager had gone about his task. Without redress, "there is much reason to apprehend that the Indians will be forcibly driven from the gold region, unless they are immediately prohibited from appropriating its mineral wealth." Goodman summed up the spirit of indignation expressed against any type of federal power when he declared that white intruders would continue to dig "unless stopped by the executive power of Georgia."[25]

For the intruders, however, the use of violence did not upset them as much as the discrimination they faced at the hands of federal troops. They protested the ways in which the troops categorized whites. When Wager's troops removed white Georgians but allowed other whites who had connections to the Cherokees to remain at the mines, his decisions flouted the rampant spirit of white-male egalitarianism present in Jacksonian America. By taking such an approach, the federal troops had essentially created and enforced a hierarchy among the gold miners and placed those from Georgia at the bottom. By allowing whites within the Cherokee Nation to take gold, the federal government had, through the actions of its troops, demonstrated their low opinion of Georgia's backcountry residents. Despite the fact that they had no right to the gold, once the offended intruders faced expulsion from the gold region, they cried foul. Only the protestations of "men of Influence and standing" among the intruders prevented them from having "mischief done" to the Indians.[26]

The fact that the intruders grounded their complaint against the federal government in terms of political equality is important. When voting rights had been liberalized in late 1824, the legislature used whiteness as the indicator by which equality was measured. Therefore, the actions of federal authorities to not recognize that equality showed intruders that the state and not the federal government guaranteed equality. The men who wrote to Gilmer connected their expulsion to the presence of federal troops, and at least one intruder claimed that he would only submit to the power of the state. These Georgians intruding on Cherokee land understood fully the importance of the contest for sovereignty between the state and the federal government and how they could benefit from the confusion it caused. They understood that if the state won that contest, then their idea of equality would be upheld and they, or other white Georgians, would be allowed access to the gold mines. The continuation of a federal presence meant further indignity and a lack of respect for egalitarianism. If the Cherokees remained, and as long as the federal government continued to uphold Cherokee sovereignty, the white man's chance was in danger.

Whiteness was not the only reason that the state eventually requested the withdrawal of federal troops. The legal conception that Georgia's politicians and jurists held regarding the Cherokee Nation fundamentally changed once the extension law took effect on June 1, 1830. Prior to its enactment, Georgians reluctantly saw the Cherokee Nation as somewhat autonomous, an unsustainable *imperium in imperio* that not only relied upon the federal government to enforce the various Intercourse Laws regulating commerce but also was dependent upon federal troops to maintain its borders. After June 1, a striking reformulation of the ways in which Georgians thought about Cherokee lands occurred. In a letter to the governor, Augustin S. Clayton, a judge for the western circuit based out of Athens, referred to the gold region as the "Cherokee nation" but corrected himself and termed it "the states property." Another jurist, J. W. Jackson, concurred: "The Indian title is permissive—at the permission of Georgia alone—the, soil, and the mines within it, are Georgia's." Gilmer began calling the gold region "public property" owned by the state. This shift is key, for it demonstrates that Gilmer had begun to see the relationship between the disputed territory and the state as synonymous with the federal government's relationship with its western territories. In those situations, the federal government had a great deal of authority to disburse land to settlers or corporate entities. Such a reformulation allowed state officials to act as though they had sovereignty over the territory formerly known as the Cherokee Nation, even though Cherokees still lived there. And it also demonstrated that Gilmer had started to formulate a policy about how to shape the settlement of the disputed territory.

Such a reformulation of the disputed territory in the minds of Georgia's leaders allowed them to claim another victory in the contest for sovereignty because it allowed the governor to maintain a states' right footing when dealing with the president. In other words, the extension law had done away with the government known as the Cherokee Nation. Because it no longer existed, there was no longer any need for the federal government to continue the enforcement of the Intercourse Laws. "The government of the U States had no authority to enforce the non-intercourse laws," Gilmer informed Jackson, even though he had asked federal troops to do precisely that.[27] Therefore, Gilmer used this reformulation when it served the interests of the state and his party but resorted to a more measured tone when dealing with his subordinates. When several militia units wanted to muster for the purposes of going into the gold region and arresting Cherokees who were mining for gold, Gilmer urged his officers to follow the law: "It is not considered a criminal offence for the Indians to dig for gold in the lands occupied by them and that they are not liable to an arrest." In this respect, Gilmer proved something of a realist. He understood that the Cherokees still occupied this land, and he did not want to unleash the local militia without cause.[28]

Understandably, the Cherokees fretted over the repercussions of this rhetorical shift. Elias Boudinot warned the readers of the *Phoenix* in the final May issue of 1830: "Before the next number of our paper shall be issued . . . the extension of [the state's] assured jurisdiction over the Cherokees and the execution of her laws touching the Indians, will have arrived." Once this occurred, the Cherokees understood how difficult their lives would become: "One thing we know, there will be suffering. The Cherokees will be privy to the cupidity of white men—every indignity and every oppression will be heaped upon them. . . . [H]ow will it be when full license is given to the oppressors?"[29]

Initially, not much happened. Perhaps the intruders felt emboldened and were more impudent, and the sheriff of Carroll County could have felt compelled to intercede on the behalf of the intruders more frequently, but no documentary evidence exists stating this was the case in the weeks after the extension law went into effect. Federal troops that still patrolled the region kept widespread intrusion at bay, and the Cherokees still had some protection from the actions of state actors. The real threat came from the General Assembly in Milledgeville. The state legislature had few qualms about the nature of state authority in the "public property." In the winter of 1830 the legislators exercised their belief when they enacted the supremacy law, which explicitly criminalized the Cherokee National Council and prohibited it from meeting and executing the laws of the Nation. The terms of the supremacy law forbid any person who had been authorized by the Cherokee government to collect tolls at turnpike gates and ferries. Moreover, these attacks on Cherokee institutions further undermined their national sovereignty because it could interfere with the Cherokees' ability to control who entered their land. By criminalizing the acts of John Ross and the rest of the Cherokee state, Georgia declared its sovereignty over Cherokee lands and the supremacy of its own laws. The legislature went further with the supremacy act by prohibiting all whites from residing in the backcountry unless they had sworn an oath to "support and defend the Constitution and laws of the State of Georgia" or were employed by the United States government. The law also permitted the governor to appoint an agent who could rent out to whites lots that had belonged to Cherokee families who had previously emigrated to Arkansas. Though it did not go into effect until March 1, 1831, the law precipitated a constitutional showdown.[30]

The supremacy law also limited the number of intruders residing in the backcountry, and for the first time, the state formulated the proper deportment it expected from whites who received residency permits. Not only did potential residents have to swear to uphold the state constitution, but they also had to promise to "uprightly demean" themselves "as a citizen." By explicitly stating the type of behavior the state expected from its citizens, it implied that those who behaved poorly could not enjoy the benefits of citizenship. Therefore, the "disorderly sort" and other troublemakers residing in the backcountry were not entitled to the benefits enjoyed by white citizens. Any violators of the law's provisions would stand trial for a high misdemeanor and, if convicted, would "undergo an imprisonment in the Penitentiary at hard labor for the space of four years." In effect, the state had given itself leeway to act against miners in its efforts to provide order in the gold region.[31]

Perhaps intruders believed that the state would never attempt to limit its own citizens in the disputed territory, and therefore state authority was preferable to federal intervention. By laying out explicitly what the law expected of its white citizens, though, the supremacy law gave the state a great amount of authority to create the kind of community that order-obsessed leaders envisioned. The legislature made it clear that it was not interested in creating a hierarchy that divided the white population by class or its connection to the Cherokees. Instead, it sought to create a community whose members demonstrated they deserved the wealth in the gold mines by their ability to conform to the law and to the expectations of citizenship. The supremacy act did more than just lay out plans for the white backcountry community. It also made explicit the type of hierarchy that white Georgians expected by criminalizing the actions of the Cherokee Nation. In one fell swoop, the legislature claimed victory in the contest over sovereignty, it criminalized the actions of the Cherokee Nation, and it provided a way for the governor to create a community that abided by the law and protected whiteness.

The supremacy law put into practice what the intruders in the borderlands had requested: state authority that could protect and even privilege whiteness. Such a brash expression of state sovereignty, in spite of its dubious constitutionality, compelled Gilmer to prepare the way for the state to take the lead in the disputed territory. To hammer home the point that it was now the supreme authority in the region, the state announced its more forceful articulation of state sovereignty by requesting the withdrawal of federal forces. Gilmer knew that if Jackson complied, it would signal that the state had assumed suzerainty over Cherokee land, its inhabitants, and, more importantly, the implementation of the Intercourse Laws. In a letter to the president, Gilmer laid bare his frustrations with the current state of affairs. Having sent a proclamation into the backcountry preventing anyone, white or Cherokee, from taking gold from the "ungranted lands," Gilmer complained: "Before these proclamations reached the part of the state occupied by the Cherokee, the U. States troops had driven from it all persons except Indian occupants." Though his objection appeared to disapprove of the army's efficiency, he instead was protesting Jackson's "exercise of power," which he did not find constitutional, especially in the wake of the extension law.[32] A scant five months after he had personally requested the assistance from Wager's troops from Fort Mitchell, Gilmer now informed the president that such an action went against his constitutional scruples. By the end of October, when U.S troops had largely cleared the mines of intruders, Gilmer wrote to Jackson formally asking for a withdrawal of federal troops, arguing that with the implementation of the extension law, the federal government could no longer enforce the Intercourse Act within the state's "rights of jurisdiction." Though Gilmer recognized that Jackson had sent the troops for "the preservation of peace," a gesture he "truly appreciated," he still had to ask the president to "withdraw the troops as soon as it can be convenient." Jackson did not tarry, and by the following month, November 1830, the troops had been sent to their winter quarters.[33]

The final reason for the hasty withdrawal of the federal troops came from Old Hickory himself. At different times throughout his presidency he advocated the rights of the states, though Jackson also expressed an ardent nationalism. He also harbored many of Jefferson's sentiments regarding the expansion of the yeoman's frontier. In Georgia, he had the chance to put both beliefs into practice. In his annual message to Congress in December 1829, Jackson asked Congress to appropriate funds to subsidize the removal process. Though it created a political imbroglio, especially among northern evangelicals and abolitionists, who rejected the bill's inhumanity, the following year Congress set about drafting legislation that would allow Natives living east of the Mississippi to "voluntarily" exchange their land for a like amount of acreage in territory beyond the river. By the end of May 1830, Congress had finalized the legislation and, on the last day of the month, Jackson signed the Indian Removal Bill into law. The bill also appropriated a half million dollars for the express purpose of removal.[34]

Though the Indian Removal Act strengthened the federal government's hand when it came to Indian policy, it did not necessarily mean that Jackson would continue to use the army to uphold Native boundaries until removal occurred. Thus, when Gilmer contacted the president and requested the withdrawal of federal troops in October 1830, he agreed. At the president's behest, Secretary of War Eaton ordered those forces stationed in the Cherokee Nation to strike from Camp Eaton and enter winter quarters, and each company returned to its normal base of operations. Having them return to their winter quarters was a clever and open-ended way for Jackson's administration to appease the Georgians. The troops were leaving, much to the chagrin of the Cherokees, but because they had not been ordered off permanently, it left open the possibility that they might return in the spring. Gilmer claimed credit for the withdrawal of the troops and harbored no illusions about the possibility of their return. He understood that the federal government, under Jackson, would no longer enforce the Intercourse Acts within the state's limits. In effect, Jackson had taken Cherokee affairs out of the hands of the Office of Indian Affairs and put them into those of Georgia's elected officials. Even though Jackson had consented to the troop withdrawal, he had not left his administration completely helpless to enforce order or prevent intrusion. As late as 1835, small numbers of federal troops from Fort Mitchell still patrolled the Cherokee border. The governor of Georgia could request their aid or compel them to leave. Lewis Cass, the secretary of war, wrote to Governor Wilson Lumpkin that year explaining this relationship: "The commanding officer of the United States troops, now at Fort Mitchell, has been directed to march into the Cherokee country, whenever you inform [him] that his services are no longer required where he is now." Further, Lumpkin could withdraw those forces "by communicating [his] views to the Commanding Officer."[35]

To prepare for removal, Jackson authorized the Office of Indian Affairs to begin conducting "voluntary removal." Though Cherokees had begun moving to Arkansas in 1794, it was not until the ratification of the Treaty of 1819 that Indian agents began to officially encourage and pay for voluntary removal to that territory. Even then, the Cherokees hesitated to enroll. In 1830 about five hundred Cherokees arrived in Arkansas, many of them making part of the journey in their own keelboats. By the end of 1834, federal enrolling agent Benjamin F. Currey had convinced more than one thousand Cherokees to take federal assistance and leave for Arkansas while another two hundred did so at their own expense.[36] Still, these numbers were small and the amount of cajoling it took to convince Cherokees to leave their homes made the task slow and tedious. It became apparent that it would take an incredible amount of coercion to make Cherokees remove voluntarily.

It was convenient for Jackson, then, to let the state have its way in the disputed territory. Rather than commit federal troops, an expensive proposition for the spendthrift president, he would allow Georgia to bear the expense and the political fallout. By October 1830, the federal government's interposition between the intruders and the Cherokees had come to an end. Though the switch in policy seemed to originate from Gilmer, the passage of the Indian Removal Act and Cherokee resistance saw President Jackson concede to the state's demands. That the state and federal government were now working in tandem to expedite the removal process in Georgia came as a shock to the Cherokees, who looked to the courts for relief.

William Wirt, the attorney whom the National Council had hired in the summer of 1830, brought two cases before the Supreme Court, *Cherokee Nation v. Georgia* and *Worcester v. Georgia*. In *Cherokee Nation*, Wirt wanted the Supreme Court to issue an injunction against Georgia's extension law to prevent the state from asserting state law in Cherokee territory on the basis that the Cherokee Nation, through numerous treaties with the federal government, was a sovereign, foreign power. Chief Justice John Marshall and most of the court's seven justices disagreed. Rather than the Cherokee Nation being an independent state, Marshall declared in his famous formulation, the relationship between the Cherokees to the United States "resembles that of a ward to his guardian." Through his decision, Marshall was attempting to delineate the nature of the federal-Indian relationship as it pertained to the Cherokees, and while he was willing to deny them their injunction, he readily admitted that the federal government, and not the states, controlled Indian policy.

In spite of the court's insistence that Georgia had no right to extend its jurisdiction over the Cherokee Nation, the court was powerless to prevent it because the court did not have jurisdiction in the matter. According to Marshall, the bill of injunction filed by Wirt would have required the court "to control the legislature of Georgia, and to restrain the exertion of its physical force." Such an act, according to Marshall, lay outside of the court's purview and would have constituted a gross misapplication of the court's power: "The propriety of such an interposition . . . savours too much of the exercise of political power to be within the proper provinces of the judicial department."[37]

The 1831 *Cherokee Nation v. Georgia* decision seemed to have been a major setback for John Ross and his government. But Marshall's ruling implied support for another suit that would fall within the court's jurisdiction. It did not take John Ross and William Wirt long to find such a case.

* * *

As the withdrawal of the federal contingent from the disputed territory commenced, Jackson moved to make the federal government less visible in its dealings with Cherokees. By doing so, he had opened a path for the state to commence with a more violent ordering of the backcountry that also allowed him the opportunity to advocate for states' rights. Jacob Scudder, the owner of the land where Major Philip Wager's small contingent had built their barracks, received word from the governor that the state had requisitioned the use of Scudder's property to house a newly created state military force. "The Legislature now in session has authorized me to raise a Guard for the protection of the gold mines, and enforcing the laws in the Cherokee territory," Gilmer wrote Scudder. Noting that the "quarters erected by the U.S. Troops have been placed in your charge," Gilmer apprised Scudder that the new Guard would garrison at the fort on his property.[38] With the creation of the Guard, the state would do what the federal government would not: use violence to convince the Cherokees to leave so it could bring the white man's chance into being.

5 / The Georgia Guard and the Politics of Order, 1830–1832

In the middle of January 1831, a column of forty men trekked north along the federal road and stopped where it intersected with the Upper Alabama Road near the Etowah River. They had reached their post, an inn owned by a War of 1812 veteran named Jacob Scudder whose considerable ambitions had led him to construct an inn on a small creek that emptied into the nearby river. His inn had been inhabited by members of the Fourth U.S. Infantry. Those men had built a small barracks while they set about expelling whites who had been mining for gold from Cherokee country. Those quarters had been abandoned in 1830, when President Andrew Jackson released those troops to their winter quarters. In their place came the small contingent of armed men dispatched by the governor called the Georgia Guard. When they arrived at their post, they rechristened the barracks Camp Gilmer. At their new post, the Guard found a small blacksmith shop, stables, and other outbuildings. The barracks had eight small rooms with one ramshackle fireplace, and half of the rooms had dirt floors, though Scudder had the floorboards in his possession.[1] From Scudder's Inn, the Guard proceeded to go about its task of "protecting the gold mines," which involved confronting white intruders and intimidating Cherokees. The Guard's task of regulating the social environs of the gold mines made it the central actor not only in the latest Supreme Court cases but also in the next gubernatorial election in the fall of 1831.

When it mustered into service in January 1831, the Guard consisted of a scant forty men. Few thought that so few men could cause so many problems. To demonstrate caution and to show the voters of Georgia that he spent their money wisely, Governor George R. Gilmer had even reduced the size of the force by a third, down from the sixty men that the legislature authorized. Even though he desired to bring order into the disputed territory so that white settlers could be granted property, his decision to unleash the Guard had far-ranging consequences that ultimately doomed his reelection bid. The Guard's actions, like those of the federal troops, became political flashpoints once it became known that they, too, targeted whites.

In addition to the actions of the Guard, the election turned on two additional proposals that Gilmer made. Rather than sticking to the tried-and-true method of a land lottery for any land that contained gold, Gilmer instead proposed an expansive set of internal improvements that he would fund through state ownership of the gold mines. Such a proposal ran afoul of the state's usual method of land distribution and went against the governor's own insistence on private property ownership. In addition, Gilmer countered one of the sections of the extension law that made it illegal for Cherokees to testify against white citizens in state courts. Gilmer, who desired order above all else, challenged that idea and therefore the entire notion of white superiority. State-sponsored violence, Indian testimony, and state ownership of gold mines doomed his reelection bid. The Clark opposition charged him with attempting to limit the "white man's chance," and they fought to keep the gold mines open for a democratic distribution. Whiteness and how the state would best protect and expand the legal prerogatives enjoyed by the state's white citizens proved central to the outcome of the gubernatorial election of 1831. When voters went to the polls in November 1831, the returns show that voters could no longer trust Gilmer or the Troup faction to protect whiteness in the disputed territory.

The problems wrought by the Guard began soon after their arrival at Scudder's Inn. Only a few days after they mustered for duty, John W. A. Sanford, the Guard's commander, dispatched Charles H. Nelson and a squadron of fourteen guardsmen on a march to the upper mines "with instructions to destroy every species of gold-digging machinery, to raze every camp or building heretofore occupied by the miners, and to drive from the Nation all that class of people" still intruding on the gold mines. On January 17, Nelson and his small detachment returned to the newly minted Camp Gilmer and brought with them troubling news. In his report to the governor, Sanford applauded Nelson for the completion of his march but, regrettably, had to add that Nelson and his men ran afoul of "difficulties of the most serious and embarrassing nature."[2] These embarrassments haunted Gilmer and ultimately doomed his political program and his vision for an orderly settlement of the disputed territory.

In the autumn of 1830, a state militiaman and self-proclaimed "humble individual" who only wanted to serve the "Common good" wrote to Gilmer hoping to convince the governor that the gold mines needed a military force to secure their treasures. "Till Some Troops under [Georgia's] own authority are put out, for the individual purpose of Surpressing all Whether Indian or White man," the plunder of the mines would continue. The letter's author, Charles H. Nelson, had no compunction about stating that the presence of the federal troops served as more of a "protection than a detriment" to the intruders because those troops had no knowledge of the backcountry. The "hordes of Lawless white[s] that infested the Territory," according to Nelson, needed only to "find a place of Some Secrecy (and they are abundant) to pursue their depredations." Employing troops from Georgia in the gold region would fill any gold seekers with "greater terror" and compel them to "respect that authority for which they now feel so much Contempt." Nelson argued that a force of two hundred mounted men would suffice. Gilmer heeded much of Nelson's advice and even named Nelson a colonel and subcommander of the newly minted Georgia Guard, a decision he would later regret.[3]

With the passage of the supremacy law in December 1830, the state legislature and the governor announced their intention of using state-sponsored force to bring into being their version of a well-ordered society. The state's new forceful implementation of its sovereignty did more than extend jurisdiction into the backcountry. The law also sought ways to outlaw the Cherokee government and regulate the people living in the gold region. The supremacy law proclaimed it unlawful for anyone "under pretext of authority from the Cherokee tribe" to convene "for the purpose of making laws, orders, or regulations." The law further empowered the state to eject all whites residing in the gold region unless they swore an oath upholding the state's constitution and acquired a residency permit from a state agent. This provision did not extend to any white women or white men under the age of twenty-one (legal minors), federal agents or employees, or those who rented Cherokee land legally from the state. Those arrested for disobeying the law faced a stint in the state penitentiary doing hard labor.[4] In the battle over sovereignty in

George Rockingham Gilmer, governor of Georgia, 1829–31 and 1837–39. A member of the Troup faction, Gilmer articulated a strong states' rights position that encouraged the use of the Georgia Guard to use violence as a way to expedite Cherokee Removal. George Mandus, *Portrait of George Rockingham Gilmer* (1960). Courtesy of the Georgia Capitol Museum, Object ID 1992.23.0027 what Georgia considered its land, Gilmer had confidently seized control by criminalizing the efforts of the Cherokee National Council.

To enforce the law, the legislature empowered Gilmer to create a military unit that could enforce the law's provisions. Gilmer had previously declared that he wanted civil law to create order, but the sheer scope of the intrusion made that desire unrealistic. With the legislature's cooperation, the supremacy law relied upon force first and civil authority second. To enforce the supremacy law, the legislature requisitioned twenty thousand dollars for a sixty-man militia unit called the Georgia Guard "for the protection of the gold mines," a catch-all phrase that furnished the Guard with expansive police powers, including the regulation of white intruders until civil authority could provide permanent order. The final version of the legislation took effect on March 1, 1831.[5]

Gilmer wasted little time and began recruitment efforts soon after the bill's passage. He selected Charles H. Nelson as the Guard's second-in-command but asked the more even-tempered John W. A. Sanford to command. In two weeks, the roster had been filled, and the forty recruits headed north to establish their headquarters. Of those men who volunteered, nineteen came from areas that did not adjoin the Cherokee Nation. Including Sanford, three men came from Milledgeville and the rest of Baldwin County, while Wilkes County, the home of Charles H. Nelson, supplied six additional recruits. Clarke and Jackson Counties sent a total of ten men to the Guard. The majority of the men serving came from border counties. Sixteen men enlisted from Hall County, another five from DeKalb and Gwinnett. That most of the men who joined the Guard lived in close proximity to the Cherokees should not be surprising.[6]

In a letter to the governor commenting on recruitment, Sanford raved about the physical and moral qualities of his men. He beamed when discussing the constitution of his troopers, especially their "hale and athletic" countenances. In addition to their physical appearances, each potential recruit had to supply testimonials of their good character. Most importantly to Sanford, each of the men had an abundance of "that most essential requisite of the soldier—*courage*." The commander of the Guard also had the benefit of choice when he selected his soldiers. Noting that a flood of recruits offered their services "with astonishing eagerness," he had the luxury of choosing only those who exhibited the "best character." By prizing character, Sanford demonstrated a great deal of discretion when selecting his outfit. He also shared many of the governor's fears about the compatibility of a military unit and a democratic society. Sanford and Gilmer could both point to the upstanding character that distinguished the guardsmen and the care with which they were chosen. In this way, the Guard, from the outset, was rhetorically distinct from the intruders, who had been characterized as degenerate and near-savage white men.[7] Those men in the Guard would need character in abundance when they began their activities. The men who joined had to have known that their assignment would prove difficult and dangerous. And their first foray into the disputed territory demonstrated just how unpredictable their time would be. The difficulties of a "serious and embarrassing nature" that Nelson and his small detachment got themselves into set the tone for the Guard's tenure in the disputed territory.

Leaving from their barracks at Scudder's Inn, the small group under Nelson's command crossed the Chestatee River at a place called Leather's Ford and made their way into the gold region. They soon arrested eleven white men engaged in mining. As they made their way back to Camp Gilmer with their prisoners, they met unexpected resistance. The "friends and former associates" of the arrested men "resolved upon their release" and ambushed the Guard as it headed back across the Chestatee. Sanford's account of the event at this point became confused. He first learned that the attack happened by surprise, and Nelson only became informed of the melee when "the Sergeant commanding the rear, brought intelligence of it being attacked." In the same letter, Sanford made it appear that rather than a surprise attack, the guardsmen passed through a gauntlet of miners, fifty or sixty in number, who had placed obstacles in the river. Ordering his troops not to provoke the miners, Nelson advised his men to maintain "a cautious and circumspect deportment."[8]

Maintaining composure proved difficult for the guardsmen, especially in light of the actions of one particular miner. Called "the vilest of the vile" by Sanford, this nameless miner raised the ire of the Guard when he "professed the utmost contempt for Georgia, her laws, her officers, [and] denied her jurisdiction over this territory." Such an affront to the state's sovereignty angered one of the guardsmen, who moved to silence the intruder. Sensing the attack, the assembly of miners, "as if by preconcert," began hurling rocks, sticks, and "every species of missile" they could find at the Guard. In the ensuing fight, the man who had verbally abused the state received several bayonet wounds. Sanford expressed remorse when he learned that the wounds were not mortal and the intruder "was not likely to experience the fate so richly merited by his infamous life." Perhaps the intruders began the encounter at

Leather's Ford and hoped that their show of communal solidarity would intimidate the Guard, but they certainly came out on the losing side.⁹

The intruders, after suffering at the hands of the Guard, sought the protection of civil authorities. Soon after the fight at Leather's Ford, the miners swore affidavits before a judge, the first step in filing charges against individual guardsmen for their actions in the brawl. The miners' version of events differed greatly from that in Sanford's official report. Mark Castleberry, an intruder involved in the scuffle, in a statement made to a Hall County justice of the peace, offered an alternate interpretation of events at Leather's Ford. The Guard, in Castleberry's account, began hostilities when another intruder, Ligon, the so-called "vilest of the vile," asked Sergeant Henderson about the fate of the prisoners being hauled off. Henderson and the men under his direct command had lingered behind their comrades to "get their Canteens or Flasks filled with spirits" and did not want to answer the man's question. When one of the guardsmen replied that Ligon could not ask questions, the intruder replied testily that "he would speak when he pleased." To quiet the dissent brewing among the miners, Henderson threatened to "blow a load thro' Ligon" and presented his cocked musket, aimed squarely at Ligon's head. Ligon backed down, claiming that he did not have a musket with which to defend himself; Henderson rode off to find his superior officer. When Henderson, Nelson, and the rest of the Guard returned, the miners had crowded together while the guardsmen searched for Ligon. In his stead, they found a man who resembled him, and Nelson and the rest of the troops "thrust him with their Bayonets severly three or four times and ordered the old man to surrender." When he refused, the wounded old man, Taylor, was stabbed again at Nelson's order. Despite his wounds, Taylor turned and ran toward the safety of the crowd of intruders, so Nelson commanded his men to fire. One of the musket balls struck Taylor, who cried out that he "was a Dead man." However, once the Guard left, the intruders found that Taylor had survived the Guard's "butchering."¹⁰

The two different versions of the violent encounter at Leather's Ford highlight the fraught and violent encounters that occurred in the disputed territory. That the two different groups had two very different explanations for the violence that occurred should not be surprising. Sanford had a reason to make it appear that the miners had premeditated their attack against the Guard; the miners had sufficient motive to claim that they had been the innocent victims of the Guard's abuse. Although the truth of what precipitated the violent encounter probably lies somewhere between the two stories, it seems that people in Hall County did not believe the Guard's story. A man named Robert Mitchell wrote to the governor imploring him to believe the citizens rather than the Guard. Mitchell informed the governor that "a great many of the most respectable men in this county who think you should be fully apprized of the conduct of the Guard... toward the people of this county" supported the information presented to the governor in the affidavit. Gilmer was having none of it. In his reply to Mitchell, the governor urged him to drop any type of investigation into the incident and instead to encourage the people of Hall County to unite in the goal of protecting the gold mines.[11]

The violence wrought by the Guard appeared to bother the guardsmen little. Rather than retaliations against their patrols, the stern actions taken at the ford brought a reprieve to Sanford and his men. "Its good effects have already been experienced, for I understand that no less than seventy of these desperate and abandoned wretches have suddenly disappeared from their former haunts," he informed the governor. In spite of the apparent retreat Sanford witnessed, the Guard's duty became more difficult because a "hue and cry against the guard for its conduct" had spread "far and wide thru the country."[12] Other Georgians agreed and warned Sanford regarding the Guard's precarious situation. In Hall County, Hines Holt Jr. apprised Sanford of the "hostile feeling twords the guard in this County" but urged Sanford to continue his firm stance toward the intruders: "The most rigid & uncompromising course will be the most speedy & effectual method of allaying it." More appalling to Holt, however, was the way in which the Guard's actions led backcountry residents to disparage "the Legislature who passed the Laws, the Gov. who sanctioned them, and the Guard who were endeavoring to support them most outrageously vilified & abused." This critique, which had echoes of the statement Ligon had directed at the Guard at Leather's Ford, directly implicated the legislature and the governor in the violence being directed at those men.[13]

The men who had been attacked did not confine their assault on the Guard to the ford or to courts of law. They also went to the press. The state's press, like so much of the newspaper business in the 1830s, widely circulated their issues and did not hide their partisan leanings. The *Georgia Journal*, in particular, was the most prominent paper because it was printed in Milledgeville, the state capital, but it was also friendly to Gilmer and the Troup faction. It only printed the official version of events that Sanford described to Gilmer. The *Georgia Athenian*, on the other hand, proved more than willing to print alternative versions of the event, which were eventually picked up by the *Cherokee Phoenix*. In these accounts Ligon was branded "a man of worth and respectability" who was dealt with in a very "abrupt and uncourteous manner." Moreover, this report claimed that perhaps only fifteen or twenty men were present at the ford, not the sixty Sanford suggested. Last, the intruders who penned the article, including Robert Ligon, saw no weapons and wrote that it was the hostility of the Guard that provoked violence. The abuse directed at the intruders did not end there. The prisoners were made to ford the river in late January, and the cold had a visible effect. Another of the sergeants of the Guard crossed the Etowah River and struck a man with the butt of his musket when that man would not open a gate for him.[14]

Sanford began to express concern regarding the "extreme repugnance" that whites in the disputed territory expressed toward the actions of the Guard and warned the governor of the likelihood of a violent outburst by the intruders: "Nothing, in my opinion, prevents its violent manifestation, but the paucity of their number." In a letter to all of the state militia commanders in the border counties, Gilmer encouraged the formation of militia companies to aid the Guard with the expulsion of "vicious & refractory white men" residing with the Cherokees, who, because of their poor character, would no doubt resort to violence when confronted by the Guard. Gilmer even wrote to Nelson to help sustain his commander in the face of withering criticism. In periods of "high party excitement," Gilmer warned, "all public men, especially if their stations are elevated on employment connected with important interests," should expect "abuse & calumny." In spite of the public criticism, men of their standing "should be wanting of patriotism if such treatment drove us from serving our country." By supporting Nelson, Gilmer acknowledged the commander's usefulness despite his violent tactics.[15]

The Guard's presence in the backcountry, designed to put the region on the road to orderly settlement, instead further destabilized an already precarious region. As Gilmer suggested, it also created an increased amount of partisan conflict. As the Clark faction's opposition to the Guard continued to mount, Sanford and Gilmer struggled to salvage its reputation, and their own. Sanford reassured Gilmer that he and his men would continue to carry out their charge despite "popular clamor or vulgar misrepresentation." As the weather in January and February worsened, Sanford could only take solace in the fact that the Guard had achieved some measure of support in the backcountry. The Guard's conduct "as far as it has been rightly understood or properly explained has received the *decided* approbation of the most *orderly* and *respectable* portion of the community." Sanford's meaning was unmistakable. The "orderly" portion of the white backcountry population who observed the law and resisted the temptation of digging for gold appreciated and supported the actions of the Guard. Those who sought to break the law spread false information regarding the Guard's activities and therefore deserved prosecution under the supremacy law. Only when the disorderly population respected the law and those who enforced it would the disputed territory know order.[16]

Sanford's attempt to coerce respect for the law became increasingly difficult because of poor weather and a cadre of intruders who had no intention of being denied quick riches. After the incident at Leather's Ford, the Guard continued to patrol the gold region. Through March, however, it had little success apprehending intruders. Much of its frustration stemmed from the wariness of the miners. They had become astute observers of the Guard's movements, and their network allowed for rapid communication to warn prospectors of the Guard's approach. In one expedition in early March, Nelson and a squad of guardsmen had difficulty rounding up any intruders because of the "vigilance of their spies, who watched our movements and conveyed intelligence of them to the gold-diggers." Even under cover of darkness, the intruders remained vigilant of the Guard's whereabouts and managed to help one large gathering of intruders slip through Nelson's trap. When they arrived in the intruders' camp, the troopers found only emptiness and silence: "Not a light to be seen—not a mattock to be heard—nor a human being to be found," lamented Sanford.[17]

The class dimensions of Gilmer's stance are difficult to ignore. Gilmer insisted on getting the wrong sort of people out of the disputed territory so he could replace them with the right sorts of people. Again, he turned to the Georgia Guard to do this by renting out fractional lots to prospective settlers. This program began in December 1830, when the legislature passed a law instructing the governor to prepare for a land lottery that would distribute Cherokee lands in the disputed territory. Before the state held the lottery, the commander of the Guard rented out fractional lots in the Cherokee Nation to white citizens. The commander, John W. A. Sanford, not only ensured that his command had sufficient supplies and carried out its orders regarding clearing the gold mines, but he also had the responsibility of renting out fractional lots in the newly formed border counties and on land vacated by Cherokee families who had "voluntarily" emigrated to Arkansas. Many of Sanford's duties, in fact, revolved around renting land and keeping the peace between Cherokee residents and their new neighbors. "I have, as Agent on part of Georgia been directed by His Excellency the Governor to rent certain Creek and Cherokee improvements laying within its limits," Sanford wrote to the Cherokee agent Hugh Montgomery. Only three months into his tenure as commander of the Guard, Sanford had netted $7,570 for the state by renting out fractional plots. By the end of 1831, more than 208 separate families moved into the backcountry. The land was rented only to men, though 134 had wives and they brought with them 610 children. In all, more than 950 Georgians rented land from the state and moved into the disputed territory. While the vast majority farmed, others made their livings as merchants, blacksmiths, mechanics, millers, wheelwrights, and one man as a shoemaker.[18]

The people who rented land from the Guard exemplified the type of settlers that state leaders wanted to reside in the disputed territory. To fill the land with more orderly settlers, the legislature passed the 1830 lottery act, which was designed to strengthen the agrarian nature of the state, which would, most Georgians agreed, create order. The majority of the 1830 lottery legislation dealt with the qualifications for surveyors, the oaths they would take, and the penalties imposed on those who would attempt to stop them. Section 13 stipulated the number of draws open to each state resident and added additional chances for Revolutionary War veterans, widows with dependent children, and orphans. Although the legislation was inclusive, it also included stipulations that prevented members of the "disorderly" population from enjoying the promises of Cherokee land, including whites who had "either directly or indirectly" aided "a certain horde of Thieves known as the Pony Club," or individuals who "may have dug gold, silver, or any other metal," or those who hired other people to do so. It also included Cherokees as members of the disorderly community. To ensure that no Cherokee could retain their land, the legislation stipulated: "That no person or persons who are residents on any part of the lands contemplated to be disposed of by this act, shall be entitled to a draw or draws under any of its provisions."[19] The lottery legislation grouped disorderly whites and Cherokees into the same undesirable category: neither were fit to bring about order and were therefore excluded from receiving land from the state.

Of course, the land Sanford rented out to settlers was still claimed by the Cherokee Nation. The fact that Sanford specifically mentioned that he rented out Cherokee improvements again undermined the state's claims regarding Cherokees and their agricultural practices. For years, both U.S. and state leaders had encouraged removal because of the

Indians' "wastefulness" regarding land use. Now the state profited handsomely from improvements made by Cherokee farmers and rented out to whites. Not satisfied with Chief Justice Marshall's ruling in *Cherokee Nation v. Georgia* regarding the status of the Cherokee as a "domestic, dependent nation," the states' rights jurist Augustin S. Clayton sought to strengthen the governor's legal position when it came to appropriating Cherokee land. Proclaiming that the Cherokees had no right to the land because of their inefficient agricultural practices, he urged the governor to consider the relationship between the state and the Cherokees as that between "Landlord & tenant." Because the Cherokees could not claim fee simple ownership of the land and because their "*ordinary* method of cultivating lands" proved wasteful, they could not claim the land according to the law of nations. So on the one hand, Georgians felt entitled to Cherokee land because Americans practiced a superior form of agriculture, but the state rented out Cherokee improvements, including plowed fields, corn cribs, homesteads, orchards, and fenced pastures to settlers who would benefit from the industriousness of the supposedly inferior Native farmers.[20]

The model of "landlord and tenant" put into place by Clayton allowed the Guard to evict those who were not paying rent to the state—namely, the Cherokees—but also intruders. When the weather turned warmer, a portion of the Guard, this time led by a different officer, Sergeant Jacob R. Brooks, resumed operations to expel the enemies of order. Once again, the Guard sought to expel those of poor character and explicitly targeted the remnants of the Pony Club. Vowing to "expel the Pony Club from the Cherokee Territory," Brooks announced publicly his intention to remove white families who could not claim "GOOD CHARACTER" and vowed to protect the Cherokees "from the aggressions of Bad White men." The *Cherokee Phoenix* soon attacked Brooks's position. After all, the paper claimed, the Guard had hand-picked those who could rent the improvements and intimated that the state was responsible for the longevity of the Club: "Has the Club been rooted out of the territory? Have they not rather been introduced into the nation?"[21]

The Guard sought out not only intruders and the Pony Club but also any other whites who violated state law. In August, the governor received a report that made him think about whites from out of state. "Since the state has extended her jurisdiction," warned one concerned backcountry resident, "the violation of her Commercial laws is a matter of every day occurrence." The supremacy law required all merchants who wished to trade within the Cherokee Nation to acquire a permit. The nominal licensing fee had more to do with Georgia's insistence on sovereignty—and therefore its own enforcement of the Intercourse Laws—and less to do with making money from the fees. Savvy merchants from Tennessee realized their advantage and swung into action. An assortment of "peddlars, waggoners, citizens . . . from Tenn[essee] are constantly in motion violating the laws of Georgia" because they crossed the border, set up their shops in Georgia without acquiring the proper permits, and sold "all manner of produce and Merchantdz foreign and domestic . . . they durst not sell at home without paying a high price for license." To cut down on illicit trade, Sanford had to spread his forces thin, so he had less control over his men and the officers. By the end of the month, his men had commandeered two smaller outposts in addition to their headquarters, including one that had previously served as a station for missionaries. Hoping that less centralization would help his men better patrol the "circumjacent & intermediate country," Sanford soon came to see the distance between him and his men as a detriment because he lacked direct control over their actions. The new strategy proved effective. A week later, Sanford reported to Gilmer on the Guard's successes; since their arrival at its new posts, the Guard had entirely ceased trespass upon the mines.[22]

From January to August 1831, the Georgia Guard had set out to control the social world of backcountry whites. Having clashed with miners at Leather's Ford, chased reported intruders all across the disputed territory, rented out lots to settlers from Georgia, and expelled merchants from Indian country, the Guard had effectively done its duty. However, white intruders did not constitute the Guard's sole set of responsibilities. Sanford and his men increasingly came into contact with Cherokees, especially as they ramped up their efforts to install white citizens on fractional lots. According to an early summer report in the *Milledgeville Federal Union*, the Guard had practiced "undue and unlawful severities over the Cherokees, and others residing on the Cherokee soil." The paper's editor attributed such behavior to a lack of oversight by the government because of the distance between Milledgeville and the Guard. Though the editor never enumerated what the abuses entailed, Gilmer, who lacked detailed reports from Sanford, could not mount a sufficient defense of the Guard. Rumors that an out-of-control military force acting on its own accord in ways "not sanctioned by the government" proved worrisome. If accurate, the Guard's "improper violence" offended the "honor of the State, as well as the principles of humanity," and required the punishment of the offenders.[23] Sanford balked at such claims. Responding on August 1, Sanford's account of the Guard's movements made them seem nothing short of demure. The mines "have been visited" by the Guard, Sanford wrote, "and have been found generally free from intrusion." He reiterated that the Guard would not lower its vigilance as it worked to limit the intruders from operating at a "greater magnitude." In spite of Sanford's insistence that the gold mines were free from intruders and that his men had acted appropriately, political opposition to their actions continued to mount.[24]

As the Cherokees waited for the Supreme Court to make a ruling, they did not remain idle. Even though they claimed sovereignty, the supremacy act had outlawed any meeting of the National Council and prohibited the Cherokees from enforcing national laws. The Guard, furthermore, often appeared in Cherokee towns and villages. Such appearances were not random but, rather, concerted efforts by the Guard to exert Georgia's power over the region and its inhabitants. In early February 1831, Nelson led a contingent of the Guard into the Cherokee village of Coosawattee, where he appeared "in his military costume, with his sword hanging at his side." The armed company "in such military array, with muskets, pistols, swords, and all the implements of warfare, even to a drum dangling at the side of one of their number," sought to tear down a toll gate on the federal road but instead arrested the operator. The Cherokee Constitution of 1827 authorized agents to collect tolls on roads leading into the Nation, though such structures implied sovereignty. "These are fearful times indeed," warned Elias Boudinot, "if an honest citizen, attending to his business in his own premises, and in time of peace, may be invaded by an army!" In October, the Guard rode to New Echota, hoping to catch members of National Council. The Guard, though, had been misinformed; the Council instead convened in Tennessee. Others reported even more invasive attacks by the Guard that interrupted solemn religious services. Some of the Guard under Nelson rode to the Baptist station at Tensewatee, where the Reverend Duncan O'Bryant was baptizing Cherokees. The Guard, "claiming to be possessed by the spirits," tried to trample the small congregation so they could baptize their horses. Once in the water, the Guard purportedly mocked the baptismal sacrament.[25]

As chapter 2 demonstrates, the Cherokees did not remain impotent or passive in the face of intrusion. Coordinated efforts by the National Committee proved difficult because of the Guard's aggressive efforts to arrest the council. To register their discontent with the lottery and the fact that the state planned on disbursing Native ground to whites, the Cherokees sought to exert some control over who could pass through their territory. If they could not collect tolls because of the harassment directed at tollbooth operators, they could attempt to forestall the surveying of Cherokee land. When the first surveyors lugged their instruments into the backcountry, the Cherokees found and arrested them. Some surveyors also ran into trouble with Cherokee patrols, but by the beginning of July all but seven of the thirty-two surveying teams had reported back to Milledgeville, where they complained of "high mountains and big rattlesnakes," but little else. One surveyor, F. A. Brown, did run into trouble when he met up with the Cherokee leader David McNair. As the two men walked down the federal road, deep in conversation, the pair passed three more Cherokee men, all of whom appeared armed and, Brown assumed, to be "horse hunting." Instead, McNair and the three men arrested him. "Brown, you know that this land belongs to us," McNair warned him, "and that Georgians are taking it from us: No power on earth has the right to do this." Claiming that he had orders from the National Council to arrest the surveyors, McNair took Brown and his aides into custody for violating the Intercourse Laws that prohibited the surveying of Indian country. Though he asked to be taken to a county court in Georgia where Brown knew he stood a good chance of a release, the Cherokees instead took him to Athens, Tennessee, where he went before a magistrate. The state judge recused himself from deciding on a question of Indian policy and sent Brown to a federal judge in Knoxville. Prior to his departure, a superior court judge intervened and ordered his release because, he argued, Tennessee's courts did not have jurisdiction for an event that occurred in Georgia.[26]

That did not mean that the governor expected the Guard to rest on its laurels when it concerned the Cherokees. Though he still equivocated over the degree of force he expected the Guard to employ when it came to expelling whites from the gold mines, the governor gave the Guard free reign when dealing with the Cherokees. Though Gilmer acknowledged that the Guard should "keep the Indians quiet," he also recognized that "their rights should not only be respected, but protected with vigilance from violation." Gilmer then ordered Sanford to assure anxious Cherokee leaders that the "disposition of the State" focused on the "arrest of every white man who may commit crimes affecting" the Cherokee. Such magnanimity did not come free, of course: "The State requires of the Cherokee submission to its authority, and is bound in return to protect them," Gilmer informed Sanford.[27] The "protection" offered by the Guard was only extended to a certain element of the Cherokee population, namely those who had submitted to state law and had agreed to enroll "voluntarily" for deportment to Arkansas.

Those Cherokees who did not submit to state authority had to face the Guard's behavior. In early September 1831 a detachment of guardsmen shot at two Cherokee boys whom they suspected of digging for gold. During its pursuit of the two boys, the Guard came across another man who promptly "took to his heels." To prevent his escape, Sergeant Brooks ordered his men to fire. The first two shots missed. A third shot struck the man and wounded him "dangerously." On the same patrol, the Guard came across another man and shot him "thro' the body," a wound the guardsmen "suppose[d] to be mortal." Such flagrant actions reinforced the insecure and untenable situation forced upon the Cherokee Nation. It bears notice at this point the difference between how the Guard treated Cherokees who were found near the mines and white Georgians. White Georgians were arrested and taken to state courts; Cherokees were shot at and killed. When it came to enforcing the supremacy law, the Guard had become judge, jury, and executioner.[28]

Attacking individual Cherokees was one thing, but for the state to assert supremacy, it had to develop a strategy to deal with Cherokee leaders. For that reason, Gilmer also instructed the Guard to gather as much information as possible to solve a fundamental contradiction in the way he viewed Cherokee society. In one version, Gilmer saw the Cherokee people as a divided society controlled by a mixed-race elite. Gilmer "consider[ed] it of some importance" for Sanford to take note of the "particular history of the Chiefs of mixed blood who are at present influencing the conduct of the Cherokees." The governor believed that a cabal of elites, who used the skills taught to them by Christian missionaries and northern antislavery agitators, had long delayed removal efforts. Their chokehold on power allowed them to control the Nation through arbitrary measures and "assumed authority." For Gilmer, the government of elite leaders had gained power by submitting other Cherokees into "slavish dependence," which they had, no doubt, learned from their "intercourse with vicious white men." Contrary to that view, he likewise believed that Cherokees remained mired in savagery and custom. "Upon examination, it will be found that the Aboriginal people are as ignorant, thoughtless, and improvident, as formerly," he argued.[29]

Sanford agreed, believing that the character of whites who interacted with Cherokees in the past—and those who currently acted in nefarious ways—made all the difference. In his reply to the governor, Sanford agreed that the offspring of "vicious" white men, known for their "infamous practices" during the Revolutionary War, had indeed corrupted the Cherokees. Rather than join the American cause, these men had allied with the Cherokees and emulated their deeds of "horror & bloodshed" against white families living on the "unprotected & defenceless Frontier." The current Cherokee leaders, whom he claimed descended from these colonial-era "monsters of iniquity" who were "guilty of every species of crime and abomination" known to "human society," now sought to sustain a nation in the midst of the state. One need not speculate to see that the point Sanford wanted to make was that, in his eyes, these leaders were not Cherokees at all. In fact, they were something different altogether, neither white nor Native, but certainly a portent of the type of society that would continue if the Cherokees were allowed to stay. Georgia could not relinquish its sovereignty, Sanford argued, or it would permit an immoral, violent, and racially ambiguous community to subject state citizens to further outrages.[30]

If Gilmer and his agents operating in the disputed territory saw Cherokee leaders as a problem that needed solving, they understood that much of the political support enjoyed by the Cherokees in Congress came from northerners. Much of their support was a political reaction against President Andrew Jackson's removal program, though they were also motivated by antislavery sentiment. Enforcing the supremacy law became an expeditious method of dealing with those supporters, or anyone else, as the most efficient way for the Guard to undermine the authority of the Cherokee Nation because it allowed the Guard to expel any white who had failed, or refused, to acquire a residency permit from the state. Their immediate targets, northern missionaries who had political connections to politicians opposed to removal, became a point of controversy across the United States. When six missionaries, led by Samuel Worcester and Elizar Butler, refused to swear an oath of loyalty upholding state law, the commander of the Guard bristled: "I have not faith however that any thing short of the strong arm of the Law will remove those obstinate & incorrigible *Christian pretenders*." The campaign of intimidation launched against the missionaries brought scorn down on the state.[31]

Beginning in March 1831, the Guard commenced its harassment of various ministers stationed throughout the backcountry. On March 7, they arrested Samuel A. Worcester, marched him more than one hundred miles, but then released him on a judge's order. Upset that their tactics had not persuaded the ministers to flee back north, the governor unleashed the full fury of the Guard. "Spare no exertions to arrest them," he urged Sanford. "If they are discharged by the Courts, or give bail, continue to arrest them for each repeated act of continued residence in violation to the law." Since they had chosen to ignore the laws, Gilmer implored the Guard to "make them feel their full weight." The Guard's campaign of intimidation against the missionaries came to fruition in early July, when Gilmer ordered their arrest for violation of the supremacy laws. The operation that corralled the ministers occurred simultaneously with the Guard fanning out across the Nation and taking the ministers from their homes. Having refused to swear loyalty to the state, Worcester, a Congregationalist minister, and the other missionaries dispatched by the American Board of Commissioners for Foreign Missions found themselves in the custody of the Guard, chained to their horses and being dragged off to stand trial for their insubordination at the Gwinnett County courthouse. Recounting his arrest, Worcester admitted that it began peacefully enough and that for the duration of his confinement at Camp Gilmer, most of the Georgia Guard treated him with civility and some with kindness. Most of his abuse came at the hands of the Guard's two ranking officers, Charles H. Nelson and Jacob R. Brooks.[32]

Brooks arrested Worcester, but when the minister informed him that his wife was ill, Brooks allowed the minister to stay with his family for an additional night. The next morning, Worcester and Brooks were joined by another prisoner, J. J. Trott, and the two were forced to march almost ten miles. When a Methodist minister from Tennessee passed his arrested peers on the road, Brooks let loose a "tremendous torrent of curses," which "could not be exceeded by any thing which the most depraved and polluted imagination could deceive," and ordered the minister to "flank off." When another minister, Wells, refused to leave the side of the arrested men, Nelson beat him on the head with a stick. When they stopped for the night, the ministers, chained "two by two," passed an uncomfortable and humiliating evening. The next day, a minister arrested from another part of the Cherokee Nation, Elizur Butler, suffered the most abusive treatment at the hands of the Guard when they fastened a chain around his neck with a padlock and secured it to a horse. When he stumbled in the darkness, the horse dragged him by the neck. Taking some pity on the minister, the guardsmen placed him on the back of a horse he shared with a soldier. The horse eventually stumbled under its load, and the two men went tumbling, though the guardsman, having suffered at least two broken ribs, was the worse for wear.[33]

When the bedraggled ministers finally staggered into prison at Camp Gilmer, Brooks warned them: "This is where all the enemies of the State of Georgia will have to land—there and in hell." The arrest occurred on July 7, and for the next eighteen days the ministers could not leave their cell nor did they see a judge. In spite of the initial cruelty, Worcester admitted "most of them treated us with civility and kindness." Almost two weeks after their arrest, they appeared before the inferior court at Lawrenceville in Gwinnett County for a trial. All of them were convicted, though they all posted bail. Having promised to reappear in Lawrenceville at the next session of the superior court, the ministers left the courthouse and returned to their families and congregations.[34]

Even though Gilmer felt that backcountry whites were the source of most of the problem in the gold region, he still felt ambivalence regarding the use of violence against them. His outlook allowed him to extend the state's "protection" and "forbearance" to those Cherokees who obeyed state laws, but he had little sympathy for whites who did not behave accordingly. "I owe it to the sovereignty of the State, to punish with the utmost rigor, the injurious and insolent conduct of the whites who deny its power and oppose its authority," he wrote to Sanford, including the ministers. When the Guard used the full extent of the power granted it, though, Gilmer became horrified when it exceeded what he saw as appropriate. When the governor read "statements from Worcester . . . charging Col. Nelson and some of the guard with the use of irons in confining them, and other illegal and unnecessary severe measures," he balked. Though he immediately discounted the missionaries' story because of their "flagrantly criminal conduct," he soon learned from a trusted source the accuracy of the report. Gilmer reminded Sanford that the use of irons did not conform to the law, and in the future he should remind the troops under his charge that "no other severity is authorized by the law." Even if Gilmer desired order and had endorsed the Guard to use its "full weight" against the ministers, he had little stomach for the violence undertaken to secure his ideal society.[35]

Gilmer's strategy of implementing order in the backcountry, predicated on the cooperation of landholding white men who would implement civil law to secure their property, had proven more difficult than he imagined. Instead of a gentler civil law, he found himself willing to implement order at bayonet point because whites of whose character and conduct he disapproved continued to flout the state's sovereignty. When he authorized the Guard to use whatever measures they saw fit to arrest the ministers, he soon regretted the decision because of the lengths the guardsmen went to detain and berate peaceful men. Though perhaps it was acceptable in Gilmer's mind to use irons to confine a slave or a hardened criminal, their use on ministers appalled the public. Almost immediately, the cry to remove Nelson and halt the actions of the Guard made it necessary for the overzealous commander to tender his resignation. Gilmer, surprisingly, did not accept it. "I have uniformly found you exceedingly active and faithful in the discharge of the public service which has been assigned to you," he wrote to Nelson. He continued, "Although I have not altogether approved of the means which were employed on one or two occasion, in enforcing the laws, I have never doubted but that your object was the performance of what you considered your duty." Yet Nelson's interpretation of his duty obviously differed from Gilmer's, who reminded the colonel: "Confinement is never to be rendered severe upon prisoners for the purpose of punishment."[36]

The governor's condemnation of violent tactics came too late to stem the growing political discontent marshaled by the opposition. The "disgraceful and savage" treatment that the ministers received by the Guard, with orders from the governor, was without peer "in the annals of limited government." It would have been acceptable to apprehend the ministers, for the *Macon Telegraph* admitted that they were fugitives, but to "blackguard, beat, chain, and drag ... ministers of the Gospel" proved intolerable. Moreover, opposition to his policies transcended state factionalism and spread beyond the state's boundaries, where Christian opponents saw the Guard's brutality as a sure sign of southern arrogance. "At the hands of Georgia Guards," wrote one editorialist in Massachusetts, the ministers "received treatment, which could be justified only toward the most desperate of felons." Wondering why the Guard's officers had not been put on trial for their abuses, the editorial declared that unless Georgia had "gone to the depth of degradation," it would prove impossible for "any officer of the law thus to use his authority." The editor had to wonder "in what state we must henceforth consider Georgia—whether as civilized or savage."[37]

Gilmer did try to extricate himself from the growing political mess by claiming that he had limited control over the Guard. He argued that those who opposed the brazenness of the Guard were "entirely mistaken as to my power over the Guard." "I have no authority to punish them whatever may be their conduct," he reasoned, because the guardsmen "are neither soldiers nor subject to military law." Gilmer scrutinized the law that created the Guard and concluded that it prevented him from punishing individual guardsmen; only citizens could file suit against them. Even though the Guard had a distinct martial bearing, Gilmer tried to argue that his chosen avenue for employing order did not constitute a true military outfit. The Guard, rather than a regiment of militiamen who imposed order through martial law, were substitutes for "sheriffs and Constables" because they could act "more efficiently." Such a fine distinction was lost upon many of his detractors, who began to see the Guard as an instrument of abuse symptomatic of the governor's overbearing style of rule.[38]

Gilmer's executive style came under a higher degree of scrutiny than usual because 1831 was an election year. The biennial gubernatorial contests agitated partisan spirits. Combined with the promise of the land lottery, the election of 1831 offered up a high level of excitement and competition. Hoping to improve his abusive image, Gilmer sought to offer clemency to the convicted ministers. Eventually, he floated the offer of an official pardon if the ministers would leave the state; only four of the ministers took his offer. Worcester and Butler rejected his overture and began their stint in the state penitentiary, an outcome that "entirely satisfied" the governor. Though his military force, the Georgia Guard, had rather successfully protected the gold mines, it had done so in a way altogether inconsistent with egalitarianism and white superiority. Instead, the Guard's mission to clear the gold mines meant that it indiscriminately carried out its charge. Their attacks on miners, ministers, and Indians made them appear to voters, ironically, as prejudiced because they did not treat all whites equally. Rather than a racial hierarchy, it had established a moral hierarchy where law-abiding citizens were rewarded with leases and lotteries while law-breaking residents were beaten and jailed.[39]

By that point, mid-September, the governor's clemency came too late to do much political good as the election of 1831, pitting Gilmer against Wilson Lumpkin, had reached fever pitch. The divisive issues separating the two candidates came down to initiatives each supported for the direction of the state's economy and for landownership in the disputed territory. More importantly, the parties squabbled over the implementation of order and the sanctity of whiteness, two ideas tied intimately in the political discourse. During his time as governor, Gilmer made two proposals that raised serious opposition to his reelection. First, he advocated state ownership of the gold mines. Second, he floated a proposal in his first year as governor that Indians should be allowed to testify against whites in state courts, if only to make it easier to convict white intruders. Such out-of-touch proposals made it easy for the Clark party to paint the Troup band as elitist and proponents of an integrated, biracial society, much like the kind developing in the disputed territory, where cooperation rather than superiority had become custom.

Both of the governor's proposals came in October 1830 in an address to the legislature and not during the immediate lead-up to the election.

Gilmer certainly championed landownership by white residents in the backcountry, and the land lottery in particular, but he did not want the land that contained gold distributed in a similar fashion. The governor, instead, desired to implement a plan calling for state ownership of the gold mines. He had two reasons for this. First, he believed that the proceeds from publicly held gold mines could do much to alleviate the problems of the state's poor. If the mines proved "exceedingly profitable," he argued, "the State will be enabled thereby to relieve the people from taxation, improve the public roads, render the rivers navigable, and extend the advantages of education to every class of society." Such a plan would benefit all members of society. Freed from the burdens of taxation, they could spend their money improving their land, thereby "adding to the riches of the country," instead of having their money "drawn from them to be placed in the public treasury." The gold mines, for Gilmer, could provide the state with untold riches; a panacea enabling the governor to implement a wide-ranging program of internal improvements, education, and tax reform. With the proceeds from the mines, the state would pay the laborers who worked in the mines (or the rent to the slave owners who leased the labor of their chattel), pay for a system of public schools for poor whites, improve the state's transportation network, and lower the tax burden of its citizens. Part of Gilmer's reasoning for state, rather than individual, ownership rested on his understanding of poverty. Gilmer did not believe that poor whites who won land that contained gold would be able to retain their republican simplicity and would instead turn to immoral profligacy. State ownership, Gilmer believed, would usher in a broad-based economic growth that would modernize the state's economy and work toward eradication of generational inequality.[40]

Denying individual ownership of the gold mines had another benefit for Gilmer: it would protect the morals of the region's inhabitants. A gold lottery would only injure the public good, he argued, because it would encourage people to speculate wildly. In true republican fashion, Gilmer feared the introduction of corruption that would accompany the sudden wealth that some might gain. "The community would be highly excited by the hope of acquiring great wealth, without labor. The morals of the country would be in danger of corruption," not only because of the temptation to speculate in gold mines, but because those individuals lucky enough to win would quit upright habits. "Regular industry and economy would for a time be suspended by restless idleness, and imaginary, as well as real and unnecessary expenditures," Gilmer said. If a lottery gave away gold mines to those with poor character, the acquisition would only exacerbate their moral shortcomings and fuel the demise of the republic. The common good required a virtuous citizenry not tempted into prodigality by gold. Gilmer, in other words, sought to use the power of the state to save poor people from themselves by imposing government ownership of the gold mines to ensure that individual morality would not be corrupted.[41]

Lumpkin's supporters immediately sprang into action and charged Gilmer and the rest of the Troup faction with elitism. "Oh! No—," one editor chided the governor, "It will turn your heads you poor folks to become so 'suddenly' rich!" Rather than take the gold for themselves, poor men should "let your rich neighbor, who drives his carriage and drinks his wine, have it." Lumpkin's supporters also wanted to look out for the common good but thought that Gilmer's approach was more befitting a "monarchy or aristocracy—where the nobles may oppress their subjects and wallow themselves in ease and luxury." Such a condition, however, "does not suit a republican people, for the very import of the form *republic* implies the wealth and prosperity of the people," and not a select few. For Lumpkin and his supporters, the fate of the republic hinged on the liberty of white men to pursue happiness as they saw fit. They drew on patriotic themes to connect the sanctity of private property and Lumpkin's campaign. One editor urged the candidate's supporters to help Lumpkin pilot the "staunch republican-built boat" and channeled Oliver Hazard Perry: "DON'T GIVE UP THE GOLD MINES!"[42]

Lumpkin's offensive against public ownership of the gold mines countered Gilmer's moralist tones. It would not be the people who succumbed to moral decay because of the gold mines but, rather, government agents charged with managing the mines' operation. Such agents "would deem it God's service to purloin, embezzle, and swindle the State out of the last particle of gold to be found in the country." Lumpkin declared that large stores of public money in the coffers of the state bank posed the real threat to the morality of the people and would seduce state leaders into corruption. When the gold reached the Central Bank, "the work of corruption" would really begin. Estimating that the mines would produce nearly four million dollars over the course of a decade, a corrupted governor with so much disposable income could raise an "army of thirty thousand men" and "compel obedience" from the rest of the state. Such a course could not come to pass. Public ownership of the gold mines would prove nothing short of a catastrophe for the state and would set the state on a course that would end its republican character: "A good Executive would endeavor to prevent an influence inimical to republicanism, so adverse to public morals and so destructive of the true interests of the country."[43]

Lumpkin also expressed less concern over any moral failing that the poor may have possessed. Poverty did not derive from a lack of morals but from bad luck or unfortunate circumstances. Not a few "worthy citizens" could use the riches of the gold mines to "carry independence, and comfort, and happiness" into the homes of "honest and patriotic" men who just happened to be poor. A gold lottery, one editor estimated, would spread happiness and independence to more than one thousand households. Rather than allow the state to hoard the gold, the government should scatter wealth, "with a bountiful broad-cast, over the whole population!" The editor of the *Federal Union* reminded his readers that the interests of the government should never be separated from those of its citizens. The "best mode of building up public institutions, is, first, to establish, on solid foundations, the prosperity of the people." What less fortunate Georgians deserved, Lumpkin's supporters cried, was a "white man's chance" to better themselves and their families. A lottery for gold claims would ensure such an opportunity and, in the process, would preserve the proper relationship between the people and the state government.[44]

What was this "white man's chance"? Certainly, there was a connection between chance and lottery. Each citizen had a chance to win, so it fit it very well with the zeitgeist of Jacksonianism. The phrase also speaks of opportunity. Those individuals who won then had a chance, an opportunity, to become successful. The spirit of the white man's chance was equality and opportunity. At its heart, then, the white man's chance was about the relationship between white citizens and the state government. For the white man's chance to flourish, the state government had to create the conditions for economic opportunity and democratic equality. The settlement of the disputed territory was the fulfillment of the government's promises to whites. It would expand their economic opportunities by limiting the chances of Cherokees to maintain their nationhood. If legalistic maneuvers were not sufficient, the use of violence as a way of creating the white man's chance was permissible. Hence, the desire for order and sovereignty was inseparable from the white man's chance.

In this rendering, the state government played a key role. To fulfill the white man's chance, it had to expand rights and privileges to whites while limiting those of nonwhites. Therefore, it was convenient for Lumpkin's supporters when Gilmer made another proposal that potentially limited the legal prerogatives enjoyed by whites. In his annual address to the state assembly in October 1830, Gilmer made a serious gaffe when recommending legislation he hoped the state assembly would consider. He proposed the repeal of a state law that prohibited Indians from testifying in state courts against whites. Politicos across the state raised their eyebrows in wonder; Lumpkin and his associates pounced. "If Indians are allowed to testify against white men, under the present state of our Indian relations, what is to become of the white people" in the border counties?, wondered the *Federal Union* editor. Such a proposal would put whites at the mercy of Indians in court and set a dangerous precedent concerning the right of free blacks or even slaves to testify against whites.[45] Gilmer's proposal obviously struck at the heart of the legal prerogatives enjoyed by white Georgians, though the governor himself never explained his proposal. Perhaps he wanted to make it easier for Cherokees to aid in the prosecution of disorderly whites, but he never specified.

His lack of public defense hurt him and his faction. Georgia's election of 1831 contained within it many of the hallmarks that characterize the Second Party System. The Troup faction's discussion of internal improvements, moral reform, and a supposed disdain for the poor predicted its turn toward the Whig Party later in the decade. The Clark faction's insistence on the sanctity of private property and the equality—indeed, the superiority—of white men easily meshed with the vision of society put forth by Andrew Jackson's Democratic Party. As Georgia's political system began coalescing into the political structure that would shape national politics for the next three decades, it also contained within it peculiarities all its own. For example, nullification was still an important point of contention not only because of Georgia's proximity to South Carolina, but because there was a distinctive awareness among state leaders and the Cherokees that Georgia had nullified federal law when it passed the supremacy act and extended its sovereignty over the Cherokee Nation.[46]

As voters streamed to the polls in October 1831, they largely rejected Gilmer's proposals and the use of force in the backcountry. The injury to the "white man's chance," especially the governor's efforts at instilling moral reform by prohibiting private ownership of the gold mines and hinting at Indian testimony in state courts while using a military force as a political tool all combined to spell certain defeat for Gilmer. In the border counties, especially, voters rejected Gilmer. In the six border counties, Lumpkin accumulated overwhelming majorities that mirrored the returns in the rest of the state. Of the 7,647 votes cast in the border counties, a paltry 2,399 went for Gilmer, just over 31 percent. Lumpkin received 5,248 votes, or nearly 69 percent of the votes cast.[47] For voters, Gilmer's vision for the disputed territory clashed with their expectations. The promise of Gilmer's vision—that all of the state's citizens, even the poorest, would have a free education and a modern, market-based economy all paid for by the riches found in the gold region—was rejected handily by voters. Unlike his opponent's democratic posture on the gold mines and the rights of white citizens to own them, the promise offered by Gilmer and the rest of the Troup faction denied many Georgians a path to respectability that they craved.

When Wilson Lumpkin took the oath of office in December 1831, he showed how little he had learned from the mistakes of his predecessor. During the campaign, Lumpkin's supporters chastised the Guard for the heavy-handed measures it used with white residents to enforce the law. Lumpkin promised a continuation of those policies: "The executive should be vested with full power, promptly to control the agents who have been or may be selected to maintain the authority of the laws" in the backcountry. Though a member of the party opposed to the nullifiers, Lumpkin reiterated the right of the state to extend its authority over the Cherokee territory. Framing the issue as a "moral duty" to extend the state's authority into the Cherokee territory in order to "save that part of our State from confusion, anarchy, and perhaps from bloodshed," Lumpkin called on the white residents to help him extend order: "Until we have a population planted upon the unoccupied portion of this Territory, possessed of all the ordinary inducements of other communities to sustain our laws and government," chaos would reign.[48]

As the new year dawned, Lumpkin made good on assuming control of the Georgia Guard. The legislature reaffirmed the portion of the supremacy law allowing the governor to provide for the punishment of backcountry criminals. In spite of the fact that he had chastised the Guard as an unconstitutional force and patronage tool, he willingly continued it. In late December, he nominated John Coffee to the post of commander of the Georgia Guard. Coffee accepted. In early January, the transfer of command occurred when Coffee arrived at Camp Gilmer.[49]

The beginning of 1832 brought renewed troubles for the Cherokee, but also hope. With Lumpkin entrenched in office, a land lottery began in October. Once the names of the "fortunate drawers" had been made public, thousands of them flocked to claim their winnings. This posed innumerable difficulties for the Cherokee who were evicted from their own farms when a white lottery winner arrived.

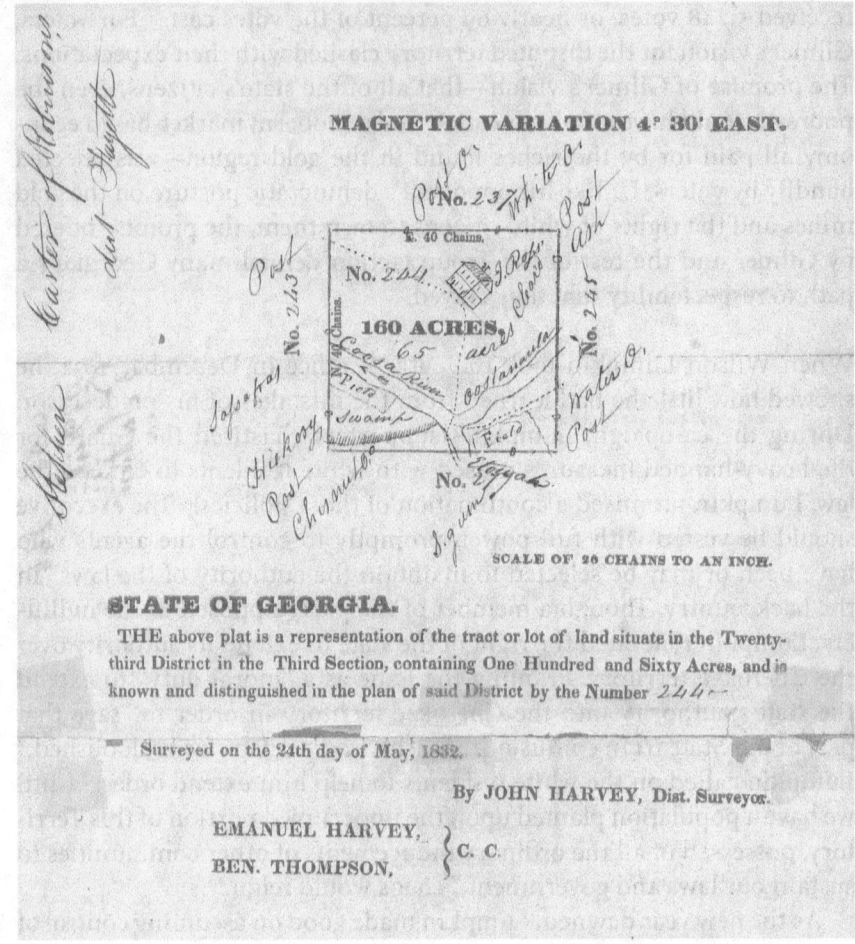

The 1832 land lottery gave Native land to white settlers. The plat above was won by Stephen Carter and entitled him to the land and improvements, even the home, of the Principal Chief of the Cherokee Nation, John Ross. "Cherokee County plat issued to Stephen Carter," February 14, 1832. Courtesy of Georgia Archives, RG 3-3-26, ah00616.

The lottery law prohibited whites from evicting a Cherokee family from their home, so white families would either begin a confrontation and force the Native family off or build nearby and deny the rightful landowners use of their land. The first week of December 1832 brought a large number of lottery winners into the Cherokee Nation like "great flocks of pigeons that hastens to the ground in search of food," despaired Elias Boudinot. "Every lot has been hewed and as many paths beaten" in search of the precious metals dusting the region's streambeds. "To this invasion of our property we protest; and we state to our readers, our right to the lands." Though outraged, Boudinot cautioned his countrymen: "Let us therefore calmly await and see if the Government will not yet acquiesce . . . or whether the government will choose to have their laws nullified by a state as the easiest mode of releasing itself from enforcing them."[50]

Boudinot's patience, along with that of the rest of the Cherokees, had been stretched thin for nearly a decade by the aggressive behavior of the State of Georgia and its citizens. When the U.S. Supreme Court met in February, the realization of the Cherokees' hopes came to fruition when John Marshall and the rest of the court sustained the case brought by Samuel Worcester. The minister's arrest and imprisonment, the court argued, were illegal because the State of Georgia had no legal claim to extend its sovereignty or legal institutions over the Cherokee Nation. The extension and supremacy laws, therefore, were null and void; Cherokee sovereignty had been confirmed. The State of Georgia, however, had no intention of heeding the ruling. Instead, Lumpkin encouraged whites to enter the Cherokee Nation in search of their claims. The governor went so far as to recommend to Coffee that if he could gather sufficient testimony proving John Ross and other chiefs were conspiring to undermine Georgia's laws, he could arrest them and haul them to Athens for trial.[51]

The creation of the Georgia Guard in December 1830 sent a clear message to the Cherokees and intruders alike. Georgia's leaders expressed their willingness to use violence to impose state sovereignty in the borderlands, and they would not tolerate deviation from those laws. By connecting the undesirability of intruders and Cherokees in the white republic, the governor took an important step in making the problem one not solely based on race. When the Guard began acting, however, it found that implementing a white republic through aggressive means proved just as difficult for state troops as it had been for federal forces. State-sanctioned violence used against intruders went against the prevailing frontier ethos that stressed white male equality. The Guard's

This deed formalized the land transaction that Carter had won in the land lottery. Absent, of course, is any recognition of Cherokee sovereignty or permission for this transaction to proceed. Cherokee County land grant issued to Stephen Carter, February 14, 1832. Courtesy of Georgia Archives, RG 3-5-29, ah00619.

white victims presented a compelling portrait of the powers of the state run amok, even to those who espoused a states' right platform. Though Lumpkin had run on a platform denouncing the Guard and the governor's efforts limiting the "white man's chance," he continued the unit when he took office and signaled an acceptance of violence against whites in the pursuit of order.

6 / The Georgia Guard and the White Man's Chance, 1832–1836

In April 1832, a recent appointment to Wilson Lumpkin's Georgia Guard, William W. Williamson, ventured into Cherokee country. Passing through unfamiliar country, Williamson happened upon Amicalola Falls, a waterfall he reckoned "the most majestic Scene that I have ever witnessed or heard of." But Williamson was not on the hunt for the sublime. Instead, he had been dispatched by the governor to ascertain the Cherokee response to the *Worcester* decision and the interest in the government's voluntary removal program. What he learned bothered him a great deal, for it spelled trouble regarding the state's efforts to extend its sovereignty over the Cherokee Nation. In small mountain communities, Williamson saw the joyous reception when the Cherokees heard the news of Chief Justice Marshall's decision. The Cherokee leaders with whom he conversed believed "Congress would compel the President to send an Armed force" to uphold the ruling. Williamson warned the Cherokees against such a hope. The other states, Williamson cautioned, would not "resque" the Cherokees lest they risk "Civil War & disunion." If President Jackson did send an army to "whip Georgia into her duty," Williamson predicted that the Cherokee people "would be swept of[f] the Earth before any assistance could arrive." These last remarks seemed to convince at least some Cherokee leaders "that a large portion of the Georgians wanted only a small pretext to exterminate them."[1]

Williamson's warning to those Cherokee leaders—that extermination was on the minds of many Georgians—no doubt confirmed to them the ultimate direction in which state actions had been heading. The Georgia

Guard under Gilmer had acted in a relentless fashion to destabilize Cherokee community. With the new governor installed in Milledgeville, the potential reprieve that he had offered because of his previous criticism of the Guard dissipated with Williamson's journey into the disputed territory. That a state agent was openly discussing Cherokee extermination as one possible outcome of the crisis over sovereignty presaged the type of actions that Lumpkin would encourage his Guard to undertake. They did not disappoint.

Williamson's journey through the Cherokee Nation, however, had other pretexts. Ordered to judge the degree of acceptance of a federal plan to encourage voluntary removal, Williamson traversed rough terrain without a guide or a translator. Forced to "turn Indian" to complete his goals, Williamson was nevertheless found out and "committed to jail," ostensibly by the Cherokee Lighthorse.[2] He did not specify what he meant when he "turned Indian," though perhaps it meant he donned Indian attire. Williamson's efforts to disguise his appearance underscored several important aspects of life in the disputed territory, both of which proved troubling to state leaders. That it was possible for a white man to shed himself of his identity, at least visually, underscored the anxieties of state leaders who demanded order and social clarity. The malleability of whiteness, especially the ease with which it could be amended or shed entirely, likewise spoke to the discomfort state leaders had with acculturation: Indians who appeared white, spoke English, adopted Christianity, and owned African slaves had created a constitutional republic. Yet acculturation did not occur solely in one direction. White criminals and intruders, acting outside the bounds of civil society, behaved "savagely," a trait that had been reserved in America's rhetoric for Natives. The blurring boundaries between American whiteness and Cherokee savagery made it possible for a white man to pass himself off as an Indian and vice versa. For state leaders, this affront to civilization had to end so that proper and natural order could resume. To achieve such ends, the removal of all of these "savage" elements became necessary and urgent.

As Wilson Lumpkin settled into office after his hard-fought campaign in 1831, the victorious leader of the Clark faction looked to secure his electoral coalition in the border counties. Having promised to conduct a lottery of Cherokee land and, perhaps more importantly, to distribute land that potentially contained gold, Lumpkin had to figure out what to do with three different groups: First, white intruders who scoffed at state and federal laws and remained in the disputed territory; second, the political class of the Cherokee Nation, which was divided on the prospect of removal; and third, the majority of Cherokees, who lived in small communal villages in land claimed by Georgia and who spoke little English.

In 1831, President Jackson appointed Benjamin F. Currey as the superintendent of Cherokee emigration. When he arrived at the Cherokee Agency near Calhoun, Tennessee, in late September, he set to work.[3] Throughout 1832 federal negotiators ramped up efforts at "voluntarily" removing individual Cherokees from their homes and deporting them to the Arkansas Territory. In April 1832, Currey reported that more than 130 Cherokee had enrolled for emigration, but he soon became frustrated by his lack of progress and noted that opposition to removal was stiffening. Moreover, some Cherokees who had gone to Arkansas had, by 1834, returned to their homes in the Cherokee Nation. Much of the opposition to the voluntary removal program, Currey noted, came from white men who had intermarried into the Cherokee Nation. "Vagabond white men are constantly intermarrying with squaws who will oppose my terms unless they themselves can be accommodated with reservations," he complained to one official at the Office of Indian Affairs. In exchange for renouncing Cherokee citizenship, some Cherokees tried to bargain with the federal government for fee simple ownership of a plot of land, or a reservation. These negotiations proved tedious. In late May, Currey once again wrote to his superiors in Washington regarding problems arising from his enrollment efforts. Most of the resistance to enrollment came from "*white men intermarried* with Cherokees." The resistance became so heated that Currey pleaded, "Can you devise any proceeding which can be taken to put a stop to these unwarrantable interferences?" If allowed to use troops, he could "punish under martial law" those who interfered, because, he claimed, "all regular constitutional government is abdicated here."[4]

Even though Currey made it seem as if a small number of Cherokees resisted voluntary removal, the Cherokees were, in fact, divided on the issue. The head of the Cherokee Nation, Principal Chief John Ross, opposed removal and staked his political future—and his people's permanency east of the Mississippi River—on continued opposition. Ross stressed national unity rather than accommodation. His rivals, led by The Ridge and other elites, saw accommodation and removal as key to Cherokee persistence and, indeed, survival. The state and federal government obviously sided with the latter. Because state and federal policy had converged, both sought to intimidate John Ross and other political leaders opposed to removal and protect those who advocated for it.[5]

Uncertainty regarding voluntary removal also prevented many Cherokees from leaving their homes. Though enrollees had access to government aid, tobacco, firearms, and food to make the trip west more tolerable, and a promise of land upon their arrival in Arkansas, they already had land where they were. Because of the political in-fighting and the undesirability of moving, the large majority of Cherokees did not opt for relocation. When Currey set out for Arkansas at the head of a contingent of émigrés in April 1832, he departed the Cherokee agency at Calhoun, Tennessee, with 200 Cherokees, plus 40 whites, and 108 blacks. Such a breakdown suggests that many of these early enrollees were Cherokee slave owners. By the end of the year, Currey had managed to relocate only 626 Cherokees. However, without the aid of the Georgia Guard, he would have relocated far fewer.[6]

The Guard that mustered into service during Lumpkin's first term, led by John Coffee, both protected those Cherokees who had enrolled and forced others into enrollment camps against their will. Such a strategy helped them widen the schism between pro- and antiremoval forces within the Cherokee polity. Because the Guard was not a part of the official military structure in Georgia, it became a useful tool at Currey's disposal to hasten his voluntary removal scheme. In March 1832, William M. Davis, a federal enrolling agent, wrote to Secretary of War Lewis Cass regarding a scuffle that occurred between the Georgia Guard and a militia company from Tennessee. At an enrollment camp in Tennessee, the Guard had been "stationed for the purpose of keeping order" at the behest of Benjamin Currey to protect the emigrants and their property from overzealous Tennesseans. Archibald Turk, a colonel in the Tennessee state militia, led a group of "privately armed" men into the camp immediately preceding a church service where they forced their way through the Guard "purposely to bring on a disturbance." Once the service ended, Turk "commenced a quarrel with the commanding officer of the guard" by deriding Coffee and his men with "the most abusive epithets, threatened to drive them beyond the limits of the state of Tennessee & presented a cocked pistol and bayonet at the breast of the officer." The guardsmen seized their own muskets, and a standoff ensued with nervous Cherokee families in the crossfire. Only the "great forbearance and prudence" that Currey demonstrated prevented bloodshed from occurring.[7]

Turk and his armed band soon left the camp but threatened to raise another party to "drive the Guard back into Georgia." He made good on his promise. The next day he arrived with an even larger armed posse and "paraded them upon the opposite bank of the river," a threatening demonstration that served as a warning to the Guard. Both Currey and Coffee heeded the message, decided "to forbear quelling the disorder by force," and returned to safety. The "disorder" caused by Turk and his party of Tennesseans came about not because of the presence of the Cherokees who had enrolled but because of the presence of the Guard. Even though they had crossed into Tennessee at the behest of a federal agent, their jurisdiction did not extend into neighboring states. The agent who recorded the brinksmanship had other ideas about who caused problems for the Cherokee. "Abandoned and unprincipled whitemen, who are numerous in this country, and who infest their camps night and day, for unworthy purposes," posed the real problem. To alleviate the tensions, he requested a "strong Guard of the troops of the United States," who ought to be posted in the Cherokee backcountry. Although the Guard had nearly set off a confrontation between Georgia and Tennessee, the importance of this incident is the fact that the Guard, acting at the behest of federal agents, had been present in Tennessee to protect enrollees from whites. This duty was so pressing that they crossed state lines to perform it.[8]

For those Cherokees who did not cooperate, the Guard did not provide a protective mantle. Instead, the Guard sought out Cherokees to harass, intimidate, and arrest. The most audacious action sanctioned by Coffee, according to the *Cherokee Phoenix*, was the attempted arrest of John Ross, though the guardsmen failed and "came off without a prisoner." Lumpkin encouraged Ross's arrest, along with that of Joseph Vann and other Cherokee leaders, which he found necessary in order to maintain "the authority of the state." The *Phoenix* also reported that Coffee and his men continued their assaults on individual Cherokees found in the gold region. They shot one man, Nickojack, clean through the arm and leg because he was suspected of digging for gold. Newspapers as far away as New York began printing stories of the Guard's "horrid barbarity." In May, the Guard apprehended Teesaskee and his wife for gold prospecting. To secure their release, the couple had to agree to enroll as emigrants; rejection meant imprisonment. Teesaskee rejected the offer of enrollment, so he and his wife went to prison in Lawrenceville for an indeterminate amount of time. Another Cherokee man, Robin, also faced expulsion from his homeland when he was caught digging for gold. When he refused to enroll, the Guard instead decided to whip him: "The Guard tied his hands fast, and led him to a tree, and inflicted fifty stripes on his back for the offence of digging his own gold." Robin had the reputation of being a poor man who worked hard for his living and managed to maintain some dignity in the affair. He informed the editor of the *Cherokee Phoenix* that the "stripes were put upon him with some degree of moderation"—suggesting white male effeteness. Coffee and Williamson did not stop there. The Guard turned to outright intimidation and coercion to hasten the removal process. Jesse Raper had lived along the Chestatee River for twenty-four years before a man named John Reaves, a lottery winner, expelled him. Afterward, he inquired about enrollment with Currey. Raper's family agreed to go but only if Currey swore they would be paid for their loss of property. Promise secure, Raper and his family signed up for enrollment but soon found themselves penniless and "forced into some public waggons . . . by the Georgia guard," bound for an enrollment camp. Rachel Rice suffered similar treatment when she was "forced from [her] home by the troops under Maj. Curry." From Rice's account of her expulsion from her property, Currey appeared to be working with the Guard and directing, or at least encouraging, its actions.[9]

Hetty Vance also suffered at the hands of the Guard. Previously, Vance had watched as a lawyer from Georgia took the slaves belonging to her late husband because the lawyer claimed she owed him payment to administer the estate. Not content with the slaves, the lawyer soon thereafter received a warrant for her arrest. The lawyer contacted the Guard, who promptly arrested Vance upon her release from jail and confined her at their headquarters for four days. Elizabeth Ware watched as her husband fled their home "owing to the oppressive character of the laws of the state towards the Citizens of the Cherokee Nation." Anxious over her isolation and exposure, Ware claimed that she became "subject to the abuse of the Georgia Guard," who she believed burned down her house with all of her worldly possessions inside.[10] Not only had the Guard begun implementing "voluntary" removal policy, but they did so in a way that targeted the most vulnerable members of Cherokee society. Vance, a widow, had no family or neighbors to protect her; Ware's husband had to leave his family.

Many of the Guard's abusive actions toward individual Cherokees and the more extreme instances of arson showed that the expulsion of Cherokee families motivated the Guard. Not only did its actions reinforce the federal government's "voluntary" removal policy, but it also helped expedite state acquisition of Indian land. As the "fortunate drawers" began to move into the backcountry to claim their winnings from the land lottery of 1832, many anticipated vacated land and an absence of Cherokee residents. Arriving at their lots, most of the lottery winners encountered Native inhabitants who expressed little desire to move. Lumpkin apprised Coffee in April: "You will in a very short time find many of our citizens disposed to be engaged in exploring and examining the Cherokee Country with a view of ascertaining the most valuable lands [and] mines." The governor went on to warn the commander about the influx of white claimants and their potential risks to the rest of the community: "*Gold digging; defacing public landmarks; arbitrary law triumphing over the civil authority; anarchy and confusion*, cannot long remain before civil war will ensue." Lumpkin urged Coffee to prevent undue violations, which included individuals who mined illegally or violated "the rights of the Indians." Not wanting to precipitate a war, Lumpkin requested "that the deportment of every officer and citizen of Georgia should be such as to silence the slander of our enemies." Unfortunately for the governor, the Guard did not excel at behaving well.[11]

By the end of 1832, in fact, the increased amount of violence, on the part of the Guard and the lottery winners alike, began to worry the governor. Lumpkin sought to deflect blame away from the state and toward those who opposed removal. "It is quite obvious," Lumpkin advised President Jackson, "that the enemies of the Union are doing all they can to give us trouble with Cherokees." Such flagrant partisanship led the governor to believe that Washington was rife with conspiracy and corruption, pitting the state and the Jackson administration against an antiremoval faction led by northern congressmen and the nascent Whig Party, "who are acting in concert with the enemies of good order & Government." Worse for Lumpkin, newspaper editors, even citizens from Georgia, "are at this moment engaged in the unhallowed work of fan[n]ing the embers of strife between the Cherokees & the Government of Georgia." In some areas of the disputed territory "where but few whites have settled," Lumpkin noted "a spirit of disregard & insolence to our laws" emanating from the Cherokees. Though he believed that the lottery winners could help generate and sustain order in the disputed territory, in its current state the residents of the area lacked "sufficient moral force" to "maintain the supremacy of our laws."[12]

The legislature had seen enough of the Guard and its antics. When it met in December 1832, its members voted to curtail the size and power of the Guard and moved to organize new counties so that lottery winners could impose civil authority. In the debate over how to bring order to the disputed territory, the legislature had grown tired of a divisive paramilitary force that was not accountable to the state government. Rather than a continued reliance upon this strategy to bring order, the state legislature instead encouraged the "fortunate drawers" to lay the foundations of civil society. The Guard had its numbers reduced from forty to ten men as a result of the Assembly's new policy. Moreover, its expansive mission of protecting the gold mines that gave it a great degree of latitude under Gilmer shifted to protecting "each and every Indian in his and their persons, and also in the enjoyment of their personal property," from any "trespass, or offence." In other words, the Guard was now supposed to prevent the lottery winners and intruders from harassing Cherokees. The General Assembly had created a problem. On the one hand, it wanted lottery winners to take possession of their winnings. On the other hand, it did not want those settlers to take possession of Cherokee improvements.

However, the Guard had already been protecting *some* Cherokees—those who had agreed to "voluntary removal." Other Cherokees, no doubt, would continue to suffer harassment at the hands of the Guard, intruders, and lottery winners alike. The new legislation codified what the Guard had already been doing, though it prevented the Guard from acting in such an aggressive capacity. Since early 1832, the Guard had protected those Indians who had enrolled while it intimidated those who resisted. The new legislation asked the Guard to continue that course but further stipulated that once the Cherokee country had been organized into counties, the legislature would automatically discharge the Guard.[13] When the legislature had first authorized the Guard in 1830, it did so with the understanding that its mission of protecting the gold mines would eventually culminate with the introduction of civil authority. Sanford and Coffee, though, expanded the scope of their mission beyond the mere protection of the mines.

The same law that limited the Guard's size and changed its mission also reaffirmed the supremacy of civil authority when it organized ten counties within the Cherokee Nation. In each of the ten new counties, the legislation specified the place of voting and the location of the inferior court and the frequency of its meeting; it also created new superior court circuits and established the frequency with which each would meet. The citizens of each new county had to elect five inferior court justices to settle minor disputes and officers of the court. To facilitate land sales, the citizens of each new county had to elect a surveyor. Undergirding the organization of each county, the militia district served as the most basic unit of local governance. Each district elected two justices of the peace as well as a militia captain to make ready the district's male population for military service.¹⁴

Only two days after the legislature had reduced the size and scope of the Guard, the governor sent a message to Williamson notifying him that he had been made commander of the ten-man force. Likewise, Lumpkin informed Coffee that though he appreciated the colonel's service, the state no longer required his efforts. Before he let his commander leave, however, he let him know that he felt the legislature had made a grave mistake: "I am left without authority, or legal direction of any kind, to protect the gold mines or fractions or put down Cherokee assumptions by the guard or any other authority, civil or military." The lack of authority given to the Guard, he declared, left settlers vulnerable to reprisals: "The legislature have utterly refused to afford this protection to the settlers in the new country, and with great and urgent reluctance at the very last moment, appropriated the money to sustain the little guard of ten men."¹⁵

The limitations imposed on the Guard had consequences. Since the Assembly frowned upon settlers expelling Cherokees, it ensured that whites and Cherokees would live in close proximity to one another. As a result, state leaders now fretted over the possibility that prostrate settlers and their families would be massacred in record numbers. What resulted was an all-encompassing paranoia on the part of politicians that white Georgians were about to be victimized by savage Cherokees, which again strengthened their desire to hasten removal. Part of the legislature's hesitation in disbanding the Guard completely—and Lumpkin's fear for borderland settlers—arose from the mysterious death of the Bowman family. In the waning days of December 1832, Lawson Bowman and the rest of his family met an untimely end when they burned to death inside their cabin. The *Cherokee Phoenix* sought to unravel the mystery and concluded that the deaths were unfortunate accidents, not the result of malicious behavior. What little property remained had not been trifled with, which led the new, antiremoval editor Elijah Hicks to conclude that Georgia could not justify the case as one of murder. In spite of Hicks's argument, the Georgia Guard began a manhunt for Native perpetrators. When they learned the whereabouts of their quarry, the Guard "rushed to the Indian settlement with the spirit of Samson" to apprehend the supposed criminals. Just before Christmas, the Guard, "like a lawless storm," chained eight Cherokee men to horses and hauled them to county court for trial, where they were released by the judge for lack of evidence.¹⁶

Williamson had an alternative explanation. In his initial report to the governor, he declared that "a most daring & Violent Murder" had been

"Committed by the Indians of Salacoe town" against Bowman and his family. According to Williamson, the "entire Family was inhumanely butchered and the Dwelling consumed by Fire," which was an effort to hide the gruesome nature of their crimes. Though he suspected Cherokee perpetrators, Williamson admitted that little animosity existed between the Georgians and Cherokee residents in that area. Unable to find a motive for the murder but unwilling to believe that the tragedy had been an accident, he concluded, "There must have been some personal difficulty between this unfortunate Family & the Indians."[17]

To solve the mystery, the Guard arrested an Indian of "infamous character" named George Took (or Tooke). Once Took was arraigned, two other Cherokees testified against him and implicated him and a coconspirator in the murders. According to the informants, Took and his accomplice planned on stealing property from the Bowman family, but when they entered the house under cover of darkness, Bowman grabbed his gun, "and a fight ensued." Eventually the two Indians overpowered Bowman and proceeded to kill him, his wife, child, and mother-in-law and "split open each head with an axe." Having finished their grisly work, the two Cherokees plundered the house and sold the goods to Creek Ben, a noted fence who disposed of the property. Held in jail in DeKalb County beginning in January 1833, Took waited for his trial to commence in Murray County in September. The judge postponed the September hearing when the lawyers could not agree upon a jury. When authorities sent him back to the DeKalb County jail, his guards stopped one evening and rested at a farmhouse. Took laid down "feigning sickness and ... extreme bodily pain." Writhing on the ground, he managed to slip the shackles over his head and off his ankles and made his escape through an open door. The sheriff offered a reward of one hundred dollars for Took's apprehension, but by the following month he still eluded capture. Civil authorities did not track him down for another two years, when he was arrested in Cherokee country. During his capture, the sheriff's deputy "was forced to shoot him," a doctor had to amputate one of his limbs, and members of the Georgia Guard had to patrol the jail to prevent another escape. Even on his deathbed, Took did not confess to the Bowman murders, though he did openly admit to killing Duck, a fellow Cherokee.[18]

The mysterious death of the Bowman family and Williamson's suspicion of foul play may have convinced the legislature to continue the Guard out of fear of other attacks. Though Lumpkin feared further violent outbreaks, he did not think the Bowman family's demise signaled encroaching doom: "I cannot believe however that this horrible act has originated from any things like a concerted plan from any considerable number of the Cherokee." Rather than fret over Cherokee reprisals, Lumpkin wanted the Guard to concentrate its efforts at fracturing whatever remained of Cherokee resistance to removal.[19]

Though the Guard had been significantly reduced, it did not abandon its mission of protecting those "good" Cherokees who vouched for removal. Indeed, by February 1833, Lumpkin had begun designating certain Cherokee residents who could keep their land. One man whom the governor stipulated as a recipient of state largesse was William Hicks, the former Principal Chief of the Cherokee Nation and a proponent of removal. After the lottery, Hicks's land had not been drawn, so Lumpkin ensured him that he was entitled to it because of his model behavior. Lumpkin deemed Hicks a positive example who had "uniformly respected the laws and authority of Georgia & treated her officers & citizens with kindness & respect, and is therefore entitled to our special regard and respect." Further placating the former chief, Lumpkin assured Hicks that he and his "friends" who felt similarly regarding removal would be "safe and free" from the "threats or abuse of any and all pretended government emanating from John Ross and his followers." In exchange for their protection, Lumpkin required that Hicks and other Indians who shared his point of view on removal continue to exert their "moral influence in a peaceable and persuasive manner." In other words, Hicks had to vouch for removal at great expense to his personal security. Such a stance was simply good politics for Lumpkin. Cherokee "protection" proved an effective tool for widening schisms within the Cherokee polity in order to further expand the white republic.[20]

Those Cherokees who did not support leaving their homes became exposed to physical abuse of the worst kind. In July 1833, the sheriff of Coweta County, David Dukes, prowled across the Cherokee Nation, searching for his lottery claim. Rumors from Coweta County circulated, claiming that that the sheriff had vacated his post because of serious debts, though the Cherokees whom he met with had no way of knowing of his pecuniary troubles. He "called" at a house occupied by two women, Oosunaley and Foster. When he discovered that the women's husbands and other male relatives were nowhere in sight, he "attempted the monstruous crime of rape" against Oosunaley because of her "delicate condition." Foster grabbed the sheriff by the boot and dragged him off her friend two separate times. When it became apparent that his efforts had been foiled, Dukes pulled out his pocketbook "and offered his injured hosts satisfaction," meaning he sought to pay them off. To his surprise, the women grabbed the pocketbook and tried to destroy it. Enraged, Dukes produced a heavy horsewhip, which he employed with ruthless efficiency "until Algiers itself would sicken at the stripes inflicted."[21]

The two women went to the magistrate in the newly created Murray County, who informed the women of the impossibility of receiving Indian testimony intended for use against a white citizen. Few Georgians had reason to believe the women's story when Dukes himself went to the press and published his version of events. He claimed that the women had invited him to sit down near their house to eat apples. After nearly twenty minutes, Dukes realized that his handkerchief was missing from the pocket of his overcoat, and, along with it, his pocketbook containing eighteen dollars. He accused the women of stealing his money but discovered his pocketbook, minus the money, stashed beneath a bundle of calico cloth. This sent him into a rage. Producing his whip, he beat one women "four or five times," until she turned over the rolled-up bank notes. When he tried to leave the scene, the other Cherokee woman grabbed the reins of his horse, until Dukes struck her twice. Dukes had not finished with the two women, though.[22]

Two days later the sheriff returned to the scene of the crime. While conversing with a third Cherokee woman who spoke English, he tried to justify his previous actions and declared that he had acted in such a brutish way because he had been robbed. At that point, the woman he had accused of stealing his money threw a stick at Dukes. Enraged, the sheriff leapt off his horse and "gave her ten or twelve severe cuts with the whip."[23] Dukes's account, and the unexplained return visit to the scene of the crime, made it seem that the sheriff sought to return to the isolated farmstead to justify his crimes and lay blame at the feet of the Cherokee women in order to protect his reputation. The extension and supremacy laws made it impossible for Cherokees to receive justice within the state legal system, and because Gilmer's proposal to allow Native testimony against whites had proven abhorrent to voters, the women had no legal recourse. Indeed, the stress and frustration that Cherokees had been living with since 1829 boiled over, but all the women could do to make manifest that frustration was itself a harmless action: they threw a stick.

It is important to remember that by the summer of 1833, the state had extended its authority over the Cherokee Nation and had gone ahead and created new counties out of that territory. Because of that, Georgians like David Dukes, who had won land in the 1832 land and gold lotteries, were now, according to the state and federal government, legally entitled to roam through Cherokee land to claim their winnings. This put them in direct contact with the current Cherokee residents who wanted to stay on their land. The epicenter for this contest occurred in Murray County, which contained the Cherokee capital, New Echota. Issues of sovereignty that had plagued federal, Native, and state leaders in the 1820s and early 1830s likewise plagued Murray County's officials as they sought to extend Georgia's version of order. But not everything in the county's body politic proved unified. For some Georgia residents living in the disputed territory, the Cherokees still exerted far too much sway in the course of events and wanted a firm hand to deal with the threat to their homes and families. Others in Murray County understood that because the lottery winners had begun claiming their new homesteads, the de facto expulsion of the Cherokees had already begun and the state should limit violence on the part of settlers.

Into the mix in 1833 came the next gubernatorial election and a statewide convention that met to determine a more equitable system of representation in the state legislature. These two contests allowed voters to further the white man's chance in new ways. State politics in the late 1820s and early 1830s had been embroiled in the prospects of state sovereignty and how best to enact the expulsion of Native populations from within the state's claimed territory. Although state politics had been vitriolic, it strayed from national norms because the competing factions had been built around personality and patronage networks rather than political issues. The election of Andrew Jackson shifted national politics in dramatic ways, not least of which, the development of the Second Party System, encouraged the growth of party politics and widespread voter participation. State politics likewise shifted, though in more subtle ways. Because the two factions within the Georgia polity supported the president and especially his removal policy, local concerns became the driving force of party loyalty. Beginning with the 1831 gubernatorial election, where Gilmer put forth a campaign grounded in a state's right to create internal improvements based on the public ownership of gold mines, the factions within Georgia began to align with the Second Party System. Wilson Lumpkin and the Clark faction, by 1833, had begun calling itself the Union Party, and their sympathies rested mostly with the national Democratic Party. The Troup faction, formerly led by George Gilmer, called itself the State Rights Party and sympathized with nullifiers in South Carolina as well as Whigs who stressed the benefits of internal improvements. Much of their political contest played out in the partisan press, which stoked voter turnout and public discourse. Some

Georgians paid lip service to decorum and evinced some trepidation about two-party politics, as evidenced by toasts made at public events. In Savannah, for example, one toastmaker implored the legislature to "secure prosperity to the State . . . by a devotion to the practical purposes of Internal Improvements, by burying the intrigues of faction in Canals, and exploding the vapours of metaphysical politics by Steam Engines and Rail Roads."[24]

Instead of a robust program of internal improvements, however, the state assembly gave voters a clarification about whiteness. In the lead-up to that year's gubernatorial election, the state legislature became involved with Cherokee acculturation in an effort to protect the prerogatives of whiteness. In its 1833 session, the legislature gave some Cherokees a chance to renounce their "savagery" in favor of "civilization." Essentially, the law allowed some multiracial Cherokees to swap their Cherokee citizenship for state citizenship, a process that would allow them to keep some of their land. To do so, the legislation stripped multiracial Cherokees of legal rights unless those individuals swore before a clerk of the superior court that they wished to be considered white rather than Indian. Once that occurred, the head of the family "shall be entitled to all privileges which are granted to such white men." Aside from making elite Cherokees choose an identity for political purposes, it also prevented Cherokees from hiring whites or slaves belonging to whites to work their land. Failure to comply with this section of the law meant that the Cherokee landowner had to forfeit his or her property "as though such improvements had never been occupied by such Indian." The law voided contracts between whites and Cherokees and, in order to hurry voluntary removal and strengthen the accommodationists, declared that preventing or intimidating any Cherokee from enrolling became a misdemeanor. Again, the state recognized that Cherokees made improvements to their land but denied them the use of it for participating in market activities that it had criminalized. All of these were efforts to hurt the elite Cherokees who continued to oppose removal. Called the Cherokee Protection Law, it provided the governor with the authority to designate "some fit and proper person as agent" to enforce this law.[25]

The man Lumpkin turned to was none other than William N. Bishop. Indeed, Bishop was a man on the rise who typified not just the rough-and-tumble world of Jacksonian political operatives but also the violent nature of life in newly settled areas. Bishop did not win a lot in the land or gold lottery, but he did purchase a tract of land that contained the buildings belonging to the Moravian mission at Springplace. Moving to his new home, he claimed ownership of the mission and its outbuildings. He quickly became a figurehead in local politics and ingratiated himself with the Union Party and publicly denounced nullification. From the newly created Murray County, Bishop had been appointed an agent who could rent out fractional lots that were not given away in the lottery to white settlers. But he noticed threats to the white polity that could not go unchecked. What troubled him most was "tolerably divided" county between those he deemed the "white" party, who threw their support behind Lumpkin and the Union Party, and the "Indian" party, who supported the opposition.

The name for his political opponents originated during the campaign for the constitutional convention that sought to readjust how state congressional seats were apportioned. Though a similarly named measure dealing with the tariff had worked its way through the U.S. Congress, Georgians dealt with an altogether different manner of reduction: decreasing the number of representatives and senators in the state house as a means of defraying costs and promoting more equitable representation. This was a deliberate attempt on the part of the Union Party to again show their democratic bona fides and weaken the State Rights Party, whose traditional base of support had been the coastal region. Advocates saw the measure as "resting on principles of the purest democracy" because it apportioned state-level representation to the free white male population and not the "federal" count that included three-fifths of a county's slaves—voters saw the governor as a champion of the prerogatives of white settlers. Fourth of July revelers and Union Party supporters toasted the wisdom of the convention for recognizing "that the free white population alone is the proper basis of representation."[26] Proposed by Lumpkin's Union Party, the measure was designed to weaken the Troup faction's traditional geographic base, the lowcountry. Moreover, most of the delegates hailed from the Union Party. The new system created new Senate districts and reduced the number of senators by half to thirty-six. It also ensured that each county had at least one representative in the lower house, which was important to Lumpkin as he derived much of his support from scantily populated counties in the northern part of the state. The convention then awarded additional seats to the most populous forty counties but limited the maximum number of representatives per county to four. When Georgians went to the polls in October, 57 percent of voters in the new counties carved out of the Cherokee Nation supported the scheme; 61 percent of border county voters supported the reduction measure. With widespread support in the backcountry, the reduction measure cruised to victory.[27]

Not everything went Bishop's way in Murray County. In the lead-up to the election, Bishop capitalized on the fact that one State Rights Party candidate for convention delegate had a Cherokee wife. This fact should have made the vote in Murray County a lopsided one, but that did not occur. When the returns for the county's delegates for the convention became public, Bishop's concerns became palpable. For the convention, he informed the governor, the Union Party had run "two respectable white men" who won the election by only a single vote each. However, they had to forfeit their spots because, Bishop admitted, there were irregularities concerning an "oath laid down to residence." The law convening the reduction convention required that delegates had resided in their respective county for at least a year and in the state for seven. In other words, those "respectable white men" had lied, their neighbors had turned them in, and they forfeited their convention seats.[28] Murray County instead sent delegates from the "Indian party." After the two delegates withdrew from the convention race, Bishop lamented the ascendancy of the "Indian party" at home. In a letter to the governor, he claimed that one of the new candidates was a man of "Infamous character" who had been a counterfeiter and a "Poney club man." According to Bishop, Cherokees were preventing whites from plowing their fields or sowing corn, thereby robbing them of their ability to support themselves and their families, in the hope of expelling "all citizens who are true to the State Laws and policy so that they can remain in power." For Bishop, a man who had spent time attacking intruders while a part of the Georgia Guard, who had made public pronouncements against the Pony Club, and who reveled in violence directed at Cherokees, the prospect of a political alliance between his enemies seemed likely. The new owner of the Springplace mission openly asked for violence to be employed as a means of intimidating his enemies. Bishop wondered if Lumpkin could "suggest any plan to intimidate these Chiefs[.] I should like to be in possession of it early."[29]

By calling his opponents the "Indian party," Bishop drew on the fear of recent settlers who thought Indian opposition would prevent them from claiming their land, or, if they did claim it, would encourage widespread reprisals. The explicit racializing of the parties was a savvy move on Bishop's part. It demonstrated that he understood the power of whiteness as it related to politics in the disputed territory, and it again connected his partisan affiliation to the protection of white Georgians, their property, and their superiority. Bishop was certain that white residents in the newly created counties would soon experience danger firsthand, especially when rumors of despotic Cherokee leaders interfering with Georgia's wholesome, benevolent civil institutions and democratic processes ran rampant. Warning the governor of the threats posed to the nascent courts in Murray County, Bishop once again warned the governor of a scheme afoot. He issued a stern warning: county officials had appointed a land agent "who is completely under the influence of the Head men of the Cherokee." The new land agent, furthermore, had an altogether "Infamous character," who reportedly passed counterfeit money and had been suspected of sympathizing with the reviled Pony Club. "Our chance for Legal Justice is Doubtful," Bishop worried. Most troubling to Lumpkin's supporter, though, were rumors that the land agent had plans "to drive a Large portion of our citizens from the country" with an "Indian Possy." Without aid from the state, "this part of Cherokee will shortly be a scene of confusion." Lumpkin sought to assuage the anxieties of his constituents and reaffirmed them that "the Supremacy of the laws of Georgia should be maintained."[30]

Bishop never let down his guard when it came to the infiltration of civil offices by his enemies. To safeguard Murray County from the "Indian party," he sought measures to protect fellow settlers. "I also wish to know," Bishop inquired, "if we raise a volunteer cavalry company if we can have arms without the usual number [of recruits]?" That the state mandated a sixty-man minimum for a new militia company did not deter Bishop from seeking special treatment from the legislature. In the end, however, they had to follow the law and could not incorporate their militia because they could not muster the minimum number of men. Even Benjamin F. Currey, the primary federal enrolling agent, championed Bishop. He recommended to the governor the appointment of Bishop, or someone with similar energy (Currey also mentioned Charles H. Nelson as a candidate for command), "clothed with full power to employ the necessary force civil or military in a summary manner from whose decisions there shall be no appeal to inferior or superior courts." Bishop's hopes were dashed when the legislature did not requisition funds for him and his men or offer the Murray County militia more extensive authority when it met later that winter.[31]

Bishop was undeterred. If he could not use force to compel order, he would do all he could to make sure that the Union Party proved victorious in electoral contests. Believing that the county was "tolerably divided" between the "Indian Party" that supported the State Rights

Party platform and the "white party" that supported Lumpkin, Bishop reported confidently that Lumpkin would win votes in the upcountry: "I believe we will be able not withstanding their [sic] is two parties to give you a large majority next fall in this County."[32] The vote for the reduction measure suggested that Lumpkin would also cruise to victory in his own election. Bishop correctly predicted the mood of the voters, who showed just how much they approved of the State Rights Party and its possible alliance with Natives at the local level. Of the 150 votes cast in fledgling Murray County in October 1833, 120 (80 percent) went to Lumpkin. A similar story played out in the nine other new counties, where Lumpkin tallied nearly 62 percent of the votes cast. In the border counties, the results mirrored those in the Cherokee counties, where 63 percent of voters supported the incumbent. That residents in the disputed territory still flocked to Lumpkin's banner, demonstrating their affection for the man who had rammed through the gold lottery and vowed to protect the white man's chance.[33]

In spite of Lumpkin's victory in the gubernatorial election in 1833, Bishop was still convinced that an imminent threat to white settlers existed. Others agreed with him. Over the next two years, Bishop maintained strong support in the backcountry as white settlers grew everfearful of Indian attacks. Though he suffered a setback when his militia company failed to make muster, he and fellow settlers sought ways of ordering their world and protecting their families. In May 1834, a committee of concerned citizens from Cherokee County, chaired by the up-and-coming Howell Cobb, made a series of proposals to the governor. Exposure to "assassination & other lowley violence" compelled Cobb to encourage other duty-bound "white settlers of this country to adopt some strong & energetic measures upon this all important subject." A series of nine proposals offered by Cobb's committee suggested unyielding measures to deal with threats to "the lives of our white citizens . . . daily and publicly made by the Indians." Cobb worried that civil law could not provide adequate protection to the county's white citizens "unless aided by military force from the state or the general government" that could "aid the civil authorities in executing the laws of the state." Without that protection, white settlers would be forced into a "disgraceful but necessary retreat" and would therefore have to "surrender . . . the country to the original savage occupants." Or, barring unexpected help from the government, citizens would take care of matters themselves. If, for example, a Cherokee murdered a white person within the county and was not turned over to civil authorities, white residents would apprehend

Wilson Lumpkin, governor of Georgia, 1831–35, put both the land and gold lotteries into place by combatting Gilmer's scheme of public ownership of the gold mines. J. T. Moore, *Portrait of Wilson Lumpkin* (1964). Courtesy of the Georgia Capitol Museum, object id 1992.23.002.

three Cherokee men and *"put them to death as an atonement."* Such a proposal dramatized the seriousness with which whites in the borderlands took threats and rumors of violence, but they also had to realize how untenable such a proposal was. It smacked of vigilantism, which many Georgians had disapproved of in the milder form taken by the Slicks. Such measures circumvented the court system and caused justice to devolve away from civil institutions and toward a dystopia plagued by disorder and lawlessness.[34]

Most of the anxiety from settlers came from what they called Cherokee effrontery. "Do the people on the East of the Chattahoochie suffer large able bodied young men to stroll about the settlements, a gang of ten or a dozen with bows & arrows shooting small birds?," wondered one resident of Murray County, John Brewster. Such a statement failed to disguise his own insecurity at the sight of youthful Cherokee prowess, which prompted other white settlers in Murray to move their "wives & children into some of the old country" before returning to defend home and hearth. Aside from the "protection of white inhabitants," Brewster believed that a "strong system of military police" had become necessary because he feared the return of the Pony Club thieves, who "are realizing with their Cherokee confederates a handsome profit." In early April, a petition from citizens in Cherokee County arrived on Lumpkin's desk imploring the governor to "have organized & sent to our relief a Company of Mounted Men." In early May, Bishop had begun prodding the governor to authorize such a force, suggesting, "Thirty Men raised in this country Mounted and Armed with Muskets could answer every purpose." "We are . . . in the beginning of war," a committee of Murray County residents predicted, and they requested "arms as well as men" to fend off any forthcoming attack.[35]

With a large Cherokee population still living on the land that had been given to the lottery winners, he had to create some way for Georgians to impose their will. But he did not believe that war loomed. Most of the fuss came from residents who were "extremely alarmed" at the pronouncements of a Cherokee child who had told white settlers that her people had begun stockpiling weapons and ammunition.[36] Much of the governor's hesitancy—what he called "calm and peaceful measures"—in deploying a military force came from past experience and his fear that a martial strategy would "supercede the civil authority by the interposition of the military." Federal troops and the first iteration of the Guard tended to compounded violent tendencies in the disputed territory and, worse, often targeted uncooperative whites, which made such forces political liabilities. Still, with the threat of an all-out Indian attack looming, Lumpkin proposed to meet force head on.[37]

To do so, he took two steps. First, he encouraged the new counties to raise volunteer militia units so locals could more effectually protect themselves and their neighbors. "Where the population will admit of it in the new counties," Lumpkin wrote to U.S. Attorney General John

Forsyth, "I am endeavouring to effect the organization of Volunteer companies to be placed under the command of prudent and intelligent men, who will be furnished with arms from our public arsenal to meet any emergency which may possibly occur." A show of military might would prevent the state from being "harassed by the enemies of good order, and all civil government." Even though he doubted the rumors plaguing the backcountry concerning an impending attack, the governor was not about to let white men and women suffer from a lack of preparedness.[38]

It soon became apparent, though, that the good citizens of the Cherokee counties were less interested in joining the militia and fighting in an Indian war than they were in having others fight in their stead. With such a small population, that attitude meant that neighborhoods and entire militia districts went undefended. Knowing that he had to at least appear prepared, Lumpkin took the advice of Benjamin F. Currey, who again pleaded for the rapid organization of a mounted guard "to keep the peace & aid the civil authorities in the execution of the law." It stands to reason that Currey wanted a state-supported unit because he had found in them a very convenient way to add additional Cherokees to the rosters of those who left "voluntarily." The governor still resisted a more forceful action, but he did take an important second step when he named Bishop and Charles H. Nelson as enforcement agents to coordinate between state militia commanders and local civil authorities to better waylay criminals and prevent violent outbursts. In November, Bishop aided local sheriffs in the hunt for a murderer, James Graves, and a Cherokee criminal, John Hog Smith, who had escaped from jail in Cass County. The two also used local militia units to expel Cherokee residents who would not vacate property claimed by lottery winners.[39]

Much of the fear exhibited by white settlers stemmed from the fact that no Guard existed in 1834. William Williamson's ten-man unit, the third such force created by the state and also the smallest, had not been renewed. In the December 1834 session of the legislature, a select committee in the House warned the rest of the legislature of "alarming disorders and disturbance in the Cherokee country" that would surely lead to war if the General Assembly did not take firm measures to prevent it. To prevent the outbreak of violence, legislators allowed the governor to enlist forty men for special duty in a new Guard. Relying upon the "energy, watchfulness, and discretion" of the governor to create a military force if the "exigency to demand it" arose, the law left the timing regarding the company's creation and its oversight to the governor, perhaps as a way to distance legislators from any political fallout from its operation. The legislature placed almost no restrictions, either financial or operational, on the force, though it did stipulate that the governor had to remain watchful for the corruption accompanying a standing military force, though it placed no limits on the amount of time or money that could be spent creating order.[40]

Lumpkin did not immediately muster the Guard into service, mostly because no immediate emergency arose. The man he wanted to appoint as the commander, Bishop, had also become embroiled in a political scandal that made it risky to do so. Rather than brashly appoint a supporter embroiled in a political scandal, he waited to see how political opponents shaped their reaction to Bishop's behavior. One Union Party supporter in the backcountry urged Lumpkin to name Bishop the commander of the Guard but warned that he would be pilloried for such a decision. "If the command of the guard is given to him," one adviser informed the governor, "you may expect to be abused for it." It would prove a difficult decision, but the adviser told Lumpkin to steel himself. After all, "what have you done for the benefit of the people since you went into office for which your enimies have not slandered you?"[41]

The incident that gave Lumpkin pause occurred in February 1835, when Bishop, acting in his capacity as the governor's agent, acted to expel Joseph Vann and his family from their home near the Springplace mission, Bishop's new home. He warned the family that they had to leave. When they refused, he arrived at their home at the head of twenty-five armed men to compel them to do so. Accompanying Bishop's posse was the lottery winner Joshua Holder, who came armed with the deed he had won. It soon became apparent that Bishop also had a tangential interest in expelling not only the Vann family but also a white man who rented one of their rooms, Spencer Riley. Bishop and his men forced themselves into the house, yelling at Riley to leave. The terrified family huddled in an adjacent room while the Georgians commenced shooting. Spencer barricaded himself in a stairwell; Bishop's men fired over a dozen shots to dislodge him. One ball struck Riley's musket, which splintered, the remnants of which lodged in his head. Bleeding profusely, he demanded to know who had fired the last shot. Bishop replied, "The state of Georgia fired that gun!" Though Bishop's testy assertion proved partly correct—he had been named the governor's agent when it came to apprehending fugitives and therefore acted on behalf of the state—he had little authority to dislodge peaceful Cherokee residents from their homes. His antics signaled just how comfortable he felt using violence to create a form of order that, for those on the receiving end, appeared like lawlessness.[42]

Such viciousness directed at a legal resident of the Cherokee country no doubt angered Riley's friends, who were not inconsiderable in state politics. This obviously made the appointment of Bishop as commander of the Guard a sticky situation for the governor. It soon grew worse. During the fracas, Bishop encouraged his men to "kill the d—d rascal, we have no use for nullifiers in this county." The overtly partisan nature of his assault on Riley made Bishop a liability. The violent rivalry between the two men did not end in Joseph Vann's living room, either. Bishop's version of events appeared in Union newspapers, where he claimed that Riley "was a bully for his party" whose "violence and rancor" forced Bishop to act in such an aggressive manner. The aggrieved state agent only hoped that his character and reputation had not been tarnished beyond repair.[43]

In spite of Bishop's troubles and the political headaches such a partisan caused for the governor, Lumpkin felt compelled to award the command of the new Guard to Bishop. Lumpkin was also savvy enough to realize that he needed someone with a fierce reputation in order to accomplish his goals. In May, Bishop had salvaged enough of his reputation in newspaper exchanges with Riley's friends that the governor found it appropriate to appoint him commander of the Guard. Further, the exigency required by the resolution to form the Guard had arrived in two forms. In early 1835, a delegation of Cherokees led by Major Ridge, Elias Boudinot, and Stand Watie began meeting with federal negotiators to hammer out a removal treaty. Tensions within the Cherokee Nation mounted and, soon enough, turned violent. By early summer, several Cherokees who supported removal—now called the Treaty Party—had been killed for their political stance by members of Ross's antiremoval National Party. Georgians living within the Cherokee Nation now found themselves in the midst of a violent civil strife. Second, news of a mass jailbreak by Cherokee prisoners convinced Lumpkin that a Guard could efficiently be deployed as a way to return the prisoners to jail and prevent any additional escapes. Indeed, it was Bishop who warned the governor: "The Prison doors have been broken open in Cassville—and all the Prisoners therein have made their escape. . . . Our country is now full of bloody assassins and our white Population are considerably alarmed." The combination of Cherokee violence over a prospective treaty and the escaped prisoners provided Governor Lumpkin the emergency he required to muster a new Guard.[44]

On May 28, 1835, Lumpkin finally authorized the creation of a new Guard and named Bishop its commander. Lumpkin's supporters sought to assuage the nerves of those who opposed Bishop's appointment. The Guard, they declared, would not override civil officers but would act in concert with them: "It will aid the civil authority in making arrests; in apprehending outlaws... in arresting those who may threaten the peace of the State, and giving security to the lives and property of friendly Indians from the murder and rapine contemplated by Ross and his followers." The new unit, the Georgia Rangers, consisted of forty men who had been called out for the "security, relief, and protection of our own citizens and the friendly Cherokees."[45]

With only forty men, the Rangers made a substantial impact on affairs in the backcountry. For the most part, they did not bother with white settlers, squatters, or intruders. Instead, they spent their time discerning the movements of and intimidating National Party members and searched for Indian fugitives and suspected criminals, whom they accused of aligning with Ross. Much of Bishop's time as commander of the Rangers was spent apprehending criminals who had escaped from county jails. Convinced that a conspiracy was afoot, Bishop blamed such perfidious machinations on Ross's supporters. Bishop and his men "arrested several persons charged with crime," including suspected murderers. Bishop also dispersed the Rangers "in various parts of the country to learn the lurking places of those Banditti or Band of Ross[']s Murderers." The trend of Bishop's Rangers and the Union Party leadership was to blame recalcitrant Indians, and not state policy, for the problems plaguing the backcountry—problems, in their minds, with only one solution, removal. The Rangers, at the behest of Currey, also went to the offices of the *Cherokee Phoenix* and stole the printing press. The *Phoenix*, long the mouthpiece of Ross and the National Council, had been a constant thorn in the state's side because it focused so much of its coverage on state policy and, in particular, violent actions aimed at Cherokees. By stealing the printing press, the Rangers effectively silenced the most vocal critics of the state's actions.[46]

As winter descended upon the disputed territory, the new governor, William Schley, learned troubling news regarding the conduct of Bishop's force. When the circuit court met in Murray County to verify jury lists for the inferior and superior courts, the proceedings were interrupted by Bishop, "with nearly all, or the great part of his guard," who demanded that the court accept his own list, filled with the names of his supporters. When several witnesses refused, including the judges, "his guard all set to cursing... with threats & menaces of the most violent character." When the judges ordered Bishop and his men to desist, a tense standoff ensued. Bishop was later reported to have said that if the deputy sheriff had tried to arrest one of his men, "he would have shot him through, as . . . he had his thumb upon the cock of his Pistol & his finger on the Trigger." One witness later learned that if he had attempted to intervene on behalf of the court he would have had "many balls shot through my carcuss." Bishop had previously despaired over the prospects of civil authority in the county because of the Indian Party. Now it suffered at his hands: "The fact is the civil authority is put down by him in this county.... [H]e pays no regard to the law unless it is to operate upon his enimies, then he rushes forward with his guard and takes it into his own hand." Bishop's authority had gone to his head.[47]

Bishop reveled in his growing power. By doing so he circumvented civil authority that the Guard had been designed to protect. Though a gross violation of his charge, it was not altogether surprising given Bishop's violent propensities. The same set of complaints lodged with the new governor detailed further abuses by Bishop and the Rangers in Murray County. The "tiranical movements" of the Guard targeted Bishop's political enemies, or "every body that dose not subscribe to his universal views." Maintaining the power of the Union Party became his overriding concern. When any of his friends found themselves liable for charges in court, Bishop and the Rangers "parades immediately and goes forward & brakes up the Court & scares off the party & returns with their friend . . . in triumph." After such spectacles, the Rangers and their political allies could be found "lauding the commander, comparing him to General Jackson," all because they had halted a court hearing and defeated "honest men." Men from the State Rights Party claimed Bishop imprisoned them without a trial, and he had "whip[p]ed the back of our whiteman to an awful extent & tourn asunder his garments."[48]

Though its victims definitely suffered at the hands of the Rangers, the real victim, according to some observers, was democracy itself. The man informing the governor of Bishop's actions, James Edmonson, feared for the fate of self-government if Bishop continued his antics. The Ranger's actions were "not consistant with well regulated government," he warned. He called Bishop a tyrant who oppressed anyone who opposed him, which made him a political liability. At the last election, the Union Party candidate for the House to represent Murray County had fared poorly precisely because of Bishop's threats. During the campaign, Bishop had spread rumors that, if reelected, the Union Party establishment would rigidly follow Lumpkin's use of the Guard. Even new voters in the county could not stomach voting for a policy "that would keep the citizens of a

146 / CHAPTER 6

county so appressed [sic] by a set of irresponsible vagabonds." The seemingly unrestrained power granted to the Guard had been corrupted by a political partisan, a man who saw violence as a viable option for the establishment of order in the backcountry.[49]

In spites of Edmonson's fears regarding the fragility of civil authority in Murray County, Schley did not remove or chastise Bishop. He did summon Bishop to Milledgeville in November to the General Assembly's meeting. While leaving the legislative chambers on Friday, November 6, Bishop, "walking arm in arm with another gentleman," was attacked from behind by his old rival, Spencer Riley. Striking Bishop with a large walking stick that broke during the scuffle, Riley had the advantage until Bishop produced a pistol and shot Riley in the chin. He then rained down blows on Riley with the gun's handle until witnesses separated the two combatants. Covered in blood, both of the men produced a pistol and dirk, waiting for the other to make a move. Finally, their friends pulled them away from each other; neither man had suffered severe wounds, which shocked onlookers, who were in awe of the "muscular power & desperate courage of the men." The General Assembly stopped only briefly when it heard the shot fired, but soon continued "with their business, as though nothing had happened." Even the legislature, it appears, had become inured to Bishop's violent outbursts.[50]

Without official censure, Bishop continued his ways. His downfall, though, was not long in coming. After a failed series of negotiations led by Ross had been rejected by the Senate, the Treaty Party went to work when it began talks with federal negotiators in December in the hope of reaching a favorable settlement for removal. When Currey learned that John Howard Payne, a northerner—and therefore, in his eyes, a foe—was visiting John Ross, he seized on the opportunity to strike at the opponents of Georgia's sovereignty. Currey ordered the Rangers to arrest John Ross and his guest. The only problem, of course, was that Ross lived in Tennessee, well out of their jurisdiction. With Bishop still in Milledgeville, probably recovering from his wounds, the job fell to the subcommander, Wilson R. Young, a resident of Murray County and an ardent Bishop man. Leading the Rangers across the Tennessee River to the home of the Cherokee Principal Chief, Young's command arrested Ross and Payne and took them back to Georgia. Payne, who had penned one of the most famous songs of the nineteenth century, "Home Sweet Home," overheard one of the Rangers humming the tune on the ride back to Murray County. When pressed on why he had dispatched the Guard into Tennessee, Currey justified his actions by claiming that

Payne "is of the whig party and rumor makes him an abolitionist." Not only did Currey encourage the Rangers to cross state borders, but his motives were just as politically motivated as those of Bishop.[51]

The national press widely reviled the actions of the Rangers. From Nashville, they were a "party of desperadoes"; Connecticut papers wondered why a police force was required for the "peace and good order of the Cherokee country." Would the Guard next seek to abolish the courts by intimidating their way out of punishment? That would not happen, for the governor of Tennessee, Newton Cannon, outraged that his state's sovereignty had been violated, cried foul and demanded an apology. Governor Schley came under intense pressure from the State Rights Party to abolish the Guard. Cannon pointed out the irony of the state's actions. He could not fathom how a state so devoted to the "cause of State rights, and State sovereignty" could impugn the sovereignty of another state. The legislature convened a select committee to investigate the Rangers' activity and concluded that when Lumpkin had appointed Bishop his orders he made it clear that his "military command is designed only to aid the civil authority in carrying into effect the laws of the State." Lumpkin had used his authority to limit the Guard and ensure its subservience to civil authority. The new governor had done no such thing, though he did not come under fire. The problem, then, must have been the commander. The committee agreed that the news out of Murray County made it seem that the Rangers had discharged their duty "with *pleasure* to themselves." Bishop did not learn of Ross's and Payne's arrest until he arrived at Springplace at the end of November.[52]

By arresting Ross and Payne, the Rangers had put the legislature in a difficult quandary. The state had long permitted the Guard, beginning with Sanford, to carry out federal policy. In 1832 Williamson and his men had even gone into land claimed by Tennessee to protect a group of enrollees from armed militiamen from the Volunteer State. In this case, the Rangers deprived an American citizen of his Fourth Amendment rights, which put the committee in a delicate situation: if it declared that the Guard had the authority to storm into Ross's home, the committee would have implied that Ross and Payne had no protection from illegal search and seizure, which would have implied he was the citizen of a foreign nation with its own sovereignty. If that were the case, then the state had initiated an invasion of a foreign state, a power not granted to it under the Constitution. Indeed, the state's entire course of action since it passed the extension law would have been unconstitutional. The select committee investigating the arrests had to be a citizen of Tennessee entitled to the protection of that state's laws. Having reaffirmed that Lumpkin and Schley had done their best to prevent corruption, the committee lay the blame squarely at Bishop's feet for inculcating a devil-may-care attitude among the Rangers.

That raised another problem, for it freely admitted that a well-known political partisan and supporter of the Union Party had overstepped his bounds. The committee, in its report to the legislature, took a firm stance on the outrages committed by the Bishop and his men: "Ours is a government founded upon opinion, and not force. Its laws must be executed by the good order and discretion of the people, and not by the bayonet and the sword." Furthermore, the upcountry had been put on a path that would allow civil authority to flourish. If an emergency did arise, then "our fellow citizens in that section of the country must look to themselves, and to the aid which will most *assuredly* and *speedily* be rendered them by their brethren in different sections of the State."[53] With the committee's report, the legislature voted to abolish the Rangers.

Bishop was still not done. In February, he won a landslide victory in Murray County to become the next clerk of the superior court. Of the 170 votes cast, he received an astonishing 158. In a little over three months in his post, new complaints arose of his abuse. One Murray citizen, Thomas A. Harper, experienced Bishop's "mischievous *designs* & miserable deeds of *darkness*" firsthand when Bishop and his armed supporters removed him from his post as clerk of the inferior court. Harper worried over the viability of civil law when the "tirant crouched at the head of his mobs" resisted state law. Though Bishop never was punished for his abuses, his actions against Harper only strengthened the prevailing view that Bishop relied upon violence as a legitimate tool for the creation of order.[54]

Between 1831 and 1835, the State of Georgia funded four distinctive military units called the Georgia Guard. Though each unit contained no more than forty men, the cumulative effect of these paramilitary units reached not into the backcountry but to the nation's capital. Most notorious for arresting Christian missionaries in 1831, the various iterations of the Guard not only tormented men of the cloth but also intruders, Cherokees, and eventually political opponents. Their intent was twofold. First, the Guard sought to "protect the gold mines" from any intruders or prospectors, Georgian or Cherokee. Second, as Cherokee society splintered into two opposing factions regarding removal, the Guard sought to sow discord among them and convince the opponents of removal that the safety of their people and the viability of their nation were threatened in

Georgia. Their two motivations for using a large degree of force showed just how willing the state was to rid the disputed territory of whites who behaved lawlessly and to get rid of the Cherokees. In short, violence proved a useful way to bring about the white man's chance.

Employing intimidation, violence, and imprisonment, the Guard, at the behest of the state, used remarkably similar tactics to accomplish both of these goals. After 1832, the state implemented a lottery for the scope of Cherokee territory within the bounds of Georgia. Rather than chase off intruders, the Guard shifted its overall focus to the Cherokees in order to deepen rifts within the Cherokee polity. Its actions, especially in 1835, became problematic because the commander, William N. Bishop, extended violence to political opponents in Murray County. The state legislature eventually disbanded the Guard and resolved never to institute a new one. Using small, politically motivated units to provide order to the backcountry had come to an end, but the use of force to bring about the white republic had not. In 1836, settlers exhibited a great amount of anxiety when reports surfaced that the Cherokees were on the cusp of launching an all-out assault on whites. With the Guard gone, state leaders needed a new way to protect Georgia's citizens from potential Indian reprisals and to make the last push to enforce the Treaty of New Echota.

7 / The Militia and the Coming of Order

George R. Gilmer had not given up on returning to the governor's residence in Milledgeville. His persistence paid off, and his victory in the election of 1837 saw him resume his duties at a trying time. A former hand-picked officer in the Georgia Guard, Charles H. Nelson, had raised more than a thousand militiamen and marched on Milledgeville to make the legislature pay his men, testing Gilmer's leadership. When Gilmer vetoed the appropriations bill—which he saw as a ransom—he demonstrated that the civilian authority within the state would not be dictated to by militiamen. Just as in his first term, Gilmer's overriding concern with Cherokee Removal and the simultaneous settlement of the area was the prevention of violence. Moreover, he knew that once the federal government called for state militiamen to aid in the forceful expulsion of Cherokees, thousands of armed whites would soon occupy the Cherokee Nation to begin the work of forced relocation. If he could demonstrate that he could command his military forces to demonstrate forbearance, perhaps John Ross, the Principal Chief of the Cherokee Nation, could do the same. In that spirit, Gilmer reached out to Ross and implored him to choose peace. On March 9, 1838, Gilmer wrote to John Ross requesting that the Cherokee Principal Chief urge his people to accept removal peacefully. "It requires no strong invention to imagine," Gilmer cautioned, "the suffering and distress which must be inflicted upon your people, if hunted up by an undisciplined soldiery, and forced from their homes." Gilmer even went so far as to urge Ross to "save them from the evils that threaten them" by submitting to the inevitable. Here, perhaps,

Gilmer was admitting that his state was in the wrong by declaring the possible actions of his people to be evil, but he insisted that the power of the state would not be denied: "The harsh and unyielding will of superior power, has determined that the portion of the Cherokees remaining in this State must remove to the country provided for them in the West."[1]

In spite of his insistence that the state was in the right simply because it had more power—the result of years of deliberate and violent attempts by the state to destabilize Cherokee society—Gilmer still wanted Ross to believe that his words were in earnest: "It is my anxious desire that the Cherokees should be treated with humanity." Ross adamantly refused to take responsibility for the actions of men defending their families from forceful expulsion: "Should blood be spilt . . . the blame can never rest on us." By the middle of April everything was in motion. The War Department officially called for state militia to enter service federal service, and Gilmer made the appropriate maneuvers and directed the men who answered the call to meet at New Echota. Soon, two thousand armed Georgians were marching into the very heart of the Cherokee Nation. Nobody knew if the Cherokees would rise up against the army entering their homeland or if they would cooperate with the process of forced expulsion from their homes.[2]

In early 1836, Georgians living in the counties that had been carved out of the Cherokee Nation had worked themselves into a panic. Rumors circulated regarding an imminent Cherokee attack that would drive white settlers from Native ground. The gossip originated with a young Indian girl who told whites that her people had been stockpiling arms and planned on launching a surprise attack. Governor William Schley, uncertain if any real threat existed, did not wait to find out: "Whether there be any real cause for alarm among the people in the Cherokee country, is a question not to be determined now." He refused to place the blame for the rumors at the feet of panicky settlers but did think it prudent to strip the Cherokees of personal arms: "Would it not be well . . . to all the Cherokees . . . until they are removed?" Schley fretted that the Treaty of New Echota, ratified "not by the sanction of their leaders," would encourage Cherokees to "make a desperate effort to obtain what they may consider revenge on the white people." Jackson did not approve of Schley's plan. Not only would it leave the Cherokees exposed to attacks by Georgians, but it put federal forces in the awkward position of having to defend Indians. Such a plan would make it seem that Jackson intended to uphold John Marshall's *Worcester* decision and repeat the mistakes the military had made in 1831.[3]

It also made sense that white Georgians expressed nervousness. Early in 1836, the Creek Nation in Alabama resisted Jackson's removal policy and commenced the Second Creek War. According to historian John Ellisor, the fighting was well planned, and the Creeks sought to draw other Native groups, particularly the Cherokees, into the conflict. Some of the fighting did spill into Georgia and Florida.[4] Creek warriors commenced a series of effective raids that kept federal troops busy. In addition, the Second Seminole War had also been raging for a year. It did not take a large imaginative leap for Georgians to realize that if the Cherokees did start a shooting war (or if settlers precipitated one), then the state would be surrounded by hostile Native peoples intent on keeping their land. Georgians felt surrounded by Native enemies and looked with trepidation northward. The governor and his military advisers worried about just this prospect. Schley's aide wrote to the former commander of the Georgia Guard and now major general in the state militia, John W. A. Sanford, warning of a three-pronged war: "The actual hostilities of the Seminole and Creek Indians, and the great disaffection and restlessness manifested by the Cherokees . . . admonishes the authorities of Georgia to lose no time in preparing for any emergency that may possibly arise out of our present relations with these treacherous foes." The governor also wrote to President Jackson that the Cherokees actively sought ways to join up with the Creeks and Seminoles. If the Cherokees "in a moment of desperation . . . hope that they can escape punishment by flying to the Creeks and Seminoles," the people of Georgia would be faced with a formidable, perhaps even an existential, threat.[5]

Cherokee leaders, still reeling from the passage of the Treaty of New Echota, had little interest in participating in a war against the state. John Ross and much of his government knew that organized, armed resistance of any sort would have spelled the doom of their people: "The Cherokees are deeply sensible of their peculiar and dependent situation, consequently are not ignorant that their very existence as a people, is at the mercy of the United States." Even members of the proremoval faction within the Cherokee Nation expressed horror at the precariousness they now experienced as nervous Georgians, who understood that the Treaty of New Echota demanded relocation, seemed to take matters into their own hands. John Ridge wrote to the War Department asking for federal military intervention to protect his people from violent whites. Ridge requested military protection from Georgians, fearing that when his people did leave for Indian Territory, their only possessions would be "the scars of the lash on our backs."[6] At least some Georgians agreed.

One man remarked that there remained no doubt that the Cherokees "are incited to mischief by the inhuman treatment they received at the hands of our own people." To allay the tensions and to prevent white settlers from "pulling down all the troubles upon our borders," residents in the disputed territory had to "treat them more like human beings ... and less like brute beasts as they appear to be now regarded by us."[7]

With the beginnings of the Second Creek War, most settlers did not evince the empathy requested by their neighbor. With a conflict brewing in southern Georgia and the prospect of a Cherokee conflict on the horizon, Georgians anticipated the beginning of federal operations that would culminate with removal. In early 1836, Schley informed state militia officers to ready their individual companies for a potential muster. Many responded; other militia districts began the process of forming companies anew. Cavalry troopers from Forsyth proclaimed their readiness and their desire to protect their "Country from emergencies of invasions from any quarter." Another company in Carroll County formed but learned that the state did not require their service near home and that they would be sent to south Georgia: "Every one along the line would be much disappointed in being sent off while there might be danger in our own neighborhood." Although there was disappointment from some of the new militias about where they would be stationed, the response did allay fears that Georgians would not rally to the protection of their state. Schley's preparedness paid dividends, for on May 25 he received orders from the secretary of war to "cause to be raised two thousand volunteers to be placed immediately in the service of the United States." From across the state, militia units offered their services to the governor. In Murray County, William N. Bishop's brother, Absalom, headed one company that formed for the express purpose "of going in to immediate action against the hostile Cherokees and Creeks."[8]

Absalom Bishop soon began working with a former officer of the Georgia Guard, Charles H. Nelson, to get their men into action. In January, Nelson wrote to Schley inquiring if the state required "further force to quell the lawless Savages in Florida?" Schley thanked Nelson for "this patriotic tender of services" and encouraged Nelson to get up a company of sixty mounted men. Schley went further to encourage the service of settlers in Murray County: "The necessary expense of your company, until you report to the commanding officers in Florida, will be paid by me. Let no man, therefore, be prevented from joining on the plea of poverty." It was not until June, however, that Nelson and Bishop called for recruits. By the end of the month, 111 men had joined the ranks of the newly minted Highland Battalion. Part of the delay in compiling the force probably came from the governor himself, who did not follow through on his end of the bargain. When Nelson and Bishop needed to pay for supplies, the aid promised by Schley did not arrive, so the governor encouraged Bishop to "do as well as you can on the credit of the State."[9]

When the Highlanders did finally muster into service, they did not go to Florida as Nelson wished, but to Lashley's Ferry on the Coosa River, about twenty miles south of Rome, Georgia, on the Georgia-Alabama border. The role played by the Highland Battalion in the Second Creek War was a small one, but it highlighted the efforts of state leaders who wished to punish or expel Indians, prevent racial mixing, and a potential Creek-Cherokee alliance. Bishop and his men were stationed at a key river crossing. Their strategy, predicated on "preventing the Creek Indians from coming into Georgia," sought to apprehend any Creeks who tried to flee federal agents in Alabama or else link up with the Cherokees. Schley declared the mere presence of the Creeks was an affront to state law. The legislature had prohibited Creeks living in Alabama from stepping onto state soil because of a "highly penal statue of this state, and therefore the authorities of Georgia are bound to arrest them when they violate this statute." While stationed there, Bishop's men from Murray County came into contact with federalized militiamen from Tennessee. Perhaps animosity lingered from the fact that Bishop's overeager brother had invaded the Volunteer State and that state's militia sought retaliation. Only vague details exist, but apparently Bishop's Company of the Highland Battalion engaged in a scuffle with their compatriots from Tennessee. When Schley heard of the fight, he grew upset that Bishop and Nelson had "acted improperly" toward the Tennesseans, but the evidence he had did not warrant punishment. Another report suggested that the entire tenure of the Highlanders had been plagued by problems, and the unit as a whole had "done more harm than good." Rather than have the legislature begin an investigation, and because it came so close to the actions of Bishop's Rangers, Schley wanted to disband the Highlanders altogether.[10]

Doing that proved more difficult than the governor had imagined. No one, with any degree of certainty, knew which government, the federal or state, currently employed Nelson and Bishop. The federal government acted as if the Highland Battalion was a hostile force. General Wool sent an order to General Dunlap of the Tennessee volunteers telling him to proceed immediately from his post in that state to New Echota so he could "prevent any interference on the part of the Georgia troops with the Cherokee." Further, he asked the general to "ascertain by whose authority they have been raised and stationed in that country." If they had been illegally raised, Dunlap should disband them immediately; if Georgia authorized the Highlanders, they had not been federalized, or sworn into service by a federal officer, which needed to happen. No federal officer had sworn in the Highlanders, though the state had stopped paying for the men once they reached the ferry. If he still was an officer of the state, the governor maintained that no troops from Tennessee, even federalized ones, could order them about, which had supposedly caused the late unpleasantness between the two militia companies. On the other hand, if Bishop had been federalized, then his punishment rested with federal forces. In the end, the governor worked with General Wool to recall the battalion, which deprived the militiamen of a year's worth of federal pay. After three months on the ground, the Highland Battalion had been sent packing.[11]

Even with the threat looming from a potential Creek uprising near the Cherokee Nation, the Georgia militiamen from Murray County found it impossible to cooperate with volunteers from Tennessee. Part of the problem stemmed from the continuity between the Rangers and the Highlanders. In Absalom Bishop's Highlander company, seven noncommissioned officers had been privates in the Rangers, while two served as privates in both outfits. One man, James Sample, held the position of first lieutenant in both companies. Almost the entire leadership of the Highlanders—both lieutenants, three of four corporals, and two of four sergeants—had all cut their teeth with the Rangers. Though the legislature had disbanded the Rangers, the unit reformed, for all intents and purposes, under a new name—albeit with a Bishop still in command. The high degree of continuity between the two units made it likely that the Highlanders exhibited the aggressive behavior that its members demonstrated when serving with the Rangers. Rather than defend the actions of another bellicose Bishop brother, Schley found it easier to disband the unit.[12]

As the Highlanders headed home to Murray County, Schley could congratulate himself on heading off a potentially volatile situation that would have done nothing to smooth relations between the state and the federal government. The Highlanders, though, were just the beginning in what would amount to more than 2,800 militiamen enrolled between 1836 and 1838 to ensure that the Cherokees went along with the Treaty of New Echota as peacefully as possible. The overwhelming show of force was a way to demonstrate American military power, to convince the Cherokees of the futility of resistance, and to make removal occur as rapidly as possible. After the Highland Battalion's dissolution, the state had to wrangle a large number of men for lengthy services. Learning from the fiasco caused by the Highlanders, state and federal officers also decided upon a strategy that they hoped would bring about a peaceful relocation. Rather than take recruits from the counties that had been formed from the Cherokee Nation, state and federal leaders wanted to draw on militiamen from outside of the disputed territory, the idea being that people who did not live in the area would be less disposed to act violently toward the Cherokees because they had less invested in removal.

Before these operations could commence, federal forces stationed in North Carolina and Tennessee went to work to prepare for forced migration west. General Wool, however, did not act with decisiveness, perhaps because he sympathized with the Cherokees. His Whiggish sensibilities made him question the wisdom of Jacksonian Indian policy even though he was tasked with its implementation. Such a combination made it difficult for him to carry out his orders, or at least it appeared that way. Rather than stockpile supplies, he spent much of his time quarreling with the governor of Alabama and restoring individual Cherokees to their homes and property taken from them by white settlers. Eventually the Alabama governor charged him with "usurping the powers of the civil tribunals of Alabama, disturbing the peace of the community, and trampling on the rights of the people." In other words, the governor of Alabama accused Wool of siding with the Cherokees and not his constituents in disputes over property. In July 1837, the War Department initiated an investigation into his leadership. When it came time for the governor of Alabama to prove his accusations, he could not produce any evidence that backed up his claims. In spite of Wool's displeasure with his task, he ordered the dispossession of "a great number of Cherokee" from their lands, which were given to white settlers. One officer interviewed during the course of the inquest sympathized with Wool and his refusal to push the Cherokees off their land. When asked about the character of white settlers, Captain James Morrow of the Alabama militia agreed that "a portion of the population is very respectable" but noted with disdain the "unworthy" settlers "who are there for the purpose of robbing and plundering the Indians, and have exercised every species of oppression towards them." The court found Wool guilty only of demonstrating caution and following his orders. It did not sanction the general, though it had already relieved him of command when the trial began, which it considered punishment enough.[13]

Wool's replacement, Colonel William Lindsay, demonstrated none of the general's hesitancy or uncertainty regarding his course of action. Lindsay, a much more energetic and forceful man, began his newfound command with gusto. His first effort, in fact, was to bring more men into service to begin the construction of "forts"—or stockades where Cherokees would be held after being taken from their homes but before they began their forced migration. To do so, Lindsay issued a call in the middle of 1837 for mounted infantry volunteers from Georgia and raised a regiment, nearly one thousand men, who would serve for up to a year.[14]

Called Lindsay's Mounted Militia, the men came from two of the border counties and other piedmont counties. In all, 981 men enlisted in Lindsay's regiment, along with three women, called "matrons," who performed various chores around camp. The men went to work constructing a series of forts and outbuildings designed to hold the Cherokees and keep the militiamen housed in relative comfort. The Treaty of New Echota and further agreements between the Senate and the Cherokee National Council stipulated that removal commence by May 24, 1838, about the time the enlistments for the mounted infantry expired. Lindsay knew that the men he called into service would more than likely not be available for the physical act of displacing Natives from their homes, but they could prove invaluable in laying the groundwork for that process to begin.

In spite of the overwhelming presence of federalized militia within the Cherokee territory, their operations proved entirely too peaceful for Charles H. Nelson. After the Highland Battalion had been disbanded, he sought a way of continuing his fight against Cherokees. Not to be outdone by Lindsay, Nelson raised nearly a thousand men and tendered their services to the governor. Federal and state leaders had already decided upon the strategy of drawing militiamen from the border counties, so initially his regiment was turned away. Nelson, though, persisted in his desire for Indian-fighting service. Appropriately, Nelson and the Union Party made the payment of the militias an election-year issue. In 1837, William Schley of the Union Party ran against the resurgent George R. Gilmer from the State Rights Party. At the May nominating convention of the State Rights Party (or, disparagingly, the Nullifiers or Nullies), Gilmer had received overwhelming support for another term as governor. Once again, the Union Party used the specter of the State

Rights Party's inherent elitism as a way to counteract them. In 1837, unlike 1831, it did not work.[15]

Hoping to remind its readers that Gilmer had once sought to deny access to the gold mines, the *Macon Telegraph* argued that the contest revolved around aristocracy and democracy. Gilmer and his supporters had openly declared that they "are the *weaker* in point of numbers" but that they still ran for elected office "on account of their superior wealth or smartness!" Fearing that Gilmer would "do every thing in his power to promote the views of the aristocracy" and buttress "privileged classes and orders" by placing burdens on "the shoulders of the poor." More importantly for the troubles within the Cherokee country, Gilmer's enemies declared that he sought "to exempt students at College from military duty." To hammer home the point that Gilmer fundamentally opposed a forceful removal of the Cherokees, Schley suggested that the state should pay for Nelson's regiment.[16]

When Schley called for Nelson's force in early September, just a month before the election, the message became clear: Schley and the Unionists would use force to expel the Cherokees; Gilmer would not. When news of Nelson's new force went public, John Ross warned the Cherokees "to be prepared for the worst." The governor's supporters maintained that the force was not for aggression but "for the protection of . . . our unoffending and peaceful citizens." With threats of "bloodshed and rapine" still fresh in the minds of voters, Schley's supporters urged their fellow citizens to set aside party motivations "and look to the interest of his country and to the cause of humanity" and support Schley for his "vigilance and patriotism." In a letter widely published across the state, Nelson argued that "there is every reason for alarm." Citing historical precedent, Nelson declared that violence and removal went hand in hand, at least on the part of Natives. Citizens in the disputed territory needed to "prepare for sudden conflict," and the state should aid them, for they lacked "organization or concert; arms or ammunition." If the legislature went along with Schley's plan, Nelson felt that "a suitable force" could remove at least half of the Cherokees well before the May 1838 deadline arrived.[17]

Nelson's insistence on state forces preempting federal troops demonstrated his enthusiasm. Troops would not just kick Cherokees out of their homes and send them on their way. Removal was a logistical nightmare for federal planners who had to plan for river crossings and treacherous terrain, supply the refugees, and provide protection from whites along the route. A state force could not just expel the Cherokees and expect them to make it to Indian Territory unscathed. Only federal forces had the wherewithal and jurisdiction to operate independently within each state. Nelson cared little for these humanitarian concerns, however, and many Georgians agreed with his forcefulness. Though Union Party operators reminded voters of Gilmer's past transgressions—Indian testimony and state ownership of the mines—the issue in 1837 revolved around Nelson's force and the payment of the militia.

Gilmer left his reelection bid to his supporters and returned to his boyhood home in western Virginia. States' Righters championed their candidate as "the soldier's friend" who would uphold the legislature's desire to pay for Colonel Nelson's force and not leave exposed settlers defenseless. Gilmer's supporters likewise trafficked in anti-Indian propaganda as a way of gaining votes. The *Athens Southern Banner* warned voters that the Cherokee "savage is sufficiently armed with the Rifle—the Tomahawk, and Scalping knife," and called these weapons the "proper symbol of their profession." Such pronouncements had only one possible interpretation: to tie the threat of Native violence to the laxity with which Schley and the Union Party had so far dealt with the Cherokees. When Gilmer returned to Georgia just prior to the election, he made no mention of Nelson's proposed force.[18]

It took nearly three weeks to determine the rightful winner of the election. With the final tally made, George Gilmer narrowly won the gubernatorial office again by a margin of only a few hundred votes. Voters in the border counties and the disputed territory judged him harshly and had not cast their votes in his favor. There the threat to the white man's chance was greatest, and voters perhaps remembered how Gilmer had sought to deprive individuals of the right to own land that contained gold. In the six border counties, Gilmer polled at only 38 percent and tallied 1,779 votes to Schley's 2,900. In the eleven counties in the disputed territory, Gilmer fared even worse, gaining only 18 percent of the vote. In fact, in eight of those counties he did not receive a single vote. He could muster only twenty-nine votes in the county named after him! In spite of his poor showing in the upcountry, Gilmer took office and did his best to frustrate the aggressive overtones espoused by the Unionists.[19]

The problem of Nelson's force did not disappear when the governor took office. To force the issue, Nelson saddled his entire force, nearly 1,400 men from the disputed territory, and rode to the outskirts of Milledgeville ostensibly on their way to Florida. Gilmer immediately saw through the charade. In a well-coordinated effort, Nelson's Unionist allies in the General Assembly pushed through a special appropriation of thirty thousand dollars to pay the men for their service up to that point and for their journey to Florida. It was believed that once they arrived in Florida, federal forces would take them into service and pay their salaries. Gilmer was a stickler for the law and noted that the federal government had not a made a call for militiamen from the Cherokee counties to travel to Florida. Gilmer also pointed out that Nelson's force would leave the Cherokee counties bereft of men in the case of a Cherokee uprising. If Nelson and his men truly wanted to protect their families, he argued, they should remain where they were rather than parade to Florida. Furthermore, the cost associated with paying for 1,400 men did not amuse the governor. When Gilmer made it public that he objected to signing the bill, two "very intimate friends" hinted at "great personal violence" if he continued to refuse. Gilmer balked at being held hostage by Nelson and his men and vetoed the legislation.

In a sternly worded message accompanying his veto, Gilmer made it clear that the military would not dictate state policy to him. Because the offer made by the federal government to bring in militia for the Seminole conflict had been withdrawn because federal forces had trouble enough supplying the troops stationed there, Gilmer declared that Nelson acted not on behalf of the state or the federal government. Instead of legitimate militiamen, Nelson's force should be seen "as so many individuals directing themselves according to their own wishes." Rather than caring about the common good, Nelson and his men acted in self-interested ways. The governor's veto did little to deter Nelson, who urged his men onward to Florida. Before he left, a Union majority in the legislature made him a major general of the militia and began calling his unit the Georgia Brigade. To Gilmer's annoyance, when Nelson arrived in Florida, General Thomas Jesup accepted him into service and put the Brigade to work. One of the men in the Brigade, Ira R. Foster, informed Union Party newspapers that the Brigade "is not only received, but kindly, by General Jesup," which he hoped would mortify their enemies. Moreover, the men now drew rations, forage, and pay from the quartermaster stationed there. Foster informed readers that several "Nullies" had joined the brigade and had since changed their allegiance.[20]

By the time Nelson's men had worn out their welcome in Florida, they had seen combat only a handful of times. Gilmer derisively noted in his memoir that Nelson's troops "killed one Indian squaw." General Jesup reported to the president that the Georgia Brigade had in fact engaged in "several skirmishes with the enemy," which resulted in the Georgia troops killing six Seminoles and taking fourteen prisoners. By the end of their enlistments, the War Department had to pay the Georgia Brigade

$306,000, which Gilmer felt had been paid on account of President Van Buren, who anticipated those men to "vote *esprit de corps*" for Democratic candidates. The overt political tone exhibited by Gilmer and Nelson in the squabble over paying the militia showed just how fractured the state's politics had become. With each party attempting to upstage the other when it came to protecting citizens from potential attacks, Gilmer's label, the "soldier's friend," had come under attack.[21]

The governor seemed to care little and was not about to muster the militiamen from the border counties in order to gain political favor, in spite of the urgings from his supporters near the Cherokee Nation and his opponents in the Union Party. Gilmer believed that the militiamen in that area desired to enter service not to protect their farms and families but to "enjoy the pleasures of camp and to get pay for doing nothing." The profligacy he attributed to Nelson's Brigade seemed to verify Gilmer's suspicions. Even federal quartermasters balked at the huge sums of money the Georgia troops applied for, which one quartermaster called "very large." When the Georgia Brigade's enlistments expired in April 1838, the 1,400 soldiers had filed nearly one thousand requisitions asking for back pay, transportation costs, forage reimbursements, or the cost of dead horses.[22]

By January 1838, four months before removal commenced, the pressure on Gilmer to call out the militia in the border counties increased. No matter what the governor attempted to do regarding militiamen, he came under the scrutiny of the voters. Citizens in Murray County complained that since Nelson's Georgia Brigade had departed for Florida, they had been exposed to attacks. A group of citizens in that county believed that "the time has arrived when it is indespensable to the safety of the people and property" for a company of local militiamen to enter into service. From Gilmer County, many citizens "speake of taking off their families if there is not more troops sent here"; while worried residents in Ellijay noted the "bold saucy and stubborn" behavior of the Cherokees. The embattled governor waited until he received the call from the federal government in early March.[23]

When the approval did arrive, Gilmer wasted no time alerting militia commanders. In a dispatch to the border counties, the governor alerted them to the purpose of their presence—and the pitfalls of straying from their orders. The primary design of the militias was "to give security to our citizens; to overawe the revengeful spirit of the lawless portion of the Indians; to prevent the people flying from their homes and the country upon every rumor of danger; to protect your families, neighborhoods, and the people of each county." However, the governor made it clear that if the militiamen acted violently or unjustly toward the Cherokees, the entire country would become embroiled in a war. Furthermore, he reminded the militiamen that their service stood to benefit the good of every citizen so soldiers should not seek profit from their service. He had reports that some backcountry whites, "for their own selfish and lawless purposes" sought to cause problems so they could grasp for land. He reiterated that the task of the militia, "preserving the peace of the country," was a boon for the entire state and should not be meddled with. The call in March, however, did not ask for a full-blown muster but, rather, an advance notice to company commanders that they and their sixty-man companies needed to prepare for service.[24]

Aside from wanting to follow the letter of the law—Gilmer often cited the Constitution when explaining to militia captains that he did not have the authority to call them up—neither did he wish to precipitate a bloodbath. By the following month, the slow-to-act federal government had begun to prepare for the military aspects of removal. In April, the commanding general of the U.S. Army, Alexander Macomb, ordered General Winfield Scott to the Cherokee country to oversee removal. The following day, he ordered four artillery regiments, part of the Second Dragoons, the entire Fourth Infantry, and a detachment of U.S. Marines to make haste for the Cherokee country. The orders placed more than three thousand regular troops at Scott's disposal and further reduced his dependence on capricious militiamen. Even with so many federal troops, the vastness of the Cherokee territory and the number of inhabitants necessitated a vast military operation. The same day, Acting Secretary of War Samuel Cooper notified Gilmer that Scott could call on Georgia to furnish militiamen who would serve for a maximum of three months. On April 12, Gilmer received a letter from General Scott asking him to raise two companies of mounted infantry. Joining the nearly two thousand militiamen from Georgia were another one thousand volunteers from both North Carolina and Tennessee. Former governor Wilson Lumpkin, now an enrolling agent stationed at New Echota, applauded the steps taken by Scott, especially the "large & imposing" military force he had assembled.[25]

Gilmer, of course, expressed anxiety. This prospect of violence bothered him to no end, so he decided to write directly to the citizens of the new counties that had been carved out of the Cherokee Nation. Rumors swirled that President Van Buren was secretly negotiating a proposal with Ross that would further delay removal, much to the chagrin of the governor and the white residents in the disputed territory. In Washington D.C., a Cherokee delegation led by John Ross tried once more to forestall removal, and many Georgians feared President Van Buren would cave in to the mounting pressure.[26] Gilmer, who had always been anxious about the prospect of mass violence erupting under his watch, sent a personal plea to the residents of disputed territory. This time, however, he feared that the rumors of the president further stalling removal would have dire consequences. "Let me, therefore, entreat you, to make no movement which may bring you into collision with your Indian neighbors," he wrote. "Let no alarm for your rights, or feelings of indignation at the conduct of the President lead you to acts of violence." Instead, he urged them to treat their neighbors as humanely as possible but again reiterated his core beliefs about the corrupting influence of Cherokee elites and that the state wanted to protect "real" Cherokees. Those who know the "true state of the Cherokee—the ruin and degradation which has been brought upon the unmixed Indians by their present situation—do not doubt but that it is their interest to remove to the country provided for them in the West."[27]

When the May 23 deadline came and went and the negotiations still had not produced a new agreement, Scott commenced his operation. Georgia's two regiments of militia mustered at New Echota in Murray County. Not trusting that the governor's plea for civility would register, Scott tried to drive home the expected peaceful actions of the militia. He issued General Order Number 25 on May 17. In it, he laid out the prescribed boundaries for each militia force. The disputed territory, now called the Middle District with a headquarters at New Echota, had the most burdensome job. Of the nearly eighteen thousand Cherokees, about half lived on land claimed by the state and now occupied by white settlers. He ordered that every Cherokee man taken into custody would be disarmed, though he guaranteed that their weapons would be returned when the westward trek began. Such an action left Cherokee men open to violence, but Scott stressed that the militia needed to remember the shared humanity of the Cherokees and Americans. If "a despicable individual should be found, capable of inflicting wanton injury or insult on any Cherokee man, woman or child," Scott made it the duty of the men to stop the harshness and cruelty. Scott's orders also delineated residents of the Cherokee Nation into three categories. The only Natives that the army had the responsibility of moving were those who had not been granted lifetime reservations by the states. Everyone else had to go.[28]

With those orders, the militia fanned out across the Middle District to the various posts constructed by Colonel Lindsay and his mounted militia over the previous eighteen months.[29] Gilmer noted that rather than conduct field operations, the best use of the militia involved having them garrison those forts to control the Indians housed there and to protect settlers. This way, the only immediate contact the militiamen would have with Cherokees would be at the forts and not pursuing those Cherokee who resisted or fled. Scott had no problems, though, sending the volunteers into the homes of Cherokee families to make them leave.

The army had begun preparing for removal in 1836, but that was difficult to discern from the lack of preparedness. It fell upon the army to feed thousands of civilians detained in the forts and the seven thousand troops involved in the operation. On May 22, before the operation had even commenced, an officer stationed in North Carolina noted the lackluster state of supplies in the Cherokee country. The troops stationed at Franklin, North Carolina, "are almost entirely out of provision and none can be procured in the country, so that it is impossible to remain. . . . The country is completely exhausted." If the town of Franklin and its hinterlands lacked supplies for troops, many of the camps that detained the Cherokees proved just as bereft. The best-stocked fort, Fort Poinsett, had more than sixteen thousand bushels of corn, while other forts, including a camp near Springplace and another in Paulding County, lacked any rations altogether. So the countryside may have been destitute of supplies, but the army had them to spare. It simply did not allocate the resources to those in need, which led to suffering when Cherokee families wallowed in the camps.[30]

When troops did go out into the countryside to capture the Cherokees, initial reports made the entire process seem banal. The federal officer John Gray Bynum nonchalantly noted, "I collected yesterday about 80 Indians." He expressed alarm regarding "a great deal of sickness . . . prevailing amongst the children of Indians." He boasted that he allowed women to stay at home to nurse the sick children. Militiamen from Georgia expressed a similar detachment toward their duty. Men from a volunteer company from Madison County did not reach New Echota until May 28 and were immediately pressed into service, stopping only to prepare a quick supper. They marched the entire afternoon and "traveled, taking Indians until midnight." That night, the men camped in a road "with some Indians who we had taken prisoner." Other men in the company slept in a "House with the Red people." In the morning, the expedition continued. At each house, the company commander left a small guard to watch over the prisoners, until Henry P. Strickland, a private, sardonically noted that by the end of the day the men "were all posted as guards," and no one could be spared to capture more Indians. In three days, three companies had captured 927 prisoners. Strickland continued his account, but it appeared that after their initial foray into the backcountry, his company did more guard duty than anything else. By the beginning of June he noted that the "great fatigue in collecting & guarding the Indians" had not lived up to the expectations of the men: "Volunteering have not proven unto them what it was cracked up to be." He noted that he had held up better than anticipated but admitted to missing home a great deal.[31]

General Charles R. Floyd, appointed by Gilmer to command the state militia, made a much more official-sounding report on May 27, when he related his initial successes. Crossing the Coosawattee River early the previous day, he sent out small detachments of troops in multiple directions to prevent "the escape of the Indians." He noted that his men behaved in a "prompt and energetic manner" that complied with General Order No. 25. Floyd reported on the progress made by all of the Georgia militia companies and was pleased to see that removal continued to proceed rapidly. By May 28, he noted that the Georgia troops had rounded up 963 individuals from their homes and detained them; two days later another 484 Indians had been corralled. By June 9, Floyd reported that the Georgia militia had captured 3,636 Cherokees, who had since been sent to Ross's Landing for processing and transportation. That number did not include another 400 still stationed at Rome waiting for an armed guard. The operation to arrest, contain, and deport the Cherokees still living within Georgia's borders had taken only a few weeks to complete. The incredible efficiency of Floyd's troops had, by the first week of June, cleared the Georgia upcountry of Cherokees.[32]

In spite of the ease Floyd reported when it came to capturing Cherokees, he still worried that acts of violence would go unreported and escalate the tenuous situation. He noted to General Scott, "The Indians made no resistance, but evinced generally a great reluctance to remove." Still, he wanted his men to keep him abreast of developments, especially if any "extraordinary event occur in collecting the Indians." The men were under great stress not only from physical exertion but also from the emotional strain of removing Indians from their homes and pressure exerted from the home front. One petition requested that Private William Calhoun be released from service because his wife "got into a deranged Condition" and had to be confined by her neighbors. Another volunteer, an assistant surgeon, had received information "of a domestic nature" and sought to resign, though he hesitated to ask for any "indulgence" because of "those honorable feelings" which forbade officers from leaving the service. The exhaustion and growing resistance to removal expressed by the Cherokees made some sort of violence inevitable.[33]

Rumors surfaced implying that militiamen enjoyed shooting at Cherokees who ran into the hills at the first sight of the troops. Many Cherokees, resentful of their confinement in open-aired prisons, attempted to escape. On May 28, Private F. M. Culbreath of Oglethorpe County shot and killed a man trying to leave one of the stockades. Though horrified, General Floyd said Culbreath had acted rightly and did not censure him because the murdered Cherokee had expressed "some indications of hostility." Still, he wanted to remind the volunteers that "we are not in a state of war with the Cherokee Indians, that they have not committed any act of violence; that they are moving peaceable out of the County." To maintain their honor, the troops should let the Cherokees leave without further bloodshed. He also wanted to inform the men that Culbreath's actions would not be used as precedent when deciding the fate of whites who shot Cherokees. Other reports trickled in regarding the cruelty of the militia toward their captives. Captain Derrick had to confess that one of his men, whom he considered "a very correct young man" who would "do nothing wrong intentionally," had abused an Indian woman when taking her prisoner. The private had knocked her down when the woman, who did not want to leave her home, had struck at the soldier with a stick and then tried to take his gun from him. At Fort Gilmer, the bailiff "who lately beat and half hanged an Indian" had been arrested.[34]

The most prominent complaint offered by the Cherokees at the time was not rough treatment but that they did not have enough time to secure any property that would make life in the forts bearable. One woman, Nancy Pheasant, was forced from her home by armed troops. When she and her detachment reached Calhoun, Tennessee, she had her horses, which she "never heard from afterwards," taken from her. Chowahuca "was forcibly removed . . . by authorities of the U. States" and lost quite a bit of property in the process. When the militia forced her from her property, she lost a loom and spinning wheel, a plow, several cows and sheep, and two horses. Whites drove Tesahnehe from his home and took his gun away from him—though disarmament became official policy with General Order No. 25—and Tieeskih claimed he had "been torn" from his home "by a force of armed men and dragged into camps and there kept." Chenashse "was rudely forced from her home by the soldiers" and had to leave all of her possessions behind. Others saw their livestock butchered in front of them to feed hungry troops. For example,

Sekekee saw "Jackson's army" slaughter "about forty head of hogs in my presence." One man, though, had an entirely different experience. When a white man showed up and knocked on his door, Head Thrower Watts did not fight and seem resigned to his fate. "The soldiers were taking the people," he said, "and a white man who took possession of my place, loaned me his wagon to take me into camp."[35]

Once dispossession happened, the displaced individuals were directed to the camps, where they languished. The winter and spring of 1838 had been particularly dry, and by May, temperatures in the upcountry were unseasonably warm. The Cherokee could have used the nourishment provided by stores of food or livestock, but the army denied them the use of their property. The inhospitable forts left the Cherokee prisoners exposed to the elements and caused rampant sickness. The ill-managed supplies only compounded their suffering. After Culbreath murdered one Cherokee, Scott changed his formerly stringent tone and allowed some Cherokees to obtain passes so they could return to their homes and retrieve some of their belongings. This led to a great degree of confusion. Some Cherokees with passes never returned to their forts, and soldiers believed that they escaped into the mountains. Others returned to their homes and sold what remained of their belongings to white settlers. Some fort commanders even let groups of Cherokees conduct themselves to Ross's Landing without an armed guard. Such "indulgences" were calculated to induce Natives to leave peaceably, though Floyd suspected that such a lenient attitude might result in "mischievous consequences," and he frowned upon Scott's generosity. Many of his officers, while conducting prisoners to Ross's Landing, allowed individual to leave the column to see to their property, check on the homes of their friends, or simply look on their country one last time. This frustrated Floyd to no end, who saw the leniency as an enticement for Indians to reenter Georgia. Even the state offered other Cherokees permits to remain in Georgia until September, a practice that further confounded Floyd. Soft Shell Turtle, for example, a Cherokee "of considerable influence" who had actively opposed removal, had a small band of followers who all had permits. Still, Floyd calculated that the continued presence of Indians would likely incite settlers to violence.[36]

Some problems arose at smaller posts commanded by unsupervised militia captains. At Fort Buffington and the camp at the Sixes, both commanders were accused of cruelty toward the Cherokee prisoners. Combined, the two forts housed 1,100 prisoners who greatly suffered. At Fort Means, one of the Cherokees "without any provocation" struck a soldier with a rock, so the captain of the fort immediately ordered his arrest. Other problems arose, especially when soldiers and Natives gambled together. At Fort Cumming, Captain Benjamin Watkins noted that one prisoner, Aaron Willman, had won $250 from a white man, Thomas York, and the former wanted to stay until York had settled his debt. Another captain refused to follow orders to turn over a fort to a different commander. Rather than face whatever humiliation he imagined a change of command would bring, Captain Dorsey fled the service and returned to his home in Hall County. His men followed his actions, and when a federal officer turned up at the fort, he found "one half of the men" absent, and the militia officers could not "give any account of them." The federal officer, Lieutenant Griffith, termed what he encountered "a complete mob," a far cry from the strict discipline and order envisioned by the state's leaders.[37]

Watkins encountered other cases of disorder, not from Cherokee prisoners but from his men. He placed Lewis W. Tredwell, a cavalry volunteer, under arrest for a litany of charges, including drunkenness, "the act of rioting," and "an attempt to commit murder." Other soldiers behaved in an unprofessional way and were likewise detained by officers. A. P. Bush, a private from Franklin County, reported that his captain disgraced his rank. Not only did the company move at a glacial pace while marching, but the captain absented himself from the men much of the time, and the men openly discussed his drunkenness. The men had little respect for him. While stationed at Fort Buffington, he threatened to have one of the men arrested until the enlisted men "presented their muskets at him" and dissuaded the captain from making such a poor decision. At Fort Hoskins, Floyd reported "one case of Mutiny" and several more of insubordination, which, he vowed, "shall not be suffered to pass unpunished." Even military discipline suffered as a result of removal.[38]

Floyd had been kept busier by the misbehavior of the militiaman than he had by any actions on the part of the Cherokees and therefore applauded Scott's efforts to drum the Georgia militia out of service promptly. Scott's plan had been predicated on getting the Cherokees out of Georgia, the state most ardently opposed to their presence, as quickly as possible. In fact, in North Carolina the army would not even begin the process of relocation there until the operation in Georgia had terminated. With those Cherokees out of Georgia's forts, Scott no longer required the Georgia militia. On June 19, Floyd reported to Scott that his scouting parties had scoured the countryside and could not find any traces of the nearly 9,000 Cherokee who had once lived in the territory. On June 25, Captain Derrick reported that he had sent off another 85 Indians to Ross's Landing, which put his total at 884. He remarked that those Cherokee families who had fled to the mountains would soon come in because the white settlers "feel no apprehension of danger from them," a good sign that meant the residents no longer feared an Indian uprising. By July 1, the two regiments of Georgia militia had been mustered out of service, paid, and sent home. Beginning on May 26, the militia from Georgia had rounded up thousands of Cherokee civilians, placed them in detainment camps, marched them to larger camps, and guarded them from white settlers. Though violence did occur, the lack of killings by Georgia's militias had to have pleased Gilmer, who had spent most of his time as governor fretting over the possibility of that outcome.[39]

The lack of widespread violence began with the Cherokees themselves. The historian Mary Young posits that a vibrant middle ground allowed for fruitful negotiations between Winfield Scott and John Ross, which led to a more peaceful operation. Knowing that they had been swindled out of their land, the Cherokees still refused to resist. In spite of their forbearance, some violence did occur, and several Cherokee had been shot, beaten, or killed by troops. Ross, in particular, opened up a fruitful channel of communication with Scott that paid dividends and saved lives. Young also argues that had Schley won the election of 1837, he more than likely would have placed Charles H. Nelson in the field. Such an action would have proved disastrous. His Georgia Brigade, composed of men who lived in the Cherokee counties, would have shown much less restraint than did the militia raised by Gilmer.[40]

When those Cherokees expelled from Georgia arrived at Ross's Landing in Tennessee, the first expedition of about 300 émigrés departed, but the extreme heat made the going difficult. Ross pled with the general to delay until temperatures cooled and to put Cherokees, rather than army officers, in charge of operations. Scott agreed, and it seemed like a crisis had been averted. Meanwhile, real suffering broke out in the camps: fresh water became increasingly scarce, and sickness weakened the prisoners. Not until January 1839 did those expeditions leave Tennessee, bound for Indian Territory, never to return. Though no exact count exists, scholars put the death toll as low as two thousand and as high as four thousand. More recently, Russell Thornton's careful demographic study puts the death toll as high as eight thousand. Many now believe that at least two thousand Cherokees perished as a result of lengthy imprisonment in the camps.[41]

For nearly two decades, Georgians had tried to use the extension of civil law as a tool to remove the Cherokee Indians from within the state's boundaries. By passing laws, creating new counties, and subjecting

Natives to discriminatory statutes, state leaders had shown the Cherokees that Georgia was a white man's country that would go to great ends to effect their displacement. As much as Georgians wanted the process to seem like an orderly, legal proceeding, events did not turn out that way. Instead, Georgians used military force—some of it sponsored by the state, other sanctioned by the federal government—to intimidate, corral, and relocate the minority population. Even during removal, military force trumped civil law. When a sheriff and two deputies interfered with the military's operations, Floyd had them arrested and detained. Major Pope rescued a white citizen from arrest by civil authorities, though he had no authority to do so. The message was clear: civil authority proved useful when dealing with everyday affairs in settled areas; military force and violence were necessary to create order and the essential aspects of the white man's chance when the burgeoning American empire encountered groups opposed to its expansion.

Conclusion

In the 1820s and 1830s, the State of Georgia used questionable legal tactics and a tremendous show of violence to extinguish Cherokee sovereignty, distributed the land that both political entities claimed for its own citizens, and then worked in coordination with the federal government to effect removal of the Cherokees. The point of this deliberate and targeted aggressiveness was to create a society, based on the concept of order, that could perpetuate what was called the white man's chance. The idea behind the white man's chance was that the state government should use its power to create a political and social climate that allowed white men an opportunity at—but not a guarantee of—economic success. In actions grounded in states' rights ideology, the state wielded its power to further the equality of white men by exploiting racialized others.

Although the state's actions often created partisan opposition within the state's electorate, few disputed their results. Indeed, political parties ossified around the idea of the white man's chance and how best to achieve it. The gubernatorial election of 1831 best typifies this transition toward a more formalized party structure and away from the personality-driven partisanship that dominated state politics prior to the Jacksonian era. When George R. Gilmer's reelection bid floundered on the fact that he called for public ownership of the gold mines, the opposing faction decried the maneuver as a threat to the white man's chance and solidified its political stranglehold on the disputed territory. As political coalitions became more formalized, the Georgia upcountry turned its back on Gilmer's State Rights Party and embraced Lumpkin's Union

Party. Before long, the Unionists openly championed the Democrats, whereas the State Rights Party turned toward the Whigs.

Underlying the concept of white male equality in the first half of the nineteenth century was the state's intention to create a well-ordered society that encouraged widespread land ownership, the continued subservience of nonwhites, and the perpetuation of democratic institutions. Missing from this society was any sort of racialized other who did not submit to the "superior" race. In this way, the whole notion of Cherokee national sovereignty, or of whites not having unfettered access to Cherokee land, not only flew in the face of the well-ordered society but undermined the whole concept of the white man's chance.

By 1840, it appeared as if most Cherokees had been expelled from the contested territory. State leaders applauded their own efforts on behalf of the people and their forbearance in not unleashing the terrible, violent power of the state in a campaign that surely would have touched off a war that pitted the state against the Cherokees and the federal government. This did not happen. The Cherokees chose national persistence at the expense of remaining on their homeland. Their exodus saw most Cherokees relocate to Indian Territory in what is now Oklahoma, though some went even farther afield.[1] In fact, not all Cherokees left their homeland. Many sought refuge in the southern Appalachians, and enough of a community was able to stay behind that the Eastern Band of the Cherokees now have a federally protected reservation in North Carolina. Much to the horror of many Georgians who fretted over multiracial Cherokees remaining in Georgia, some *did* stay in Georgia but had so blended into American life as to be indistinguishable from their white neighbors. By 1840, the state had granted citizenship to twenty-two Cherokee families who had stayed behind in the hope of maintaining their land and way of life. Others hid in isolated parts of the Appalachians.[2]

Although much of America's past was rooted in legal practices that sought to deny the personhood of nonwhites, exploit their labor, and deny them political rights and equality, all the while noting that the United States is a land that celebrates both freedom and equality, the actions of the state in the disputed territory highlighted these trends and their urgency in Jacksonian America. The idea of the white man's chance grew out of this concept of the United States. In early Georgia, it became the state government's responsibility to ensure that white males experienced political equality. By the 1820s, all white males could vote for both governor and president. By the late 1820s and early 1830s, Georgia's General Assembly and governors championed the idea that white men should also have some type of economic equality as well. In practice, the white man's chance depended upon the distribution of resources in an equitable fashion. Between 1802 and 1832, the state held a total of seven lotteries that gave away roughly three-quarters of the entire area of the state. In that sense, the lotteries successfully distributed lands to settlers as a way of ensuring that each white man in Georgia had the chance of economic success through land ownership. In practice, however, that rarely panned out. David F. Weiman has demonstrated that lotteries created a secondary market for land ownership. In Carroll County, for example, land had been distributed there from a lottery in 1827. By 1830, only 7 percent of "fortunate drawers" had kept their land; the rest had been sold to other settlers. The reasons for this are numerous.[3] Perhaps the lottery winners saw their land merely as a way of getting quick cash, or they lacked the small amount of money needed to pay the fees associated with land ownership. Perhaps they also knew the county's reputation as a haven for criminals and therefore sold their plot rather than risk being swept up in the violence that engulfed the county.

The land lottery of 1832 distributed land that belonged to the Cherokee Nation and gave it away by means of a system where each white male in Georgia stood to win land. This sort of redistributionism is not what typically comes to mind when we think about state-level political economy in the antebellum South. In other words, the state was doing more than engineering republican economic independence for its citizens. By expropriating Native ground, it was demonstrating that equality among whites was dependent upon the continued exploitation of nonwhites. The purpose was the creation of a certain type of society whose framework saw the state play a more active and involved role in shaping and directing economic policy with an end toward white male equality.

Framed this way, the state's actions are rendered more complicated than simply a land grab. Extending the state's jurisdiction and distributing land was a way for the state to engineer economic and political policies that sought to create an orderly society based on widespread land ownership, racial hierarchy, and the continuation of democratic institutions. Although land was at the heart of this exercise, access to that land also had to be distributed in a fair way that led to social stability. The proposed solution, the land lottery, first occurred in 1802. The lotteries were a significant piece of the social contract that the state had made with its citizens: land acquired by the state would then be turned over to white citizens in as equitable a manner as possible. Properly administered, the lottery offered a fair chance at fee simple land ownership. In this light, the white man's chance was equal treatment by the state government, thus ensuring that everyone had a similar chance of acquiring land. The white man's chance did not guarantee that they would become profitable farmers. That was not the point. What the lottery was designed to do was demonstrate how the state treated its white citizens equally. As Georgia and South Carolina lurched toward a conflict with the federal government over nullification, and as the Ultras became a more entrenched political force, states' rights became a rallying cry throughout the region. But Georgia took states' rights in a different direction by marshalling the vast resources it claimed but did not yet possess and distributing them in an equal fashion to white men as a way of bringing into being a vision of society that so many of the state's politicians longed to see.

However much the state government desired to bring this type of society into being, two serious obstacles existed. For starters, the Cherokee Nation still claimed the land that Georgia wanted to raffle off to white farmers and gold miners. Because the state had not yet gained control over the disputed territory, the state's ability to distribute lands to whites was called into question. Unable to dole out lands to its citizens meant that the nonwhites were limiting the chances of whites to get ahead. In this framing, eliminating the Cherokee claim to nationhood was also a way of protecting whiteness and the legal and political liberties enjoyed by white men.

But the presence of thousands of Cherokees posed another problem for state authorities. The state's politicians believed that the mere presence of these Natives compelled poor whites to live in the border region, drawn to the seeming lawlessness of the Cherokee Nation. The respectable class blamed the poor and transitory population for committing crimes and destabilizing life in the border region. Members of the Pony Club, for example, were lumped into this category. What started as a band of horse thieves became a more nefarious organization that jeopardized the integrity of the local government and court system. As long as disorder threatened the state's acquisition of Cherokee land, the ability of the state to acquire and distribute land was in jeopardy. For those who desired order, the lure of the frontier posed a problem to the extension of state sovereignty and good government. State leaders, therefore, took a two-pronged approach to dealing with disorder. First, George R. Gilmer turned to violence to coerce whites into compliance with their designs. The creation of the Georgia Guard in 1830 did much to cement violence as a legitimate tool of social control. It also became a useful instrument for sowing chaos and disunity with the Cherokee polity. Second, the state began raffling off land to "fortunate drawers" although the issue of sovereignty had not been decided. Such forceful measures allowed the state to act as if it had ownership of the disputed territory (which the extension law gave it), while the use of force and settlement of the region gave the state a greater say in how it created order.

For their part, Cherokees also desired stability and sought to create it by ratifying a constitution and solidifying their national claim to the land on which they currently resided. Courts and a police force attempted to punish criminals, but the scope of white intrusion onto Cherokee soil was overwhelming. The official line from Ross's government was to dissuade violent behavior by individuals and to rely instead upon treaties made with the federal government to maintain the Nation's boundaries. That position was not always a tenable one. Even with the aid of federal troops, white intruders acted with near impunity, especially after the gold rush began in 1829. The Cherokee position remained tenuous even though it was buttressed by federal policies, but after 1830, when Andrew Jackson and his supporters passed the Indian Removal Act, the prospect of maintaining their boundaries became even more uncertain. For Georgians who had long been clamoring for access to Cherokee land, the message became clear: it will soon be yours.

That does not mean that Cherokees accepted removal as inevitable or stood helplessly in the face of white encroachment. The Cherokee Lighthorse patrol exercised its authority and expelled white intruders. At one point, a group of Cherokees appointed by Ross burned down the cabins of intruders, angering whites in neighboring counties. Near Carroll County, Cherokees turned to a form of vigilante justice and began "slicking" suspected horse thieves and other members of the Pony Club. This movement, though it began in Cherokee communities near the border using a traditional means of punishment, soon had Cherokees working in concert with white neighbors who also desired stability and the end of crime and unpredictability in their neighborhoods. Moreover, the Pony Club had corrupted the institutions of Carroll County by counting the sheriff among their numbers and using intimidation to control the goings-on at the courthouse. The multiracial cooperation demonstrated by the Slicks proved anathema to the worldview of Georgia's politicos, even if the threat to the institutional integrity was at stake. Order demanded a clear hierarchy; the Slicks demonstrated that two different communities could work in concert toward similar ends.

One way to eliminate that cooperation was to turn a limited form of community-mindedness that the Slicks embodied into outright competition. To that end, the land lottery of 1832 encouraged "fortunate drawers" to move onto Cherokee land and displace the residents whose land they had won. Giving away land to individuals who could then enact small acts of interpersonal removal would set the stage for the larger process of government removal to commence. The land lottery situated these small competing claims for sovereignty as a competition for scarce resources over which individual Georgians and Cherokees had to squabble. But not all Georgians saw access to the land in such a cutthroat way. Even though state leaders appeared committed to land distribution, the presence of gold changed that calculus. Running for reelection in 1831, George R. Gilmer proposed public ownership of land that contained gold rather than holding a lottery of that land. By doing so he broke the trust voters had in their government to perpetuate equality. The white man's chance had to benefit whites equally, which the public works projects Gilmer proposed, they argued, would not do. When Gilmer lost reelection in 1831, his successor, Wilson Lumpkin, continued Gilmer's policy of using state-sponsored violence as a means of bringing about an orderly society. Government-supported violence as a means of enforcing the law also occurred at the federal level. For many years, federal agents had attempted to expel whites who had settled illegally on Cherokee land, yet the agents never met with much success. This problem only compounded after the discovery of gold. As federal troops swept white intruders from Cherokee land, those on the receiving end of federal coercion disputed the legitimacy of such coercive actions and based their arguments in whiteness. Whites who were "connected" to the Cherokee Nation—either through marriage or the multiracial products of those relationships—could stay and continue to mine. For white Georgians, the fact that some whites were being privileged above others was anathema to their worldview and their conception of whom the federal government should support.

When the Georgia Guard went after intruders, the intruders did not resort to claims about the inviolate nature of whiteness but instead politicized their grievances in the state's ferocious partisan contest. As the problem of violence became a political one, the Georgia Guard became a way for its opponents to attack the policies of the sitting governor and his faction. This salvo was not just confined to the state. When the Guard arrested the peaceful missionary Samuel Worcester, protests from across the country echoed all the way to the Supreme Court. Although the court ruled that the Cherokees had sovereignty, the court lacked standing to stop the harassment posed by the Georgia Guard. Indeed, I argue, it was precisely this sort of deliberate harassment and violent behavior that helped fracture the Cherokee polity and convinced some elites to sign the Treaty of New Echota, effectively ceding Cherokee sovereign territory to the U.S. government and making removal inevitable.

To implement removal, the federal and state governments again turned to force and coercion to make the policy a reality. From a pragmatic standpoint, the U.S. Army and the state militias were the only organizations large enough to handle the logistics involved with the relocation of thousands of civilians. They also hinted at the use of force if the Cherokees did not opt to peacefully leave their homes. The federal government saw the military as an appropriate vehicle for removal because it could better protect Cherokees from Americans along the route west. It also meant that violence between soldiers and Cherokees being forced from their homes was guaranteed. When violence did break out between Cherokees and militiamen, the force commanded by Winfield Scott easily put disputes to rest and stifled any attempt at organized resistance. Although the Cherokees who had been forced from their homes suffered in the camps built by state militias to house the displaced, they did not necessarily suffer as a result of violence directed at them from the army or the militias. Instead, their suffering came because of a lack of planning, inadequately distributed resources, and exposure. That suffering grew worse once the trek to Indian Territory began.

When Governor Gilmer called out the militia, some Georgians opposed the measure on personal, but not political, grounds. Indeed, the partisanship that had been directed toward the Georgia Guard, and its use of violence was not directed at the militia. Because the militia was a democratic institution, it did not fall prey to the partisan squabbling that had engulfed the Georgia Guard's deployment. The lack of opposition stemmed from the fact that the militia was an extension of the community's will and therefore seemingly above the partisan fray. It also signaled that the white man's chance relied upon violence to reach fruition.

Jacksonian America was raucous and violent. Mob violence, riots, beatings, duels, and murder defined much of the period. Moreover, Americans have long understood the meeting place between whites and Indians as dangerous and bloody. That violence occurred along the border between the state of Georgia and the Cherokee Nation should not come as a surprise. What is surprising is that the state government directed much of that violence, both at Cherokees and at white scofflaws. The inherent purpose of this violence, however, was motivated by political desires to extend state sovereignty as a way of creating an idealized society. Framing Cherokee Removal in the context of state-sponsored violence demonstrates that it was not just the actions of individual settlers, but the concerted policies of settler states, that used violence against Native Americans as a legitimate and legal way of acquiring their land and making them disappear.

Notes

Abbreviations

Duke	David M. Rubenstein Rare Book & Manuscript Library, Duke University, Durham, NC
Emory	Stuart A. Rose Manuscript, Archives, and Rare Book Library, Emory University, Atlanta, GA
GDAH	Georgia Division of Archives and History, Morrow
GHQ	*Georgia Historical Quarterly*
JSH	*Journal of Southern History*
NARA	National Archives and Records Administration, Washington, DC
UGA	Hargrett Rare Book & Manuscript Library, University of Georgia, Athens
UNC	Southern Historical Collection, Louis Round Wilson Library, Special Collections, University of North Carolina, Chapel Hill

Introduction

1. On Georgia's efforts to create a proactive political economy, see Heath, *Constructive Liberalism*. Georgia's system of land distribution was rooted in its treatment of American Revolutionary war veterans and loyalists. See, for example, Hall, *Land and Allegiance in Revolutionary Georgia*; and Jensen, *Patriots, Settlers, and the Origins of American Social Policy*. On the politics of the first land lottery, see Gates, "The Georgia Land Act of 1803," 1–21.

2. The two foundational texts on the nullification controversy remain Freehling, *Prelude to Civil War*; and Ellis, *The Union at Risk*.

3. On the Treaty of Indian Springs, see M. Green, *The Politics of Indian Removal*, 69–125; on the use of state sovereignty as a means of privileging state law as a means of expelling Natives, see Rosen, *American Indians and State Law*, esp. chaps. 2 and 3. Other scholars highlight various aspects that led to the expulsion of the Creeks (see,

for example, Haveman, *Rivers of Sand*, 11–41; Frank, *Creeks and Southerners*, 96–113; and Hudson, *Creek Paths and Federal Roads*, 145–66).

4. See, for example, Parsons, "A Perpetual Harrow upon My Feelings," 351–55; and Cooper, *The Lost Founding Father*, 244–49. On the Treaty of 1827, see "Treaty with the Creeks, 1827," in Kappler, ed., *Indian Affairs: Laws and Treaties* 2:284–86.

5. A growing amount of work has analyzed Cherokee culture and community both before and after removal. One of the earliest treatments, McLoughlin, *Cherokee Renascence in the New Republic*, emphasizes the political and social change resulting from a wave of nationalism in the early nineteenth century. The new political forms codified in the Constitution highlighted, according to Theda Perdue's marvelous syntheses of Cherokee life, changing gender roles that were intimately connected to the growth of race-based slavery but also demonstrated the strength of female-centered cultural traditions that helped stabilize Cherokee society in spite of the flux associated with removal and, later in the nineteenth century, allotment (see her *Slavery and the Evolution of Cherokee Society*, as well as *Cherokee Women: Gender and Culture Change, 1700–1835*).

6. Georgia's gold rush and the working culture of the mines are explored in Williams, *The Georgia Gold Rush*.

7. Historians have defined "order" in several ways. For Claudio Saunt, order equates to power. For William Novak, the well-ordered society was one in which state and local government played crucial roles in regulating the social and economic worlds of its citizens. Michael O'Brien sees order as an imagined coherence amid social and cultural dislocation, a conjecture that was unattainable (see Saunt, *A New Order of Things*; Novak, *The People's Welfare*; and O'Brien, *Conjectures of Order*).

8. Perdue, *"Mixed Blood" Indians*. Perdue persuasively argues that Cherokee cultural practices limited the impact of intermarriage. Although Cherokee country may have looked diverse, southern Indian country was mostly stable through the unifying tendencies of matrilineal kinship. In other words, Cherokees did not understand racial constructs the same way that white southerners did.

9. On the implementation of the extension law, see Garrison, "Inevitability and the Southern Opposition to Indian Removal," 107–25. Garrison's pathbreaking work *The Legal Ideology of Removal* likewise explores the ramifications of the extension law from a legal perspective. My contention—that state-level political actions and the widespread reliance on violence to enforce the extension laws and effect removal—moves in concert with Garrison's claims about the importance of state courts as weapons in the contest over sovereignty.

10. For Georgia's own nullification controversy, see Coulter, "The Nullification Movement in Georgia," 3–39, as well as E. Miles, "After John Marshall's Decision," 519–44. Other works discuss the importance of the growth of a states' right ideology within Georgia, especially among coastal elites (see, for example, J. Young, *Domesticating Slavery*). On the power of states, see Gerstle, *Liberty and Coercion*.

11. More recent work on Cherokee cultural forms has shed light on important communal behaviors that acted as important stabilizers as Cherokees weathered serious threats to their social and political institutions (see, for example, Reed, *Serving the Cherokee Nation*). Other scholars have demonstrated the ways in which boundaries acted as liminal spaces that allowed Natives, in this case under the guise of the Slicks, to work as a way of exerting influence and demonstrating sovereignty

(see Bruyneel, *The Third Space of Sovereignty*). These two works demonstrate the communal nature of Cherokee efforts to effect social cohesion on the borders of Cherokee space.

12. U.S. scholars have frequently celebrated the project of American expansionism. Frederick Jackson Turner saw American expansion and the frontier process as the force that led to democracy in the United States (Jackson, "The Significance of the Frontier in American History," 31–60). Frederick Merk, in his *Manifest Destiny and Mission in American History*, argues that a redemptive sense of mission accompanied American settlers into the West. The trend in historical scholarship, however, has been more critical of the United States' push to acquire western lands and calls into question the frontier myth. Paul Frymer's *Building an American Empire* understands expansion as a project of racial and state formation. Other recent works have demonstrated how Indian removal was not just a southern phenomenon (see Bowes, *Land Too Good for Indians*).

13. Wolfe, "Settler Colonialism and the Elimination of the Native," 387–409, quote from 387.

14. On the entanglement between the Enlightenment and racism, see Rosen, *American Indians and State Law*, 103–8. More broadly, Nicholas Guyatt explores how Enlightened Americans struggled with the idea of a multiracial society. See his *Bind Us Apart: How Enlightened Americans Invented Racial Segregation*. Jeffrey Ostler, *Surviving Genocide: Native Nations and the United States from the American Revolution to Bleeding Kansas* (New Haven, CT: Yale University Press, 2019); Adam Dahl, *Empire of the People: Settler Colonialism and the Foundations of Modern Democratic Thought* (Lawrence: University Press of Kansas, 2018).

1 / Order and Sovereignty

1. Benjamin Hawkins to James McHenry, February 16, 1798, in Hawkins, *The Collected Works of Benjamin Hawkins*, ed. Foster, 287; Josiah Tattnall Jr. to Thomas Jefferson, July 28, 1802, in Jefferson, *The Papers of Thomas Jefferson*, ed. Oberg, 38:112–14. For the story of the Wofford settlement, see Flowers, "The Wofford Settlement on the Georgia Frontier," 258–67.

2. "An Act to Regulate Trade and Intercourse with the Indian Tribes, and to Preserve Peace on the Frontiers," March 30, 1802, in Peters, ed., United States Congress *Statutes at Large*, 7th Cong., 1st Sess. The *Statutes at Large* are available from the Library of Congress's "A Century of Lawmaking for a New Nation" website: http://memory.loc.gov/ammem/amlaw/lawhome.html. Previous Intercourse Acts had been passed by Congress starting in 1790, though these laws expired every three years and needed congressional reapproval. The 1803 law did not, and it became the primary document guiding U.S.-Indian affairs for the next thirty years.

3. "An Act to Regulate Trade and Intercourse with the Indian Tribes, and to Preserve Peace on the Frontiers," 143.

4. Flowers, "The Wofford Settlement on the Georgia Frontier," 262. To be fair, the government did not have any written proof of the 1804 agreement that secured the Wofford tract in exchange for money. In 1824, Secretary of War John C. Calhoun had to write to Jefferson inquiring about the validity of the agreement. Jefferson confirmed that the Compact was indeed legit. Later that year, it was sent to the Senate for ratification. For Jefferson's reply confirming that the treaty was indeed real, see "Thomas

Jefferson to John C. Calhoun, April 25, 1824, Founders Online, National Archives, http://founders.archives.gov/documents/Jefferson/98-01-02-4211.

5. McLoughlin, *Cherokee Renascence in the New Republic*, 297.

6. Lamplugh, *Politics on the Periphery*, 104, 185–90. For the text of the Compact, see "To Ratify and Confirm Certain Articles of Agreement and Cession Entered into on the 24th Day of April 1802 [. . .]," in *Acts of the General Assembly of the State of Georgia*, 1:3–8. The full text of Georgia's legislative documents is available online at the Digital Library of Georgia (http://dlg.galileo.usg.edu).

7. "To Ratify and Confirm Certain Articles of Agreement and Cession Entered into on the 24th Day of April 1802 [. . .]," 4.

8. On permanence as an important part of European claims, see Wolfe, "Settler Colonialism and the Elimination of the Native," 396–97. Europeans relied heavily upon John Locke's ideas about land, especially his *Second Treatise on Government*. For an analysis of America's importance in that text, see Armitage, "John Locke, Carolina, and the 'Two Treatises of Government,'" 602–27.

9. For an analysis of the discovery doctrine, see Ford, *Settler Sovereignty*, 27–29.

10. On the *Johnson* case, see Robertson, *Conquest by Law*, esp. 100–116; as well as Banner, *How the Indians Lost Their Land*, 178–88. For the text of the *Johnson* case, see *Johnson v. M'Intosh*, 21 U.S. (8 Wheat.) 543–73 (1823). On the Intercourse Act, see "An Act to Regulate Trade and Intercourse with the Indian Tribes, and to Preserve Peace on the Frontiers," 139–45.

11. Gilmer, *Sketches*, 318

12. Benjamin Hawkins to James McHenry, February 18, 1798, in Hawkins, *The Collected Works of Benjamin Hawkins*, ed. Foster, 288.

13. Gates, "The Georgia Land Act of 1803," 1–21.

14. McCormick, *The Second Party System*, 236.

15. For the text of the Treaty of Cherokee Agency, see "Treaty with the Cherokee, 1817," in Kappler, ed., *Indian Affairs: Laws and Treaties*, 2:140–44; for the Treaty of Washington, see "Treaty with the Cherokee, 1819," ibid., 2:177–81.

16. Williams, *The Georgia Gold Rush*, 47–48.

17. *Milledgeville Federal Union*, July 21, 1832, 2.

18. Wilson Lumpkin to Eli Shorter and P. H. Campbell, May 2, 1835, Governor's Letter Book, February 5, 1833–June 18, 1835, Drawer 62, Box 65, Microfilm Collections, GDAH.

19. "An Act to Amend the Penal Code," in *Acts of the General Assembly of the State of Georgia*, December 20, 1817, 92–143. On legal efforts to impose white supremacy in the antebellum South, see T. Morris, *Southern Slavery and the Law, 1619–1820*; as well as Gross, *Double Character*, 61–65.

20. Lumpkin, *The Removal of the Cherokee Indians from Georgia, Including His Speeches in the United States Congress*, 1:42, 45.

21. Clayton, *The Office and Duty of a Justice of the Peace*, 5–7.

22. As the thirteenth-largest state, Georgia has the second-highest number of counties. Local lore has it that early state legislators wanted each courthouse strategically placed so that any person could make a trip to the courthouse and back home within the course of a day. On the construction of courthouses and jails in counties bordering the Cherokee Nation, see Dorsey, *The History of Hall County, Georgia, 1818–1900*, 1:16; as well as Bonner, *Georgia's Last Frontier*, 23.

23. George Gilmer to Walter Colquitt, February 15, 1830, Governor's Letter Book, November 10, 1829–June 29, 1831, Drawer 62, Box 64, Microfilm Collections, GDAH.

24. Allen G. Fambrough to George R. Gilmer, February 21, 1830, in Hays, ed., *Cherokee Indian Letters*, Works Progress Administration Project No. 4341, 1:206, Bound Volumes, GDAH.

25. Edward Telfair to Henry Knox, December 5, 1792, Report No. 37, in Cochran, ed., *New American State Papers: Indian Affairs*, 1:336.

26. *Milledgeville Federal Union*, September 11, 1830, 3.

27. *Macon Telegraph*, October 16, 1830, 3. Interposition was an important aspect of John C. Calhoun's doctrine of nullification and the entire philosophy of states' rights, which held that states had the constitutional right to interpose themselves between their constituents and the coercive power of the federal government. That newspaper editors were asking the state to interpose itself between backcountry criminals and white settlers was a pragmatic expression of the philosophical point.

28. "An Act to Alter and Amend the Second Section of the Second Article of the Constitution of the State of Georgia," November 17, 1824, in *Acts of the General Assembly of the State of Georgia*, 1:41.

29. Wilentz, *The Rise of American Democracy*, 262–63; M. Green, *The Politics of Indian Removal*, 69–125. On the vote tally, see *Georgia Journal*, November 15, 1825, 3.

30. Wilentz, *The Rise of American Democracy*, 263; Cole, *Vindicating Andrew Jackson*, 37–45.

31. "The Joint Committee on the State of the Republic [. . .]," in *Acts of the General Assembly of the State of Georgia*, December 27, 1827, 236–49. See also McLoughlin, *Cherokee Renascence in the New Republic*, 411–12; and Phillips, *Georgia and State Rights*, 72.

32. This strategy of granting allotments to Native peoples eventually succeeded in displacing the Creeks, Choctaws, and Chickasaws mostly because government negotiators could play separate tribal factions against one another and acquire favorable land cessions. On the allotment strategy, see M. Young, *Redskins, Ruffleshirts, and Rednecks*.

33. Parsons, *The Birth of Modern Politics*, 156.

34. Lumpkin, *The Removal of the Cherokee Indians from Georgia*, 1:41.

35. Recent works differ as to the actual vote tally in Georgia. Donald Cole has the Jackson vote at 19,362, while 642 voters went for Adams. Lynn Parsons notes that 19,363 Georgians cast their vote for Jackson, while none did so for Adams (see Cole, *Vindicating Andrew Jackson*, 183; and Parsons, *Birth of Modern Politics*, 182).

36. Thomas Jefferson to John C. Calhoun, April 25, 1824, Founders Online, National Archives, http://founders.archives.gov/documents/Jefferson/98-01-02-4211.

2 / Disorder in the Disputed Territory

1. Morse, *A Report to the Secretary of War of the United States, on Indian Affairs, Comprising a Narrative Tour*, 11.

2. Ibid., 32–33.

3. Johann Renatus Schmidt to Andreas Benade, November 11, 1824, in Crews and Starbuck, eds., *Records of the Moravians among the Cherokees*, 6:3193.

4. John Gambold to Theodor Schulz, June 22, 1824, in Crews and Starbuck, eds., *Records of the Moravians among the Cherokees*, 6:3125; John Gambold to Andreas Benade, August 30, 1824, ibid., 6:3167.

5. Springplace Diary, October 9, 1823, in Crews and Starbuck, eds., *Records of the Moravians among the Cherokees*, 6:3028–29.

6. See Reed, *Serving the Cherokee Nation*, xix.

7. The literature on Cherokee social change is voluminous. For those who see Cherokee social change as endemic of cultural degradation, see McLoughlin, "Cherokee Anomie, 1794–1808," 126–60. More nuanced approaches to social change have lately appeared (see Hill, *Weaving New Worlds*). On quantifying social change, see McLoughlin and Conser, "The Cherokees in Transition," 678–703. On agricultural changes, see Wilms, "Cherokee Land Use in Georgia before Removal," 1–28.

8. The idea of harmony is explored in Cumfer, *Separate People, One Land*, 25–41; and Perdue, *Cherokee Women*, 13–15. See also Daniel, "From Blood Feud to Jury System," 97–125. Julie L. Reed provides an analysis of The Ridge's transformation from a warrior to a peace-seeker as an extension of the idea of balance (Reed, *Serving the Cherokee Nation*, 30–34).

9. For a discussion of the importance of kinship ties, see Stremlau, *Sustaining the Cherokee Family*, 22–30.

10. Perdue, *Slavery and the Evolution of Cherokee Society*, 50–53. For a broader treatment of slavery in the Native southeast, see Snyder, *Slavery in Indian Country*.

11. On the Cherokee debate over allowing the federal road to pass through their lands and the resulting effects, see McLoughlin, *Cherokee Renascence in the New Republic*, 77–91; on the impact of federal roads on Creek society, see Hudson, *Creek Paths and Federal Roads*.

12. See M. Young, "The Cherokee Nation," 502–24. Other historians have explored various facets of nation building among the Cherokees. For example, Andrew Denson argues that the memorials and petitions of the Cherokee government to Congress should be taken seriously and are one expression of Cherokee nationhood (Denson, *Demanding the Cherokee Nation*, 15–51).

13. McLoughlin, *Cherokee Renascence in the New Republic*, 157–58.

14. Ibid., 223–26.

15. The Cherokee Constitution of 1827 was fully reprinted in the *Cherokee Phoenix* over the course of its first three issues (*Cherokee Phoenix*, February 21, 1828, 1). For a general discussion of the Cherokee Constitution, see McLoughlin, *Cherokee Renascence in the New Republic*, 394–400.

16. Ibid.

17. Perdue, *Cherokee Women*, 146.

18. Ibid., 144–46; McLoughlin, *Cherokee Renascence in the New Republic*, 394–400.

19. *Cherokee Phoenix*, February 21, 1828, 2; Perdue, *Slavery and the Evolution of Cherokee Society*, 48–49.

20. Hugh Montgomery to Thomas McKenny, April 23, 1825, qtd. in McLoughlin, *Cherokee Renascence in the New Republic*, 412.

21. *Milledgeville Southron*, February 23, 1828, 2.

22. *Milledgeville Southern Recorder*, March 17, 1828, 2.

23. Gilmer to William Wirt, June 19, 1830, in Gilmer, *Sketches*, 274.

24. Natalie Joy points out the ironies of the political alliance between slaveholding Cherokee and northern reformers (Joy, "Cherokee Slaveholders and Radical Abolitionists," www.common-place.org/vol-10/no-04/joy/).

25. *Milledgeville Southern Recorder*, March 17, 1828, 2.

26. "An Act to Add the Territory Lying within the Limits of This State [. . .]," in *Acts of the General Assembly of the State of Georgia*, December 20, 1828, 88–89. For additional analysis of the extension laws, see Garrison, *The Legal Ideology of Removal*, 103–25. Garrison locates the extension laws' importance in the state's execution of George Tassels, a Cherokee who had committed murder. The case *Georgia v. Tassels*, he argues, demonstrates that state courts had seized sovereignty when Tassels was executed in December 1830.

27. Featherstonhaugh, *A Canoe Voyage up the Minnay Sotor*, 2:223, 226.

28. Ibid., 2:223–24.

29. Col. Hugh Montgomery to Colonel McKenny, April 23, 1825, in "Intrusion on Cherokee Land," H.R. Doc. No. 89, p. 2; Ulysses Lewis to George Troup, January 27, 1827, in Hays, ed., *Georgia Military Affairs*, WPA Project No. 5993 (Morrow: GDAH, 1940), 5:206, Bound Volumes, GDAH.

30. Hamilton, *Men and Manners in America*, 296–97. On the ways in which life on southern steamships mirrored the southwestern frontier at large, see Gudmestad, *Steamboats and the Rise of the Cotton Kingdom*, 53–77.

31. *Macon Telegraph*, September 1, 1828, 1.

32. On the number of interracial couples in the Cherokee Nation, see tables 1 and 2 in McLoughlin and Conser, "The Cherokees in Transition," 680–81. The 1835 Census listed a total Cherokee population of 16,452, which consisted of 2,637 households, 1,454 "halfbloods" (8.79 percent of the total Cherokee population), and 1,492 "quarterbloods" (9.02 percent).

33. The 1842 U.S. Claims Commission took testimony from individual Cherokees and a witness regarding their lost property as a result of Cherokee removal. Stipulated by the 1835 Treaty of New Echota, the agents appointed by the Commission recorded the stories and valuations of lost Cherokee property and, in theory, sent those sources to Congress to approve remuneration. Agents from the War Department filed 706 claims, of which, in the end, Congress deemed only 31 to be legit; of the $2.3 million appropriated by Congress, it spent only $69,000 to restore Cherokee property. The committee responsible for doling out the funds had little by way of rationalization for its stinginess. I assume they simply refused to believe that Cherokees had accumulated so much property or they felt like Cherokees were attempting to bilk taxpayers. I take the position that stories of the victims are true and deserve attention.

34. Claim of Hetty Vance, March 18, 1842, in Chase, ed., *1842 Cherokee Claims, Saline District*, 90.

35. Claim of Tahlegalooraytee, March 20, 1842, in Chase, ed., *1842 Cherokee Claims, Tahlequah District*, 45; Claim of Young Bird, March 7, 1842, ibid., 6; Claim of Peggy Nelms, March 28, 1842, in Chase, ed., *1842 Cherokee Claims, Saline District*, 200; Claim of Goose Langley, April 12, 1842, in Chase, ed., *1842 Cherokee Claims, Goingsnake District*, 116–17; Claim of Four Killer, April 8, 1842, ibid., 98.

36. The Cherokees learned herding practices from white southerners who utilized open-range grazing, which had long been the custom in the southern Appalachians (see, for example, Aron, "Pigs and Hunters," 175–204).

37. Claim of Lacy Christy, March 24, 1842, in Chase, ed., *1842 Cherokee Claims, Tahlequah District*, 162; Claim of Atawluny, April 26, 1842, ibid., 181; Claim of Peacheater, March 25, 1842, in Chase, ed., *1842 Cherokee Claims, Goingsnake District*, 22–23; Claim of George Blackwood, March 31, 1842, ibid., 47–48; "Claim of Charle-te-he,"

April 6, 1842, ibid., 86; Claim of Whortleberry, April 16, 1842, ibid., 150; Claim of Wassassee, April 1, 1842, in Chase, ed., *1842 Cherokee Claims, Tahlequah District*, 256–57.

38. Hugh Montgomery to J. G. Williams, December 12, 1825, "Letters Received by the Office of Indian Affairs, 1824–1881," Roll 72, M234, RG 75, NARA; Claim of Thigh Walker, March 18, 1842, in Chase, ed., *1842 Cherokee Claims, Saline District*, 133.

39. Claim of William Mosely's Heirs, May 21, 1842, in Chase, ed., *1842 Cherokee Claims, Saline District*, 218.

40. Claim of Hetty Vance, May 1842, in Chase, ed., *1842 Cherokee Claims, Saline District*, 209.

41. Claim of Elizabeth Ware, March 26 1842, in Chase, ed., *1842 Cherokee Claims, Saline District*, 89.

42. Claim of the heirs of Dickes, March 29, 1842, in Chase, ed., *1842 Cherokee Claims, Goingsnake District*, 36–37.

43. Claim of Hetty Vance, May 12, 1842, in Chase, ed., *1842 Cherokee Claims, Saline District*, 211–12; Claim of Margaret Baumgarter, May 12, 1842, ibid., 205.

44. Claim of Betsey Rodgers, March 14, 1842, in Chase, ed., *1842 Cherokee Claims, Saline District*, 47; "Property of Capt. Oldfields," Valuation 72, December 21, 1833, Special File 184, Roll 51, M574, Special Files of the Office of Indian Affairs, NARA.

45. Soft Shell Turtle v. Grief Felton, April 1829, Carroll County Superior Court Minute Book, Drawer 269, Box 47, GDAH, 59–60; Claim of Bill Silk, March 15, 1842, in Chase, ed., *1842 Cherokee Claims, Saline District*, 71; Claim of Jacob Harnage, March 25, 1842, ibid., 120.

46. *Georgia Journal*, August 1, 1829, 3. Many people laid claim to the "first" gold find in the state. Beginning in 1826, hints and rumors of gold finds cropped up across the state, but no documentary evidence existed until the *Georgia Journal* article of August 1, 1829 (see Williams, *Georgia Gold Rush*, 22–25).

3 / The Slicks and the Pony Club

1. *Cherokee Phoenix*, August 5, 1829, 2.
2. Ibid., August 5, 1829, 2; September 9, 1829, 3.
3. Ibid., December 16, 1829, 3.
4. Claim of Thompson Tucker, March 26, 1842 in Chase, ed., *1842 Cherokee Claims, Tahlequah District*, 73. See also Shadburn, *Unhallowed Intrusion*, 650.
5. M. Green, *The Politics of Indian Removal*, 123–25.
6. *Augusta Chronicle*, February 11, 1829, 2. On the text of the Treaty of Washington, see Kappler, ed., *Indian Affairs: Laws and Treaties*, 2:264–68; and *Augusta Chronicle*, June 6, 1829, 2. Much of Wales's investigation into the "true boundary" consisted of interviews with white frontier residents who had long resided with the Cherokees. The *Cherokee Phoenix* posted the official report Wales sent to the current governor, John Forsyth (see *Cherokee Phoenix*, May 8, 1830, 1).
7. John Ross to Hugh Montgomery, December 27, 1825, in Ross, *The Papers of Chief John Ross*, ed. Moulton, 1:110; Hugh Montgomery to the Committee & Council of the Cherokee Nation, September 26, 1826, "Records of the Cherokee Indian Agency in Tennessee, 1801–1835," RG 75, M208, Reel 10, NARA; Hugh Montgomery to James Barbour, July 21, 1826, "Letters Received by the Office of Indian Affairs, 1824–1881," RG 75, M234, Reel 72, NARA; James G. Williams to Hugh Montgomery, July 2, 1827, ibid.

8. Hugh Montgomery to John Eaton, April 2, 1829, "Letters Received by the Office of Indian Affairs, 1824–1881," RG 75, M234, Roll 72, NARA; Hugh Montgomery to Secretary of War, March 3, 1829, in "Intrusion on Cherokee Land," H.R. Doc. No. 89, p. 8.

9. Alston H. Greene to George R. Gilmer, January 14, 1831, Box 49, Folder 11, Telamon Cuyler Collection, MS 1170, UGA.

10. "An Act to Regulate Trade and Intercourse with the Indian Tribes, and to Preserve Peace on the Frontiers," passed on March 30, 1802 by the 7th Congress, 1st Session, in Peters, ed., *United States Statutes at Large*, 2:139–46, esp. sec. 5.

11. Bonner, *Georgia's Last Frontier*.

12. Carroll County schedule, 1830 U.S. Census.

13. *Cherokee Phoenix*, February 11, 1829, 2; *Macon Telegraph*, October 16, 1830, 2.

14. The entire account of the settlers' expulsion, Chuwoyee's murder, and the subsequent events is recounted in a letter from John Ross to Elias Boudinot, in *Cherokee Phoenix*, February 17, 1830, 2. April Ford points to the house-burning and Chuwoyee's subsequent murder as the beginning of a "transformation is state discourse." See her *Settler Sovereignty*, 132.

15. Ibid.

16. Allen G. Fambrough to George Gilmer, February 8, 1830, in Hays, ed., *Cherokee Indian Letters*, 1:204; *Augusta Chronicle*, February 3, 1830, 2; Fambrough to Gilmer, February 21, 1830, in Hays, ed., *Cherokee Indian Letters*, 1:206; Gilmer to Fambrough, February 15, 1830, Governor's Letter Book, November 10, 1829–June 29, 1831, Drawer 62, Box 64, Microfilm Collections, GDAH.

17. Allen G. Fambrough to George R. Gilmer, July 12, 1830, in Hays, ed., *Cherokee Indian Letters*, 1:222.

18. Johnathan M. Davis vs. Richard Philpot, September 1828, Carroll County Superior Court Minutes, 1828–1833, pp. 1–3, Drawer 269, Box 47, Microfilm Collections, GDAH. The Leathers family were notorious members of the Pony Club and largely reviled among the Cherokees. George Blackwood claimed that in 1832 Joel Leathers, "a whiteman and a captain of the notorious Poney Club," stole a greatcoat from him at the Sixes gold mine (see "Claim of George Blackwood," March 31, 1842, in Chase, ed., *1842 Cherokee Claims, Goingsnake District*, 47–48).

19. Z. B. Hargrove to Wilson Lumpkin, July 5, 1832, in Hays, ed., *Cherokee Indian Letters*, 2:355.

20. *Macon Telegraph*, June 14, 1832, 3.

21. John Robinson vs. William and Calaway Burke, February 3, 1831, Carroll County Superior Court Minutes, 1828–1833, pp. 210–11, Drawer 269, Box 47, Microfilm Collections, GDAH; John Thomas v. Calaway Burke, April 1831, ibid., 241–43; John Thomas v. Calaway Burke, April 1831, ibid., 243–45; Arthur Alexander v. Calaway Burke, April 1831, ibid., 245–46.

22. Philip Bosworth v. Reuben Philpot, April 28, 1831, Carroll County Superior Court Minutes, 1828–1833, p. 234, Microfilm Collections, GDAH. The fight between Bosworth and Philpot resembled much of the white-on-white violence that permeated the antebellum South (see, for example, Elliot Gorn, "Gouge and Bite, Pull Hair and Scratch," 18–43).

23. Jacob R. Brooks to Gilmer, November 12, 1830, in Hays, ed., *Cherokee Indian Letters*, 2:242–43. It should be noted that Brooks was a close political ally of Gilmer's

and would soon enlist in the Georgia Guard, where he attained the rank of first sergeant.

24. Giles Boggess to Gilmer, November 15, 1830, in Hays, ed., *Cherokee Indian Letters*, 2:245; *Cherokee Phoenix*, February 13, 1831, 2.

25. William Thompson to Gilmer, December 27, 1830, in Hays, ed., *Cherokee Indian Letters*, 2:263.

26. Giles Boggess to Gilmer, November 15, 1830, in Hays, ed., *Cherokee Indian Letters*, 2:245; *Cherokee Phoenix*, February 13, 1831, 2.

27. William Thompson to Gilmer, December 27, 1830, in Hays, ed., *Cherokee Indian Letters*, 2:265.

28. *Cherokee Phoenix*, February 12, 1831, 2.

29. William Thompson to Gilmer, December 27, 1830, in Hays, ed., *Cherokee Indian Letters*, 2:265.

30. *Cherokee Phoenix*, February 12, 1831, 2.

31. Giles S. Boggess to Gilmer, December 1830, in Hays, ed., *Cherokee Indian Letters*, 2:247. State law permitted justices of the peace and sheriffs to use militia companies in the apprehension of criminals (see Clayton, *The Office and Duty of a Justice of the Peace*).

32. *Macon Telegraph*, October 16, 1830, 3.

33. Bonner, *Georgia's Last Frontier*, 34.

34. Ibid.; *Columbus Enquirer*, August 18, 1832, 3.

35. Z. B. Hargrove to George Gilmer, July 5, 1832, in Hays, ed., *Cherokee Indian Letters*, 2:355.

36. Qtd. in Bonner, *Georgia's Last Frontier*, 32–33.

37. William Thompson to Gilmer, December 27, 1830, in Hays, ed., *Cherokee Indian Letters*, 2:263; *Macon Telegraph*, October 16, 1830, 3.

38. Perdue, *Cherokee Women*, 123–24.

39. Re-creating the world of the Regulators, Marjoleine Kars's *Breaking Loose Together* stresses the social and cultural ferment of the backcountry as factors encouraging the organization and actions of the Regulators. Other accounts, most notably A. Roger Ekirch's *"Poor Carolina,"* place the emphasis on disgruntled backcountry settlers who saw the political system as one that took advantage of poor frontier farmers. Laura F. Edwards's *The People and Their Peace* illuminates the desire of the Regulators to have a greater degree of local autonomy with regard to the justice system.

40. Z. B. Hargrove to Wilson Lumpkin, July 5, 1832, in Hays, ed., *Cherokee Indian Letters*, 2:355.

41. A Cherokee law in 1811 delineated the precise number of lashes given for theft of livestock; for example: "Any person stealing a horse shall Receive one hundred lashes on there Bere Back; a Cow, fifty; or a hog, twenty-five" (qtd. in McLoughlin, *Cherokee Renascence in the New Republic*, 175). Slicking remained a part of Cherokee life even after removal. Silas W. Wilson recounted in 1938 that guilty thieves were "carried out to the whipping post or presented to the Ball Knobbers," a vigilante group in turn-of-the-twentieth-century Missouri (see "Silas W. Wilson," *American Life Histories: Manuscripts from the Federal Writer's Project, 1936–1940*, http://memory.loc.gov).

42. James Taylor Carson argues that postcontact societies should be understood in this syncretic manner. Encounter and adaptation demonstrate that individuals were not "separate nuclear units" but, rather, "contributing parts of a whole" creole society.

The amount of cooperation and cultural borrowing echoes Carson's point (Carson, *Making an Atlantic World*, xvii).

43. *Columbus Enquirer*, August 4, 1832, 3.
44. *Macon Telegraph*, June 14, 1832, 3.
45. Ibid.
46. The account of Burke's murder is recounted in the *Columbus Enquirer*, August 4, 1832, 3, and contains a more detailed, though probably more imaginative account, than that of the *Macon Telegraph*, June 14, 1832, 3.
47. *Macon Telegraph*, June 14, 1832, 3.
48. *Cherokee Phoenix*, December 10, 1829.
49. *Columbus Enquirer*, August 4, 1832, 3.
50. Lumpkin to John Coffee, July 14, 1832, in Hays, ed., *Cherokee Indian Letters*, 2:352–53.

4 / The Convergence of State and Federal Policy

1. See Balogh, *A Government out of Sight*, 153–55.
2. See John Ross to Hugh Montgomery, September 3, 1829, in Ross, *The Papers of Chief John Ross*, ed. Moulton, 1:68; Hugh Montgomery to John Ross, September 3, 1829, ibid. For Secretary of War Eaton's orders, see Thomas L. McKenney to John Ross, October 12, 1829, ibid., 1:169.
3. John Ross to Hugh Montgomery, February 6, 1830, in Ross, *The Papers of Chief John Ross*, ed. Moulton, 1:183.
4. Cherokee Deputation from the Nation to the Secretary of War, February 11, 1830, in "Intrusion on Cherokee Land," H.R. Doc. No. 89, p. 27.
5. John Ross to Jeremiah Evarts, July 24, 1830, in Ross, *The Papers of Chief John Ross*, ed. Moulton, 1:195; William Wirt to John Ross, August 9, 1830, ibid., 1:196.
6. Gilmer to John Berrien, May 6, 1830, Governor's Letter Book, November 10, 1829–June 29, 1831, Drawer 62, Box 64, Microfilm Collections, GDAH; *Macon Telegraph*, October 16, 1830, 3.
7. Gilmer to John M. Berrien, May 6, 1830, Governor's Letter Book, November 10, 1829–June 29, 1831, Drawer 62, Box 64, Microfilm Collections, GDAH.
8. For Gilmer's proclamation for citizens to remove themselves from the gold region, see Gilmer, *Sketches*, 266–67.
9. Gilmer to Commander of the United States Troops at Fort Mitchell, February 16, 1830, Governor's Letter Book, November 10, 1829–June 29, 1831, Drawer 62, Box 64, Microfilm Collections, GDAH; as well as McLoughlin, *Cherokee Renascence in the New Republic*, 432. In one of the ironies of Jacksonian Indian Policy, the U.S. Army's primary role was to prevent whites from intruding on the lands promised to Amerindians through treaties with the United States. Soldiers often resented having to take the side of Indians over whites but usually followed through with their duties. However, over the course of Jackson's two terms, the army became less a means for securing Native lands and more a tool of implementing removal.
10. Gilmer to Yelverton King, July 5, 1830, in Gilmer, *Sketches*, 279–80; Gilmer to Allen G. Fambrough, February 15, 1830, Governor's Letter Book, November 10, 1829–June 29, 1831, Drawer 62, Box 64, Microfilm Collections, GDAH.

190 / NOTES TO CHAPTER 4

11. John H. Eaton to Major General Alexander Macomb, February 24, 1830, in "Intrusion on Cherokee Land," H.R. Doc. No. 89, pp. 35–36; Major P. Wager to General Macomb, March 13, 1830, ibid., 38; *Augusta Chronicle*, March 27, 1830, 2.

12. *Augusta Chronicle*, March 27, 1830, 2.

13. *Cherokee Phoenix*, June 12, 1830, 3.

14. Archibald R. S. Hunter to George R. Gilmer, July 5, 1830, in Hays, ed., *Cherokee Indian Letters*, 1:221; William Rutherford to Gilmer, August 25, 1830, in Hays, ed., *Georgia Military Affairs*, 6:226.

15. Trenor to F. W. Brady, June 23, 1830, "Letters Received by the Office of Indian Affairs, 1824–1881," Roll 74, M234, RG 75, NARA.

16. Gilmer to Yelverton King, June 28, 1830, Governor's Letter Book, November 10, 1829–June 29, 1831, Drawer 62, Box 64, Microfilm Collections, GDAH; Gilmer to Yelverton King, July 5, 1830, ibid. Gilmer had carefully considered his options when it came to calling up the militia. He consulted at least one state supreme court judge, J. W. Jackson, who informed him that if intruders intended to trespass on the public property, he could consider it an insurrection, which would require him to muster the militia. The problem became one of defining an insurrection, which Jackson considered *"an assemblage in strength"* (see J. W. Jackson to Gilmer, August 7, 1830, Box 49, Folder 9, Telamon Cuyler Collection, UGA).

17. *Macon Telegraph*, September 11, 1830, 3.

18. Wager's report qtd. in O. Young, "The Southern Gold Rush, 1828–1836," 385; *Augusta Chronicle*, September 25, 1830, 2.

19. Major Philip Wager to Major General Alexander Macomb, September 30, 1830, in Covington, ed., "Letters from the Georgia Gold Region," 407–8.

20. *Augusta Chronicle*, September 25, 1830, 2; Hugh Montgomery to George Gilmer, September 13, 1830, in Hays, ed., *Georgia Military Affairs*, 6:228; *Macon Telegraph*, October 30, 1830, 3.

21. J. W. Brady to John H. Eaton, June 28, 1830, "Letters Received by the Office of Indian Affairs, 1824–1881," Roll 74, M234, RG 75, NARA; Elijah Hicks et al. to Captain Brady, June 26, 1830, ibid.

22. George Lowrey et al. to Andrew Jackson, March 26, 1830, in Jackson, *Papers of Andrew Jackson*, ed. Feller et al., 8:158–60.

23. For a partial list of white Cherokee residents exempt from expulsion, see Hays, ed., *Cherokee Indian Letters*, 1:230–31.

24. Archibald R. T. Hunter to George R. Gilmer, January 4, 1830, in Hays, ed., *Cherokee Indian Letters*, 1:199–200.

25. P. L. Goodman to George R. Gilmer, June 7, 1830, in Covington, ed., "Letters from the Georgia Gold Region," 402–3; Peter J. Williams to George R. Gilmer, June 17, 1830, ibid., 403–4; George R. Gilmer to Andrew Jackson, June 15, 1830, Governor's Letter Book, November 10, 1829–June 29, 1831, Microfilm Collections, GDAH; Gilmer; *Sketches*, 267; P. L. Goodman to George R. Gilmer, June 17, 1830, Roll 74, M234, NARA. Gilmer also declared federal actions against the right of the state in a letter to President Jackson: "The Government of the U States had no authority to enforce the non-intercourse laws."

26. Peter J. Williams to Gilmer, June 17, 1830, in Covington, ed., "Letters from the Georgia Gold Region," 404; B. L. Goodman to Gilmer, June 7, 1830, ibid., 402–3.

27. Gilmer to Andrew Jackson, June 15, 1830, Governor's Letter Book, November 10, 1829–June 29, 1831, Drawer 62, Box 64, Microfilm Collections, GDAH.

28. Gilmer to Yelverton King, June 28, 1830, Governor's Letter Book, November 10, 1829–June 29, 1831, Drawer 62, Box 64, Microfilm Collections, GDAH.

29. Augustin S. Clayton to George R. Gilmer, July 23, 1830, in Hays, ed., *Georgia Military Affairs*, 6:27; J. W. Jackson to George R. Gilmer, August 7, 1830, Folder 9, Box 49, Telamon Cuyler Collection, UGA. On Gilmer's view of the gold mines as public property, see his annual message to the legislature delivered on December 4, 1830, in Gilmer, *Sketches*, 289; *Cherokee Phoenix*, May 29, 1830, 3.

30. "An Act to Prevent the Exercise of Assumed and Arbitrary Power [. . .]," in *Acts of the General Assembly of the State of Georgia* (1830), 114–17, quote from 115.

31. Ibid., 115–16.

32. Gilmer to Andrew Jackson, June 15, 1830, Governor's Letter Book, November 10, 1829–June 29, 1831, Drawer 62, Box 64, pp. 146–47, Microfilm Collections, GDAH.

33. Gilmer to Andrew Jackson, October 29, 1830, Reel 16, in Jackson, *The Papers of Andrew Jackson: A Microfilm Supplement*, ed. Moser et al.

34. For the text of the Indian Removal Bill, see *Register of Debates*, House of Representatives, 21st Cong., 1st Sess. (Washington, DC: Gales and Seaton, 1830), 1135–36. The historiography of Jackson's motivation behind Indian removal is varied and contentious. Elliot Satz contended that Jacksonian policy was just another means of "control and management" of an ethnic other (Satz, *American Indian Policy in the Jacksonian Era*, quote from 292). Ronald Takaki declared Jackson the "metaphysician of Indian-hating" who engaged in "self-deception" regarding his position on Indian removal (Takaki, *Iron Cages*, 92–107). Stuart Banner detailed legal precursors to removal and equated Georgia's actions to extortion (Banner, *How the Indians Lost Their Land*, esp. 201–27). Jackson's defenders claim that his actions prevented the extinction of the Indians (see esp. Remini, *Andrew Jackson and His Indian Wars*, 278–81).

35. Lewis Cass to Lumpkin, March 23, 1835, in Hays, ed., *Georgia Military Affairs*, 6:252.

36. Cherokee Treaty of 1819, in Kappler, ed., *Indian Affairs: Laws and Treaties* 2:177–81. Because the national council opposed a similar treaty ratified in 1817, federal negotiators had to secure larger payments and more concessions before the Cherokee commenced with removal. Still, opposition persisted through 1838. On the Cherokee in Arkansas Territory, see Logan, *The Promised Land*, esp. 5–21, 23, 28.

37. *The Cherokee Nation v. The State of Georgia*, 30 U.S. (5 Peters), 1–80 (1831).

38. Gilmer to Jacob Scudder, December 20, 1830, Governor's Letter Book, November 10, 1829–June 29, 1831, Drawer 62, Box 64, Microfilm Collections, GDAH.

5 / The Georgia Guard and the Politics of Order

1. Hill, *Cherokee Removal*, 51–52.

2. John W. A. Sanford to Gilmer, January 15, 1831; John W.A. Sanford to George R. Gilmer, January 22, 1831, both in John W. A. Sanford Letter Book, Drawer 21, Reel 53, Microfilm Collections, GDAH.

3. Charles H. Nelson to Gilmer, October 20, 1830, in Hays, ed., *Georgia Military Affairs*, 6:43–44. Other backcountry residents connected to the state militia also called for a similar force (see Samuel A. Wales to Gilmer, July 27, 1830, ibid., 6:219–20).

4. "An Act to Prevent the Exercise of Assumed and Arbitrary Power [...]," in *Acts of the General Assembly of the State of Georgia,* December 22, 1830, 114–17.

5. Ibid., 116.

6. For the roster of Sanford's Guard, see John W. A. Sanford Letter Book, Microfilm Collections, GDAH.

7. John W. A. Sanford to Gilmer, January 15, 1831, John W. A. Sanford Letter Book, Microfilm Collections, GDAH.

8. John W. A. Sanford to Gilmer, January 22, 1831, John W. A. Sanford Letter Book, Microfilm Collections, GDAH..

9. Ibid.

10. Affidavit of Mark Castleberry, January 26, 1831, in Hays, ed., *Georgia Military Affairs,* 6:84–85.

11. Robert Mitchell to Gilmer, January 28, 1831, in Hays, ed., *Cherokee Indian Letters,* 3:266; Gilmer to Robert Mitchell, February 3, 1831, in Gilmer, *Sketches,* 300.

12. John W. A. Sanford to Gilmer, January 22, 1831, John W. A. Sanford Letter Book, Microfilm Collections, GDAH.

13. Hines Holt Jr. to John W. A. Sanford, June 20, 1831, File II Names, Reference Services, GDAH.

14. The competing narratives are all printed in the *Cherokee Phoenix,* March 12, 1831, 4.

15. John W. A. Sanford to Gilmer, January 29, 1831, John W. A. Sanford Letter Book, Microfilm Collections, GDAH; Gilmer to General William Ezzard et al., January 15, 1831, Governor's Letter Book, November 10, 1829–June 29, 1831, Drawer 62, Box 64, Microfilm Collections, GDAH; Gilmer to Charles H. Nelson, March 10, 1831, ibid.

16. John W. A. Sanford to George R. Gilmer, February 7, 1831, John W. A. Sanford Letter Book, Microfilm Collections, GDAH.

17. John W. A. Sanford to Gilmer, March 12, 1831, John W. A. Sanford Letter Book, Microfilm Collections, GDAH.

18. John W. A. Sanford to Hugh Montgomery, January 27, 1831, John W. A. Sanford Letter Book, Microfilm Collections, GDAH; John W. A. Sanford to Gilmer, April 1, 1831, ibid. For the list of families who rented land from Sanford (as well as a homemade remedy for diphtheria), see the last five pages of the John W. A. Sanford Letter Book.

19. "An Act to Authorize the Survey and Disposition of Lands within the Limits of Georgia [...]," in *Acts of the General Assembly of the State of Georgia,* December 21, 1830, 127–43.

20. Augustin S. Clayton to George R. Gilmer, June 11, 1830, in Hays, ed., *Georgia Military Affairs,* 6:20.

21. *Cherokee Phoenix,* March 3, 1831, 3.

22. W. J. Tavern to Gilmer, August 6, 1831, in Gilmer, *Sketches,* 279–80; John W. A. Sanford to Gilmer, August 22, 1831, in Hays, ed., *Georgia Military Affairs,* 6:85b; John W. A. Sanford to Gilmer, August 29, 1831, John W. A. Sanford Letter Book, Microfilm Collections, GDAH.

23. *Milledgeville Federal Union,* July 21, 1831 2.

24. John W. A. Sanford to Gilmer, August 1, 1831, John W. A. Sanford Letter Book, Microfilm Collections, GDAH.

25. *Cherokee Phoenix*, February 12, 1831, 2; *Cherokee Phoenix*, October 7, 1831, 3. The story of Nelson's attempted trampling of Cherokee converts is related in Linton M. Collins, "The Activities of the Missionaries among the Cherokees," *GHQ* 4 (1922): 308.

26. F. A. Brown to Wilson Lumpkin, September 15, 1831, in Hays, ed., *Georgia Military Affairs*, 6:163–72; *Macon Telegraph*, July 4, 1832, 3.

27. Gilmer to Sanford, February 4, 1831, in Gilmer, *Sketches*, 301–2.

28. John Ross to Hugh Montgomery, September 9, 1831, in Ross, *The Papers of Chief John Ross*, ed. Moulton, 1:222–23.

29. Gilmer to John W. A. Sanford, June 15, 1831, Governor's Letter Book, November 10, 1829–June 29, 1831, Microfilm Collections, GDAH; George R. Gilmer to Andrew Jackson, June 20, 1831, ibid.; Gilmer Address to the Georgia General Assembly, December 8, 1830, in Gilmer, *Sketches*, 287; Gilmer, "Message to the Legislature," ibid., 296. Ironically, many supporters of the Cherokees agreed with Gilmer's assessment. Christian missionaries reinforced the governor's observation regarding the racial divisions within the Cherokee population, though they allowed for some nuance whereas Gilmer wrote with certainty. "That the Indians of mixed blood should, *upon an average*, be in advance of the full Indians, was to be expected," the ministers resolved, "& is undoubtedly true; although some Indians of full blood are in the foremost rank, and some of mixed blood help to bring up the rear" (see "Resolution by Missionaries" January 1, 1831, in Worcester, *New Echota Letters*, ed. Kilpatrick and Kilpatrick, 85).

30. Sanford to Gilmer, August 10, 1831, John W. A. Sanford Letter Book, Microfilm Collections, GDAH.

31. Sanford to Gilmer, May 28, 1831, John W. A. Sanford Letter Book, Microfilm Collections, GDAH.; Gilmer to Andrew Jackson, December 8, 1830, in Gilmer, *Sketches*, 287.

32. On the first arrest of Worcester by the "representatives of a Christian State," see Couch, "Pages from Cherokee Indian History"; Gilmer to John W. A. Sanford, June 17, 1831, in Gilmer, *Sketches*, 314.

33. The entire account of the Guard's arrest of Worcester and his fellow missionaries is recounted in the *Cherokee Phoenix*, July 30, 1831, 1. A collection of Worcester's letters from the Camp Gilmer jail, as well as many of his subsequent letters, are reprinted in Worcester, *New Echota Letters*, ed. Kilpatrick and Kilpatrick, 95–128.

34. *Cherokee Phoenix*, July 30, 1831, 1.

35. Gilmer to Sanford, September 3, 1831, in *Milledgeville Federal Union*, September 15, 1831, 2; Gilmer to Sanford, September 3, 1831, in Gilmer, *Sketches*, 324.

36. Gilmer to Charles H. Nelson, September 5, 1830, in Gilmer, *Sketches*, 325.

37. *Macon Telegraph*, September 24, 1831, 3; *Newburyport (MA) Herald*, August 23, 1831, 2. In newspapers across the country, similar outrage was expressed. A small sample include *Ohio State Journal and Columbus Gazette*, September 1, 1831, 3; *Daily National Journal*, October 4, 1831, 3, as well as numerous others.

38. Gilmer to Reverend John Howard, September 1831, in *Milledgeville Federal Union*, September 15, 1831, 2.

39. Gilmer to Major Philip Cook, September 22, 1831, in Gilmer, *Sketches*, 328; Gilmer to Sanford, September 23, 1831, Governor's Letter Book, July 1, 1831–February 5, 1833, Drawer 62, Box 47, Microfilm Collections, GDAH.

40. Gilmer's address to the legislature in which he outlined his program for the disputed territory was reprinted in nearly every newspaper in the state. See, for example,

the *Augusta Chronicle,* October 30, 1830, 2. In spite of the fact that his address occurred in October 1830, Lumpkin's supporters did not attack the governor's position until they could score partisan points for doing so, which coincided with the start of the election cycle. The first Lumpkin commentary appeared in late July 1831, when it became clear that Lumpkin would resign his seat in Congress to oppose Gilmer.

41. Ibid.

42. *Macon Telegraph,* September 10, 1831, 2; *Milledgeville Federal Union,* September 2, 1831, 2.

43. *Macon Telegraph,* September 17, 1831, 2.

44. Ibid., September 10, 1831, 2; *Milledgeville Federal Union,* July 21, 1831, 2; and July 28, 1831, 2.

45. *Milledgeville Federal Union,* September 1831, 2. Not surprisingly, Gilmer included a heavily edited extract of his address to the legislature in his memoirs. It did not contain the portion in which he advocated for Indian testimony in court (see Gilmer, *Sketches,* 282–85). Newspapers at the time of the address, even opposition papers, did not make light of the governor's plan at the time he gave it. Instead, they waited until the election began in earnest to make use of the information.

46. On the growth of the Second Party System in Georgia, see Carey, *Parties, Slavery, and the Union in Antebellum Georgia,* 19–53.

47. *Macon Telegraph,* October 15, 1831, 2.

48. Ibid., December 19, 1831, 1.

49. "An Act to Alter and Amend the Fourth Section of an Act [. . .]," December 26, 1831, in *Acts of the General Assembly of the State of Georgia,* 143. Lumpkin had begun considering Coffee for commander of the Guard soon after the election (see Lumpkin to John Coffee, November 23, 1832, Box 49A, Folder 2, Telamon Culyer Collection, UGA; as well as Lumpkin to John Coffee, January 1832, Governor's Letter Book, July 1, 1831–February 5, 1833, Drawer 62, Box 64, Microfilm Collections, GDAH. It should be noted that the John Coffee appointed to command Lumpkin's Guard was not the same John Coffee of Tennessee who was a close confidant of Andrew Jackson.

50. *Cherokee Phoenix,* December 8, 1832, 2.

51. *Worcester v. Georgia,* 31 U.S. (6 Peters) 515 (1832). The literature on the *Worcester* decision is voluminous (see, for example, Burke, "The Cherokee Cases," 500–531; Lytle, "The Supreme Court, Tribal Sovereignty, and Continuing Problems of State Encroachment into Indian Country," 65–77; Norgren, *The Cherokee Cases*; Robertson, *Conquest by Law*; and Wilson Lumpkin to John Coffee, July 10, 1832, Governor's Letter Book, July 1, 1831–February 5, 1833, Drawer 62, Box 64, Microfilm Collections, GDAH.

6 / The Georgia Guard and the White Man's Chance

1. William W. Williamson to Lumpkin, April 28, 1832, Folder 3, Box 49A, MS 1170, Telamon Cuyler Collection, UGA.

2. Ibid.

3. Valliere, "Benjamin Currey, Tennessean among the Cherokees," 239–40.

4. For Currey's complaints about Cherokees returning to Cherokee land in Georgia, see Benjamin F. Currey to Lumpkin, December 2, 1834, File II, Reference Services, GDAH; "Abstract No. 2: Guns, Blankets, Kettles, Tobacco & Boats Delivered to Emigrants," April 1832, Letters Received from Office of Indian Affairs, Roll 75, M234,

NARA; Benjamin F. Currey to Elbert Herring, May 23, 1833, ibid.; Benjamin F. Currey to Elbert Herring, September 9, 1833, ibid.

5. On the growing divisiveness in Cherokee life regarding removal, see, most recently, D. Smith, *An American Betrayal*, 151–86; and Langguth, *Driven West*, esp. 195–218.

6. Logan, *The Promised Land*, 25.

7. William M. Davis to Office of Indian Affairs, March 23, 1832, Letters Received by the Office of Indian Affairs, Roll 75, M234, RG 75, NARA.

8. Ibid.

9. *Cherokee Phoenix*, September 15, 1832, 2; Lumpkin to John Coffee, July 10, 1832, Governor's Letter Book, July 1, 1831–February 5, 1833, Drawer 62, Box 64, Microfilm Collections, GDAH; *Cherokee Phoenix*, November 24, 1832, 2; *New York Mercury*, June 6, 1832, 5; Claim of Jesse Raper, March 11, 1842, in Chase, ed., *1842 Cherokee Claims, Saline District*, 39; Claim of Rachel Rice, March 14, 1842, ibid., 40.

10. Claim of Hetty Vance, in Chase, ed., *1842 Cherokee Claims, Saline District*, 211–12; Claim of Elizabeth Ware, ibid., 90.

11. Lumpkin to John Coffee, April 24, 1832, Governor's Letter Book, July 1, 1831–February 5, 1833, Drawer 62, Box 64, Microfilm Collections, GDAH; Wilson Lumpkin to John Coffee, June 23, 1832, ibid.

12. Lumpkin to Andrew Jackson, April 19, 1833, Governor's Letter Book, February 5, 1833–June 18, 1835, Drawer 62, Box 65, Microfilm Collections, GDAH.

13. "An Act to Protect the Cherokee Indians [. . .]," passed December 24, 1832, in *Acts of The General Assembly of the State of Georgia*, 102–5.

14. "An Act to Add Parts of the Counties of Habersham and Hall to the County of Cherokee [. . .]," December 3, 1832, in *Acts of the General Assembly of the State of Georgia* (1832), 56–62. On the history of Georgia's militia districts, see Alex M. Hitz, "Georgia Militia Districts," www.georgiaarchives.org/documents/research/Georgia_Militia_Districts.pdf.

15. Wilson Lumpkin to William W. Williamson, December 26, 1832, and Wilson Lumpkin to John Coffee, December 26, 1832, both in Governor's Letter Book, July 1, 1831–February 5, 1833, Drawer 62, Box 64, Microfilm Collections, GDAH.

16. *Cherokee Phoenix*, February 2, 1833, 2.

17. William W. Williamson to Wilson Lumpkin, December 20, 1832, Folder 4, Box 49A, Telamon Cuyler Collection, UGA.

18. *Cherokee Phoenix*, February 2, 1833, 2; *Athens Southern Banner*, March 23, 1833, 3; *Athens Southern Banner*, September 14, 1833, 3; *Macon Telegraph*, October 10, 1833, 1; William N. Bishop to Lumpkin, September 16, 1835, in Hays, ed., *Cherokee Indian Letters*, 2:446.

19. Lumpkin to John Coffee, December 26, 1832, Governor's Letter Book, July 1, 1831–February 5, 1833, Drawer 62, Box 64, Microfilm Collections, GDAH.

20. Lumpkin to William W. Williamson, February 15, 1833, Governor's Letter Book, July 1, 1831–February 5, 1833, Drawer 62, Box 64, Microfilm Collections, GDAH; Lumpkin to William Hicks, July 6, 1833, ibid.; Wilson Lumpkin to William Hicks, July 6, 1833, ibid.

21. The sheriff had drawn land in what would become Paulding County (see S. Emmet Lucas, *The 1832 Gold Lottery of Georgia*, 142; *Cherokee Phoenix*, July 27, 1833, 3; and Anderson, *A History of Coweta County, 1825–1880*, 30).

22. *Cherokee Phoenix*, July 27, 1833, 3.

23. Ibid., August 31, 1833, 3.

24. *The Georgian* (Savannah), October 31, 1833, 2.

25. "An Act More Effectually to Provide for the Government and Protection of the Cherokee Indians [. . .]," in *Acts of the General Assembly of the State of Georgia* (1833), 1:114–18.

26. *Macon Telegraph*, May 29, 1833, 2; and July 17, 1833, 2.

27. Ibid., May 15, 1833, 3. On voting totals for both the gubernatorial race and the referendum on the reduction measure, see ibid., October 31, 1833, 3.

28. Bishop to Lumpkin, April 22, 1833, in Hays, ed., *Cherokee Indian Letters*, 2:401; *Macon Telegraph*, January 9, 1833, 2. Lumpkin had appointed Bishop as a land agent in January 1833 "to rent . . . all fractions having improvements thereon, in the Cherokee Territory, not occupied by any Indians" (see Lumpkin to William N. Bishop, January 4, 1833, Governor's Letter Book, July 1, 1831–February 5, 1833, Drawer 62, Box 64, Microfilm Collections, GDAH). The convention became known as the "reduction convention," which should not be confused with the similarly named convention in the U.S. Congress to reduce tariff rates as a means to alleviate the nullification controversy. The state measure sought to reduce the overall number of representatives as a way to save money and break up the power of the low country counties.

29. Bishop to Lumpkin, April 24, 1833, in Hays, ed., *Cherokee Indian Letters*, 2:415.

30. Ibid.; Lumpkin to William Daniel, May 2, 1833, Governor's Letter Book, February 5, 1833–June 18, 1835, Drawer 62, Box 65, Microfilm Collections, GDAH.

31. Bishop to Lumpkin, April 2, 1833, in Hays, ed., *Cherokee Indian Letters*, 2:401; Benjamin F. Currey to Wilson Lumpkin, October 29, 1833, ibid., 2:459.

32. Bishop to Lumpkin, April 2, 1833, William N. Bishop Papers, File II, Box 19, Manuscript Sources, GDAH; *Macon Telegraph*, October 31, 1833, 3.

33. The 1833 election results were printed in the *Macon Telegraph*, October 31, 1833, 3.

34. Resolutions of Citizens of Cherokee County sent to Wilson Lumpkin, May 1834, in Hays, ed., *Cherokee Indian Letters*, 2:483–85.

35. John Brewster to Lumpkin, May 16, 1834, in Hays, ed., *Cherokee Indian Letters*, 2:489–93; Petition of Sundry Citizens of the Cherokee Counties for the Organization of a Guard, April 10, 1835, ibid., 3:534–36; Bishop to Lumpkin, May 15, 1835, William N. Bishop Papers, File II: Names, Box 19, Manuscript Sources, GDAH; D. R. Mitchell, John Brewster, and R. N. Holt to Lumpkin, May 12, 1834, ibid.

36. Bishop to Lumpkin, June 4, 1834, William N. Bishop Papers, File II: Names, Box 19, Manuscript Sources, GDAH.

37. Lumpkin to John Forsyth, May 30, 1834, Governor's Letter Book, February 5, 1833–June 18, 1835, Microfilm Collections, GDAH; Benjamin F. Currey to Lumpkin, November 18, 1834, in Hays, ed., *Cherokee Indian Letters*, 3:515.

38. Lumpkin to John Forsyth, May 30, 1834, Governor's Letter Book, February 5, 1833–June 18, 1835, Drawer 62, Box 65, Microfilm Collections, GDAH.

39. Lumpkin to Sheriff [of Murray County], November 12, 1834, Governor's Letter Book, February 5, 1833–June 18, 1835, Drawer 62, Box 65, Microfilm Collections, GDAH; Lumpkin to Bishop, November 12, 1832, ibid. See also the state legislature's authorization on the use of force, "Whereas, at the October Term, 1834, of the Superior Court of the County of Walker," November 12, 1834, in *Acts of the General Assembly of the State of Georgia*, 1:293–94.

40. "The Select Committee to Whom Was Referred the Communication of his Excellency the Governor of the 6th Instant [. . .]," December 20, 1834, in *Acts of the General Assembly of the State of Georgia*, 1:335–36.

41. Z. B. Hargrove to Lumpkin, in Hays, ed., *Georgia Military Affairs*, 6:257.

42. Bishop to Lumpkin, April 24, 1833, in Hays, ed., *Cherokee Indian Letters*, 2:415; T. Miles, *House on Diamond Hill*, 177–78.

43. The Bishop-Riley affair garnered nationwide attention (see *New-London [CT] Gazette*, April 29, 1835, 2). For Bishop's version of events, see *Athens Southern Banner*, June 11, 1835, 1.

44. Lumpkin to Bishop, May 28, 1835, Governor's Letter Book, February 5, 1833–June 18, 1835, Drawer 62, Box 65, Microfilm Collections, GDAH; Bishop to Lumpkin, May 15, 1835, William N. Bishop Papers, File II Names, Box 19, Manuscript Sources, GDAH.

45. *Athens Southern Banner*, June 25, 1835, 2; "The Select Committee to Whom Was Referred the Communication of His Excellency the Governor [. . .]," in *Acts of the General Assembly of the State of Georgia*, December 20, 1834, 1:336.

46. Bishop to Lumpkin, September 16, 1833, in Hays, ed., *Cherokee Indian Letters*, 2:444–45. On the Guard's raid of the *Phoenix*'s office, see Benjamin F. Currey to Lumpkin, August 26, 1835, in Hays, ed., *Cherokee Indian Letters*, 3:604, as well as Benjamin F. Currey to Wilson Lumpkin et al., September 9, 1835, ibid., 3:613–15. Local lore has it that the Guard, rather than turn over the press to Watie, instead dumped it in the Chattahoochee River, which explains why the press has never been located.

47. James Edmonson to William Schley, November 5, 1835, in Hays, ed., *Cherokee Indian Letters*, 6:279–81.

48. Ibid., 6:281.

49. Ibid., 6:280–81.

50. *Macon Telegraph*, November 12, 1835, 3.

51. The Treaty of New Echota—after a small minority of Cherokees had approved it—soon thereafter went to the Senate, where it was ratified the following spring (Perdue and Green, *The Cherokee Nation and the Trail of Tears*, 102–15; *Athens Southern Banner*, December 17, 1835, 2).

52. *National Banner and Nashville Whig*, December 7, 1835, 3; *Connecticut Gazette* (New London), December 9, 1835, 2; Newton Cannon to William Schley, December 6, 1835, in Hays, ed., *Cherokee Indian Letters*, 3:625; "The Committee to Whom Were Referred the Several Communications of His Excellency the Governor [. . .]," December 18, 1835, in *Acts of the General Assembly of the State of Georgia* (1835), 1:336–43.

53. "The Committee to Whom Were Referred the Several Communications of His Excellency the Governor [. . .]," in *Acts of the General Assembly of the State of Georgia* (1835), 1:341–42.

54. *Athens Southern Banner*, February 18, 1836, 2; Thomas Harper to William Schley, May 28, 1836, Folder 8, Box 50, Telamon Cuyler Collection, UGA.

7 / The Militia and the Coming of Order

1. Gilmer to John Ross, March 9, 1838, in Gilmer, *Sketches*, 417–18.

2. John Ross to Gilmer, April 6, 1838, in Ross, *The Papers of Chief John Ross*, ed. Moulton, 1:419; Joel R. Poinsett to the Governors of Georgia, Tennessee, Alabama, and North Carolina, May 23, 1838, in Gilmer, *Sketches*, 420.

3. William Schley to Andrew Jackson, February 13, 1836, Roll 76, M234, RG 75, Letters Received by the Office of Indian Affairs, NARA; Lewis Cass to William Schley, February 23, 1836, in Hays, ed., *Georgia Military Affairs*, 7:192A–192B.

4. John T. Ellisor, *The Second Creek War: Interethnic Conflict and Collusion on a Collapsing Frontier* (Lincoln: University of Nebraska Press, 2010), 272–77.

5. Bolling H. Robinson to John W. A. Sanford, May 72, 1836, Governor's Letter Book, Military Letters, November 28, 1835–August 2, 1840, Drawer 62, Box 65, Microfilm Collections, GDAH; William Schley to Andrew Jackson, February 13, 1836, Roll 76, M234, RG 75, Letters Received by the Office of Indian Affairs, NARA; G. Smith, *History of the Georgia Militia, 1783–1861*, 1:43–44.

6. John Ross et al. to John Wool, September 30, 1836, "The Proceedings of the Court of Inquiry in the Case of Brevet Brigadier General Wool," H.R. Doc. No. 46, p. 75; "Report of the Secretary of War," S. Doc. No. 120, pp. 607–8.

7. Wiley Williams to William Schley, December 28, 1835, in Hays, ed., *Georgia Military Affairs*, 6:298–99.

8. Arthur Erwin to William Schley, April 8, 1836, in Hays, ed., *Georgia Military Affairs*, 7:250–51; William G. Springer to William Schley, January 31, 1836, ibid., 7:99; Lewis Cass to William Schley, May 25, 1836, ibid., 7: 367b–367c; Roster of Murray County Guards, June 27, 1836, ibid., 8:178.

9. William Schley to Charles H. Nelson, January 23, 1836, Governor's Letter Book, Military Letters, November 28, 1835–August 2, 1840, Drawer 62, Box 65, Microfilm Collections, GDAH; William Schley to Absalom Bishop, June 30, 1836, ibid.

10. William Schley to General John E. Wool, August 17, 1836, Governor's Letter Book, Military Letters, November 28, 1835–August 2, 1840, Drawer 62, Box 65, Microfilm Collections, GDAH.

11. On the uncertain situation of the Highland Battalion, see John E. Wool to Brigadier General Dunlap, August 4, 1836, in *American State Papers: Military Affairs* (Washington, DC: Gales and Seaton, 1861), 7:550; William Schley to Brigadier General Richard Dunlap, August 17, 1836, Governor's Letter Book, Military Letters, November 28, 1835–August 2, 1840, Microfilm Collections, GDAH. On the short duration of the Highlander's enlistment, see "Index to the Compiled Service Records of Volunteer Soldiers Who Served during the Cherokee Disturbances and Removal in Organizations from the State of Georgia," M907, NARA.

12. The rosters of the Highlanders are located in "Index to the Compiled Service Records of Volunteer Soldiers Who Served during the Cherokee Disturbances and Removal in Organizations from the State of Georgia," M907, NARA; the roster of Bishop's Rangers is located in the Adjutant General Military Records, Vol. 1, Drawer 40, Box 16, GDAH.

13. Testimony of Henry B. Shaw, "The Proceedings of the Court of Inquiry in the Case of Brevet Brigadier General Wool," H.R. Doc No. 46, 25th Cong., 1st Sess., p. 15; Testimony of Captain James Morrow, ibid., 5.

14. In all, militia in Georgia constructed at least fifteen forts (see Hill, *Cherokee Removal*).

15. Interestingly the name "State Rights Party" was still widely used within Georgia. However, newspapers outside of the state had begun calling that group the Whig Party (see *Portland [ME] Eastern Argus*, May 30, 1837, 3).

16. *Macon Telegraph*, September 5, 1837, 3.

17. Charles H. Nelson letter, dated September 18, 1837, printed in the *Athens Southern Banner* on September 23, 1837, 3.

18. *Athens Southern Banner*, August 12, 1837, 2.

19. For election returns, see the *Milledgeville Federal Union*, October 26, 1838, 3.

20. For the governor's veto message, see Gilmer, *Sketches*, 406–9; and *Macon Telegraph*, December 11, 1837, 3.

21. "Estimate of Appropriations—Indian Hostilities," January 5, 1838, H.R. Doc. No. 65, p. 3; "Message from the President of the United States, Transmitting a Report from Major General Jesup [. . .]," July 7, 1838, S. Doc. No. 507, 25th Cong., 2d Sess., p. 6; Gilmer, *Sketches*, 410.

22. "Horses of Volunteers Abandoned to U. States," February 11, 1839, H. Doc. No. 179, 25th Cong., 3d Sess., p. 12.

23. Citizens of Murray County Petition, January 6, 1838, in Hays, ed., *Cherokee Indian Letters*, 3:657; Samuel Tate to Gilmer, February 21, 1838, ibid., 3:672; B. Griffith to Gilmer, February 27, 1838, ibid., 3:680.

24. Gilmer, *Sketches*, 413–16.

25. Alexander Macomb to Winfield Scott, April 6, 1838, Correspondence of the Eastern Division Pertaining to Cherokee Removal, April-December 1838, Roll 1, M1475, RG 75, NARA; *Charleston Southern Patriot*, April 16, 1838, 2; S. Cooper to Gilmer, April 9, 1838, ibid.; Gilmer to Winfield Scott, April 20, 1838, ibid.; Lumpkin to Winfield Scott, April 7, 1838, ibid.

26. Gilmer to Winfield Scott, May 7, 1838, Correspondence of the Eastern Division, NARA.

27. George R. Gilmer to the Citizens of the Cherokee Counties, in Gilmer, *Sketches*, 428–29.

28. An original copy of General Order No. 25 is located in the Benjamin T. Watkins Family Papers, Mss 717, OP 4, Emory.

29. For a detailed description and history of the forts, see Hill, *Cherokee Removal*.

30. John Gray Bynum to G. A. Montgomery, May 22, 1838, Record Book of John Gray Bynum, William Preston Bynum Papers #117, Series 3, Folder 35, UNC.

31. John Gray Bynum to "Sir," June 15, 1838, Record Book of John Gray Bynum, UNC; N. W. Pittman and H. P. Strickland to Henchin Strickland, June 6, 1838, John R. Peacock Papers, #1895-z, Series 1, Folder 1, UNC.

32. General Floyd to Winfield Scott, May 27, 1838, Roll 1, Correspondence of the Eastern Division; "Number of Indians in the Possession of the Georgia Volunteers for Emigration Reported to Brig. Gen. Floyd up to May 28 [1838]"; General Floyd to Lt. Colonel Worth, May 30, 1838; "Number of Indians Sent to Ross's Landing and the Cherokee Agency from the Different Posts in Mid. Military District," June 9, 1838, all located in Roll 1, Correspondence of the Eastern Division, NARA.

33. General Floyd Order No. 8, May 29, 1838, Roll 1, Correspondence of the Eastern Division, NARA; Petition of Citizens for the Discharge of William Calhoun, May 30, 1838, ibid.; General Floyd to Winfield Scott, June 6, 1838, ibid.

34. For the rumors of troops shooting at fleeing Cherokee civilians, see Order No. 15, May 7, 1838, Box 1, Folder 7, Benjamin Watkins Family Papers, Mss 717, Emory; General Floyd Order No. 16, June 1, 1838, Roll 1, Correspondence of the Eastern Division, NARA; Captain William Derrick to Brigadier General Eustice, June 4, 1838, ibid.; Charles Floyd to Winfield Scott, June 2, 1838, ibid.

35. Claim of Nancy Pheasant, March 11, 1842, in Chase, ed., *1842 Cherokee Claims, Saline District*, 25; Claim of Chowahucah, March 14, 1842, ibid., 121; Claim of Tesahnehe, March 15, 1842, ibid., 59; Claim of Tieeskih, March 15, 1842, ibid., 62; Claim of Chenahse, March 15, 1842, ibid., 54; Claim of Sekekee, February 6, 1842, in Chase., ed., *1842 Cherokee Claims Commission, Skin Bayou District*, 13; Claim of Head Thrower Watts, February 28, 1842, in Chase, ed., *1842 Cherokee Claims, Skin Bayou District*, 20–21.

36. Charles Floyd to Winfield Scott, June 24, 1838, Roll 1, Correspondence of the Eastern Division, NARA.

37. Charles Floyd to Winfield Scott, June 2, 1838, Roll 1, Correspondence of the Eastern Division, NARA; Charles Floyd to Winfield Scott, June 6, 1838, ibid.; Captain Benjamin T. Watkins to General Floyd, June 9, 1838, Box 1, Folder 4, Benjamin Watkins Family Papers, Emory; Captain Derrick to J. H. Simpson, June 25, 1838, Correspondence of the Eastern Division, NARA.

38. Captain Benjamin T. Watkins to General Floyd, June 9, 1838, Box 1, Folder 4, Benjamin Watkins Family Papers, Emory; Charles Floyd to Winfield Scott, July 1, 1838, Correspondence of the Eastern Division, NARA; A. P. Bush to Col. Turk, June 3, 1838, Roll 1, ibid.; General Floyd to Winfield Scott, June 6, 1838, ibid.

39. Charles Floyd to Winfield Scott, June 16, 1838, Roll 1, Correspondence of the Eastern Division, NARA; Captain Derrick to J. H. Simpson, June 25, 1838, ibid.; Charles Floyd to Winfield Scott, July 1, 1838, ibid.

40. Mary E. Young, "Conflict Resolution on the Indian Frontier," *Journal of the Early Republic* 16 (Spring 1996): 15–17.

41. A figure of four thousand deaths as a result of removal has long been accepted, though uncritically, by historians (see Prucha, *The Great Father*, 241n58). For a correction, see Thornton, "The Demography of the Trail of Tears Period," esp. 83–93.

Conclusion

1. On the larger Cherokee migration, see Smithers, *The Cherokee Diaspora*.

2. On the community of elite Cherokees who were granted state citizenship, see Flanagan, "The Georgia Cherokees Who Remained," 584–609.

3. David F. Weiman, "Peopling the Land by Lottery? The Market in Public Lands and the Regional Differentiation of Territory on the Georgia Frontier," *Journal of Economic History* 51 (December 1991): 835–60. Weiman posits here that the type of land won played an important role in determining whether a fortunate drawer would claim the land or sell it.

Bibliography

Primary Sources

Archival Materials

David M. Rubenstein Rare Book & Manuscript Library, Duke University, Durham, NC (Duke)

George Rockingham Gilmer Papers. Section A.
Edmund Schriver Papers (Dalton Collection).
James Taylor Papers. VII-E.
William H. Thomas Papers.
John Rodgers Vinton Papers.

Georgia Department of Archives and History, Morrow (GDAH)

BOUND VOLUMES

Hays, Louise Frederick, ed. *Cherokee Indian Letters, Talks, and Treaties, 1786–1838.* 3 vols. WPA Project No. 4341. Atlanta: GDAH, 1939.
———. *Georgia Military Affairs.* 9 vols. WPA Project No. 5993. Atlanta: GDAH, 1940.
Lucas, S. Emmet. *The 1832 Gold Lottery of Georgia: A List of Fortunate Drawers in Said Lottery.* 1838. Reprint, Easley, SC: Southern Historical Press, 1988.
Smith, James F. *The Cherokee Land Lottery in Georgia.* 1838. Reprint, Greenville, SC: Southern Historical Press, 1991.

MANUSCRIPT SOURCES

William N. Bishop Papers. File II: Names. Box 19.
Hines Holt Jr. File II: Names.

MICROFILM COLLECTIONS

Carroll County Superior Court Minutes, 1828–1833. Drawer 269, Box 47.
Governor's Letter Book, November 10, 1829–June 29, 1831. Drawer 62, Box 64.
Governor's Letter Book, July 1, 1831–February 5, 1833. Drawer 62, Box 64.
Governor's Letter Book, February 5, 1833–June 18, 1835. Drawer 62, Box 65.
Governor's Letter Book, Military Letters, November 28, 1835–August 2, 1840. Drawer 62, Box 65.
Hall County Superior Court Minute Book. Drawer 72, Box 71.
Murray County Superior Court Minutes. Drawer 93, Box 64.
John W. A. Sanford Letter Book. Drawer 21, Reel 53.

ONLINE RESOURCES

Acts of the General Assembly of the State of Georgia. http://neptune3.galib.uga.edu/ssp/cgi-bin/ftaccess. cgi?_id=7f000001&dbs=ZLGL.

UNPUBLISHED COURT CASES

Arthur Alexander v. Calaway Burke. April 1831.
Philip Bosworth v. Reuben Philpot. April 1831.
Carroll County Superior Court Minutes.
Jonathan M. Davis v. Richard Philpot. September 1828.
John Robinson v. William and Calaway Burke. February 1831.
Soft Shell Turtle v. Grief Felton. April 1829
John Thomas v. Calaway Burke. April 1831.

Hargrett Rare Book & Manuscript Library, University of Georgia, Athens (UGA)

Telamon Culyer Collection. Ms 1170.
Keith Read Collection. Ms 921.

Library of Congress, Washington, DC

MICROFILM COLLECTIONS

Presidential Papers Microfilm. *Andrew Jackson Papers.* 78 reels. Washington, DC: Library of Congress, 1961.

ONLINE SOURCES

"American Life Histories: Manuscripts from the Federal Writers Project, 1936–1940." http://memory.loc.gov.

National Archives and Records Administration, Washington, DC (NARA)

MICROFILM COLLECTIONS

RG 75, M208. "Records of the Cherokee Indian Agency in Tennessee, 1801–1835." 14 rolls.

    M234A. "Letters Received by the Office of Indian Affairs, 1824–1881." 200 rolls.

    M574. "Special Files of the Office of Indian Affairs, 1831–1862." 85 rolls.

RG 94, M907. "Index to the Compiled Service Records of Volunteer Soldiers Who Served during the Cherokee Disturbances and Removal in Organizations from the State of Georgia." 1 roll.

RG 393, M1475. "Correspondence of the Eastern Division Pertaining to Cherokee Removal, April–December 1838." 2 rolls.

Southern Historical Collection, Louis Round Wilson Library, Special Collections, University of North Carolina, Chapel Hill (UNC)

William Preston Bynum Papers. No. 117.
Chiliab S. Howe Papers. No. 3092.
Isaac Jarratt Papers. No. 3514.
Lenoir Family Papers. No. 426.
John R. Peacock Papers. #1895-z.

Stuart A. Rose Manuscript, Archives, and Rare Book Library, Emory University, Atlanta, GA (Emory)

J. Durelle Boles Collection of Southern Imprints. Ms 943.
Benjamin T. Watkins Family Papers. Mss 717.

Government Documents

Published Documents

Cochran, Thomas C., ed. *New American State Papers: Indian Affairs.* 13 vols. Wilmington, DE: Scholarly Resources, 1972.

Kappler, Charles J., ed. *Indian Affairs: Laws and Treaties.* 7 vols. Washington, DC: U.S. Government Printing Office, 1904.

Peters, Richard, ed. *United States Statutes at Large.* 18 vols. Boston: Charles C. Little and James Brown, 1845–78.

U.S. Congress. "Correspondence—General J.W.A. Sanford." H.R. Doc. No. 127 (Serial 347-4), 25th Cong., 3d Sess. (1839).

———. "Estimate of Appropriation—Indian Hostilities." H.R. Doc. No. 265 (Serial 328-8), 25th Cong., 2d Sess. (1838).

———. "Intrusion on Cherokee Land." H.R. Doc. No. 89 (Serial 197-3), 21st Cong., 1st Sess. (1830).

———. "Letter from the Cherokee Council to Col. Hugh Montgomery." H.R. Doc. No. 6 (Serial 184-1), 20th Cong., 2d Sess. (1828).
———. "Letter from the Secretary of War . . . on the Subject of the Boundary Line." H.R. Doc. No. 108 (Serial 186-3), 20th Cong., 2d Sess. (1829).
———. "Memorial of a Delegation from the Cherokee Indians." H.R. Doc. No. 57 (Serial 208-3), 21st Cong., 2d Sess. (1831).
———. "Message from the President of the United States." S. Doc. No. 65 (Serial 204-2), 21st Cong., 2d Sess. (1831).
———. "Message from the President of the United States." H.R. Doc. No. 2 (Serial 206-1), 21st Cong, 2d Sess. (1830).
———. "Message from the President of the United States." H.R. Doc. No. 2 (Serial 233-1), 22d Cong., 2d Sess. (1832).
———. "Proceedings of the Court of Inquiry in the Case of Brevet Brigadier General Wool." H.R. Doc. No. 46 (Serial 311-1), 25th Cong., 1st Sess. (1837).
———. "Removal of the Cherokees: Letter from the Secretary of War." H.R. Doc. No. 453 (Serial 331-11), 25th Cong., 2d Sess. (1838).
———. "Removal of the Cherokees West of the Mississippi." H.R. Rep. No. 1098 (Serial 411-5), 27th Cong., 2d Sess. (1842).
———. "Report from the Secretary of War." S. Doc. No. 120 (Serial 315-2), 25th Cong., 2d Sess. (1838).
———. "Report of a Committee and Resolutions of the Legislature of the State of Georgia in Relation to Certain Lands Occupied by the Cherokee Indians." H.R. Doc. No. 102 (Serial 171-3), 20th Cong., 1st Sess. (1828).
———. "Resolutions of the Legislature of Georgia." S. Doc. No. 80 (Serial 165-3), 20th Cong., 1st Sess. (1828).
———. "Supplemental Report from the Bureau of Indian Affairs." H.R. Doc. No. 11 (Serial 184-1), 20th Cong., 2d Sess. (1828).
———. "Volunteers, Militia, and Regular Troops—Comparative Expense Of." H.R. Doc. No. 271 (Serial 328-8), 25th Cong., 2d Sess. (1838).
U.S. Serial Set.
1820 U.S. Census.
1830 U.S. Census.

Supreme Court Cases

Cherokee Nation v. State of Georgia 30 U.S. (5 Peters), 1–80 (1831).
Johnson v. McIntosh 21 U.S. (8 Wheat) 543–573 (1823).
Worcester v. State of Georgia 31 U.S. (6 Peters) 515–597 (1832).

Microfilm Collections

Harold D. Moser, ed. *The Papers of Andrew Jackson: A Microfilm Supplement*. 39 reels. Wilmington, DE: Scholarly Resources, 1986.

Newspapers

Athens Southern Banner
Athens Southern Whig
Augusta Chronicle
Cherokee Phoenix
Columbus Enquirer
Macon Telegraph
Milledgeville Federal Union
Milledgeville Georgia Journal
National Banner and Nashville Whig
Newburyport (MA) Herald
Ohio State Journal and Columbus Gazette
Portland (ME) Eastern Argus
Savannah Georgian
Washington, DC, Daily National Journal

Published Contemporary Materials

Chase, Marybelle W., ed. *1842 Cherokee Claims, Goingsnake District*. Tulsa, OK: Marybelle W. Chase, 1989.
——. *1842 Cherokee Claims, Saline District*. Tulsa, OK: Marybelle W. Chase, 1988.
——. *1842 Cherokee Claims, Skin Bayou District*. Tulsa, OK: Marybelle W. Chase, 1988.
——. *1842 Cherokee Claims, Tahlequah District*. Tulsa, OK: Marybelle W. Chase, 1989.
Cherokee Nation. "John Burnett's Story of the Trail of Tears." www.cherokee.org/About TheNation/History/TrailofTears/24502/Information.aspx.
Clayton, Augustin S. *The Office and Duty of a Justice of the Peace and a Guide to Clerks, Constables, Coroners [. . .]*. Milledgeville, GA: S. Grantland, 1819. Early American Imprints, Series II: Shaw-Shoemaker, 1801–1819, no. 47639.
Couch, Nevada. "Pages from Cherokee Indian History." Address Delivered at the Commencement of the Worcester Academy, Vinita, OK, 1884.
Crews, Daniel C., and Richard W. Starbuck, eds. *Records of the Moravians among the Cherokees*. 8 vols. Tahlequah: Cherokee Heritage Press, 2010–.
Featherstonhaugh, George W. *A Canoe Voyage up the Minnay Sotor . . .* 2 vols. 1847. Reprint, St. Paul: Minnesota Historical Society, 1970.
Gilmer, George R. *Sketches of Some of the First Settlers of Upper Georgia, of the Cherokees, and the Author*. 1855. Reprint, Americus, GA: Americus Book Company, 1926.
Hamilton, Thomas. *Men and Manners in America*. Philadelphia: Carey, Lea and Blanchard, 1833.

Hawkins, Benjamin. *The Collected Works of Benjamin Hawkins.* Edited by Thomas Foster. Tuscaloosa: University of Alabama Press, 2003.

Jackson, Andrew. *The Papers of Andrew Jackson.* Edited by Daniel J. Feller et al. Knoxville: University of Tennessee Press, 1980–.

Jefferson, Thomas. *The Papers of Thomas Jefferson.* Edited by Julian P. Boyd et al. 43 vols. Princeton, NJ: Princeton University Press, 1950–.

Lumpkin, Wilson. *The Removal of the Cherokee Indians from Georgia, including His Speeches in the United States Congress [. . .].* New York: Dodd, Mead, 1907.

Morse, Jedidiah. *A Report to the Secretary of War of the United States, on Indian Affairs [. . .].* New Haven, CT: Davis and Force, 1822.

Ross, Chief John. *The Papers of Chief John Ross.* Edited by Gary E. Moulton. 2 vols. Norman: University of Oklahoma Press, 1985.

Worcester, Samuel. *New Echota Letters: Contributions of Samuel Worcester to the "Cherokee Phoenix."* Edited by Jack Frederick and Ann G. Kilpatrick. Dallas: Southern Methodist University Press, 1968.

Secondary Sources

Abbot, W. W. "Lowcountry, Backcountry: A View of Georgia in the American Revolution." In *An Uncivil War: The Southern Backcountry during the American Revolution*, edited by Ronald Hoffman, 321–32. Charlottesville: University Press of Virginia, 1985.

Abzug, Robert H. *Cosmos Crumbling: American Reform and the Religious Imagination.* New York: Oxford University Press, 1994.

Adelman, Jeremy, and Stephen Aron. "From Borderlands to Borders: Empires, Nation-States, and Peoples in between in North American History." *American Historical Review* 104 (June 1999): 814–41.

Anderson, William U. *A History of Coweta County, 1825–1880.* Newnan, GA: Newnan-Coweta Historical Society, 1977.

Armitage, David. "John Locke, Carolina, and the "Two Treatises of Government.'" *Political Theory* 32 (October 2004): 602–27.

Aron, Stephen. *American Confluence: The Missouri Frontier from Borderland to Border State.* Bloomington: Indiana University Press, 2006.

———. "Pigs and Hunters: 'Rights in the Woods' on the Trans-Appalachian Frontier." In *Contact Points: American Frontiers from the Mohawk Valley to the Mississippi, 1750–1830*, edited by Andrew R. L. Cayton and Frederika J. Teute, 175–204. Chapel Hill: University of North Carolina Press, 1998.

Balogh, Brian. *A Government out of Sight: The Mystery of National Authority in Nineteenth-Century America.* New York: Cambridge University Press, 2009.

Banner, Stuart. *How the Indians Lost Their Land: Law and Power on the Frontier.* Cambridge: Harvard University Press, 2005.

Bender, Thomas, ed. *The Antislavery Debate: Capitalism and Abolitionism as a Problem of Historical Interpretation.* Berkeley: University of California Press, 1992.

Bens, Jonas. "When the Cherokee Became Indigenous: *Cherokee Nation v. Georgia* and Its Paradoxical Legalities." *Ethnohistory* 65, no. 2 (2018), 247–67.

Bonner, James C. *Georgia's Last Frontier: The Development of Carroll County.* Athens: University of Georgia Press, 1971.

Bowes, John P. *Land Too Good for Indians: Northern Indian Removal.* Norman: University of Oklahoma Press, 2016.

Brands, H. W. *The Age of Gold: The California Gold Rush and the Birth of Modern America.* New York: Doubleday, 2002.

Brown, Richard Maxwell. *Strain of Violence: Historical Studies of American Violence and Vigilantism.* New York: Oxford University Press, 1975.

Bruyneel, Kevin. *The Third Space of Sovereignty: The Postcolonial Politics of U.S.-Indian Relations.* Minneapolis: University of Minnesota Press, 2007.

Burke, Joseph C. "The Cherokee Cases: A Study in Law, Politics, and Morality." *Stanford Law Review* 21 (February 1969): 500–531.

Carey, Anthony Gene. *Parties, Slavery, and the Union in Antebellum Georgia.* Athens: University of Georgia Press, 1997.

Carson, James Taylor. *Making an Atlantic World: Circles, Paths, and Stories from the Colonial South.* Knoxville: University of Tennessee Press, 2007.

———. "'The Obituary of Nations': Ethnic Cleansing, Memory, and the Origins of the Old South." *Southern Cultures* 14 (Winter 2008): 6–31.

Cole, Donald B. *Vindicating Andrew Jackson: The 1828 Election and the Rise of the Two-Party System.* Lawrence: University Press of Kansas, 2009.

Collins, Linton M. "The Activities of the Missionaries among the Cherokees." *GHQ* 4 (1922): 285–322.

Cooper, William J. *The Lost Founding Father: John Quincy Adams and the Transformation of American Politics.* New York: Liveright, 2017.

Coulter, E. Merton. "The Nullification Movement in Georgia." *GHQ* 5 (March 1921): 3–39.

Covington, James W., ed. "Letters from the Georgia Gold Region." *GHQ* 39 (December 1955): 407–9.

Cumfer, Cynthia. "Local Origins of National Indian Policy: Cherokee and Tennessean Ideas about Sovereignty and Nationhood, 1790–1811." *Journal of the Early Republic* 23 (Spring 2003): 21–46.

———. *Separate Peoples, One Land: The Minds of Cherokees, Blacks, and Whites on the Tennessee Frontier.* Chapel Hill: University of North Carolina Press, 2007.

Dahl, Adam. *Empire of the People: Settler Colonialism and the Foundations of Modern Democratic Thought.* Lawrence: University Press of Kansas, 2018.

Daniel, Michelle. "From Blood Feud to Jury System: The Metamorphosis of Cherokee Law from 1750 to 1840." *American Indian Quarterly* 11 (Spring 1987): 97–125.

Denson, Andrew. *Demanding the Cherokee Nation: Indian Autonomy and American Culture, 1830–1900*. Lincoln: University of Nebraska Press, 2004.

———. *Monuments to Absence: Cherokee Removal and the Contest over Southern Memory*. Chapel Hill: University of North Carolina Press, 2017.

Dorsey, James E. *The History of Hall County, Georgia, 1818-1900*. Gainesville, GA: Magnolia, 1991.

Dupre, Daniel S. *Transforming the Cotton Frontier: Madison County, Alabama 1800–1840*. Baton Rouge: Louisiana State University Press, 1991.

Edwards, Laura F. *The People and Their Peace: Legal Culture and the Transformation of Inequality in the Post-Revolutionary South*. Chapel Hill: University of North Carolina Press, 2009.

Ekirch, A. Roger. *"Poor Carolina": Politics and Society in Colonial North Carolina, 1729–1776*. Chapel Hill: University of North Carolina Press, 1981.

Elkins, Stanley, and Eric McKitrick. "A Meaning for Turner's Frontier, Part I: Democracy in the Old Northwest." *Political Science Quarterly* 69 (September 1954): 321–53.

———. "A Meaning for Turner's Frontier, Part II: The Southwest Frontier and New England." *Political Science Quarterly* 69 (December 1954): 565–602.

Ellis, Richard E. *The Union at Risk: Jacksonian Democracy, States' Rights, and the Nullification Crisis*. New York: Oxford University Press, 1987.

Finger, John R. "Cherokee Accommodation and Persistence in the Southern Appalachians." In *Appalachia in the Making: The Mountain South in the Nineteenth Century*, edited by Mary Beth Pudup, 25–49. Chapel Hill: University of North Carolina Press, 1995.

Fischer, David Hackett, and James C. Kelly. *Bound Away: Virginia in the Westward Movement*. Charlottesville: University of Virginia Press, 2000.

Flanagan, Sharon P. "The Georgia Cherokees Who Remained: Race, Status and Property in the Chattahoochee Community." *GHQ* 73 (Fall 1989): 584–609.

Flowers, Carl, Jr. "The Wofford Settlement on the Georgia Frontier." *GHQ* 61 (Fall 1977): 258–67.

Ford, Lacy K. "Frontier Democracy: The Turner Thesis Revisited." *Journal of the Early Republic* 13 (Summer 1993): 144–63.

———. "Making the 'White Man's Country' White: Race, Slavery, and State-Building in the Jacksonian South." *Journal of the Early Republic* 19 (Winter 1999): 713–37.

Ford, Lisa. *Settler Sovereignty: Jurisdiction and Indigenous People in America and Australia, 1788–1836*. Cambridge: Harvard University Press, 2010.

Frank, Andrew K. *Creeks and Southerners: Biculturalism on the Early American Frontier*. Lincoln: University of Nebraska Press, 2005.

Freehling, William W. *Prelude to Civil War: The Nullification Controversy in South Carolina, 1816–1836*. New York: Oxford University Press, 1965.

Frymer, Paul. *Building an American Empire: The Era of Territorial and Political Expansion*. Princeton, NJ: Princeton University Press, 2017.

Garrison, Tim Alan. "Inevitability and the Southern Opposition to Indian Removal." In *The Native South: New Histories and Enduring Legacies*, edited by Garrison and Greg O'Brien, 107–25. Lincoln: University of Nebraska Press, 2017.
———. *The Legal Ideology of Removal: The Southern Judiciary and the Sovereignty of Native Americans Nations*. Athens: University of Georgia Press, 2002.
Gates, Frederick B. "The Georgia Land Act of 1803: Political Struggle in a One-Party State." *GHQ* 82 (Spring 1998): 1–21.
Gerstle, Gary. *Liberty and Coercion: The Paradox of American Government from the Founding to the Present*. Princeton, NJ: Princeton University Press, 2015.
Gorn, Elliot. "'Gouge and Bite, Pull Hair and Scratch': The Social Significance of Fighting in the Southern Backcountry." *American Historical Review* 90 (February 1985): 18–43.
Green, Fletcher M. "Georgia's Forgotten Industry: Gold Mining, Part I." *GHQ* 19 (June 1935): 93–111.
———. "Georgia's Forgotten Industry: Gold Mining, Part II." *GHQ* 19 (September 1935): 210–28.
Green, Michael D. *The Politics of Indian Removal: Creek Government and Society in Crisis*. Lincoln: University of Nebraska Press, 1982.
Gross, Ariela J. *Double Character: Slavery and Mastery in the Antebellum Southern Courtroom*. Princeton, NJ: Princeton University Press, 2000.
Gudmestad, Robert. *Steamboats and the Rise of the Cotton Kingdom*. Baton Rouge: Louisiana State University Press, 2011.
Guyatt, Nicholas. *Bind Us Apart: How Enlightened Americans Invented Racial Segregation*. New York: Basic, 2016.
Hall, Leslie. *Land and Allegiance in Revolutionary Georgia*. Athens: University of Georgia Press, 2001.
Hatley, Tom. *The Dividing Path: Cherokees and South Carolinians through the Revolutionary Era*. New York: Oxford University Press, 1986.
Haveman, Christopher. *Rivers of Sand: Creek Indian Emigration, Relocation, and Ethnic Cleansing in the American South*. Lincoln: University of Nebraska Press, 2016.
Heath, Milton Sydney. *Constructive Liberalism: The Role of the State in Economic Development in Georgia to 1860*. Cambridge: Harvard University Press, 1954.
Hill, Sarah H. *Cherokee Removal: Forts along the Georgia Trail of Tears*. Atlanta: Georgia Department of Natural Resources/National Parks Service, 2005.
———. *Weaving New Worlds: Southeastern Cherokee Women and their Basketry*. Chapel Hill: University of North Carolina Press, 1997.
Horsman, Reginald. "The Indian Policy for an 'Empire of Liberty.'" In *Native Americans and the Early Republic*, edited by Frederick E. Hoxie, Ronald Hoffman, and Peter J. Albert, 37–61. Charlottesville: University of Virginia Press, 1999.

———. *Race and Manifest Destiny: The Origins of American Racial Anglo-Saxonism.* Cambridge: Harvard University Press, 1981.
Howe, Daniel Walker. *What Hath God Wrought: The Transformation of America, 1815–1848.* New York: Oxford University Press, 2007.
Hudson, Angela Pulley. *Creek Paths and Federal Roads: Indians, Settlers, and Slaves in the Making of America.* Chapel Hill: University of North Carolina Press, 2010.
Jackson, Harvey W. *Lachlan McIntosh and the Politics of Revolutionary Georgia.* Athens: University of Georgia Press, 2003.
———. "The Rise of the Western Members: Revolutionary Politics and the Georgia Backcountry." In *An Uncivil War: The Southern Backcountry during the American Revolution,* edited by Ronald Hoffman, 276–319. Charlottesville: University Press of Virginia, 1985.
Jensen, Laura. *Patriots, Settlers, and the Origins of American Social Policy.* New York: Cambridge University Press, 2003.
Joy, Natalie. "Cherokee Slaveholders and Radical Abolitionists: An Unlikely Alliance in Antebellum America." *Commonplace* 10 (July 2010). www.common-place.org/vol-10/no-04/joy/.
Kars, Marjoleine. *Breaking Loose Together: The Regulator Rebellion in Pre-Revolutionary North Carolina.* Chapel Hill: University of North Carolina Press, 2002.
Klein, Rachel N. *Unification of a Slave State: The Rise of the Planter Class in the South Carolina Backcountry, 1760–1808.* Chapel Hill: University of North Carolina Press, 1990.
Lamplugh, George R. *Politics on the Periphery: Factions and Parties in Georgia, 1783–1806.* Newark: University of Delaware Press, 1986.
Langguth, A. J. *Driven West: Andrew Jackson's Trail of Tears to the Civil War.* New York: Simon and Schuster, 2010.
Laver, Harry S. *Citizens More Than Soldiers: The Kentucky Militia and Society in the Early Republic.* Lincoln: University of Nebraska Press, 2007.
Logan, Charles Russell. *The Promised Land: The Cherokee, Arkansas, and Removal, 1794–1839.* Little Rock: Arkansas Historical Preservation Program, 1997.
Lytle, Clifford M. "The Supreme Court, Tribal Sovereignty, and Continuing Problems of State Encroachment into Indian Country." *American Indian Law Review* 1 (1980): 65–77.
McCormick, Richard P. *The Second Party System: Party Formation in the Jacksonian Era.* Chapel Hill: University of North Carolina Press, 1966.
McLoughlin, William G. "Cherokee Anomie, 1794–1809: New Roles for Red Men, Red Women, and Black Slaves." In *Uprooted Americans: Essays to Honor Oscar Handlin* edited by Richard L. Bushman and Neil Harris, 126–57. Boston: Little, Brown, 1979.
———. *Cherokee Renascence in the New Republic.* Princeton: Princeton University Press, 1986.

McLoughlin, William G., and Walter H. Conser. "The Cherokees in Transition: A Statistical Analysis of the Federal Cherokee Census of 1835." *Journal of American History* 64 (December 1977): 678–703.

Merk, Frederick. *Manifest Destiny and Mission in American History*. New York: Knopf, 1963.

Miles, Edwin A. "After John Marshall's Decision: *Worcester v. Georgia* and the Nullification Crisis." *JSH* 39 (November 1973): 519–44.

Miles, Tiya. *The House on Diamond Hill: A Cherokee Plantation Story*. Chapel Hill: University of North Carolina Press, 2010.

Morris, Michael. "Georgia and the Conversation over Indian Removal." *GHQ* 91 (Winter 2007): 403–23.

Morris, Thomas D. *Southern Slavery and the Law, 1619–1820*. Chapel Hill: University of North Carolina Press, 1996.

Nichols, David Andrew. *Red Gentlemen & White Savages: Indians, Federalists, and the Search for Order on the American Frontier*. Charlottesville: University of Virginia Press, 2008.

Norgren, Jill. *The Cherokee Cases: Two Landmark Federal Decisions in the Fight for Sovereignty*. 1996. Reprint, Norman: University of Oklahoma Press, 2004.

Novak, William J. *The People's Welfare: Law & Regulation in Nineteenth-Century America*. Chapel Hill: University of North Carolina Press, 1996.

O'Brien, Michael. *Conjectures of Order: Intellectual Life and the American South, 1810–1860*. Chapel Hill: University of North Carolina Press, 2004.

Ostler, Jeffrey. *Surviving Genocide: Native Nations and the United States from the American Revolution to Bleeding Kansas*. New Haven, CT: Yale University Press, 2019.

Parsons, Lynn Hudson. *The Birth of Modern Politics: Andrew Jackson, John Quincy Adams, the Election of 1828*. New York: Oxford University Press, 2009.

———. "'A Perpetual Harrow upon My Feelings': John Quincy Adams and the American Indian." *New England Quarterly* 46 (September 1973): 339–79.

Perdue, Theda. *Cherokee Women: Gender and Culture Change, 1700–1835*. Lincoln: University of Nebraska Press, 1998.

———. *"Mixed Blood" Indians: Racial Construction in the Early South*. Athens: University of Georgia Press, 2003.

———. *Slavery and the Evolution of Cherokee Society, 1540–1866*. Knoxville: University of Tennessee Press, 1979.

Perdue, Theda, and Michael Green. *The Cherokee Nation and the Trail of Tears*. New York: Penguin, 2008.

Phillips, Ulrich Bonnell. *Georgia and States Rights: A Study of the Political History of Georgia from the Revolution to the Civil War, with Particular Regard to Federal Relations*. Washington, DC: Government Printing Office, 1902.

Prucha, Francis Paul. *The Great Father: The United States Government and the American Indians*. Lincoln: University of Nebraska Press, 1984.

Reed, Julie L. *Serving the Cherokee Nation: Cherokee Sovereignty and National Welfare, 1800–1907.* Norman: University of Oklahoma Press, 2016.

Remini, Robert V. *Andrew Jackson and His Indian Wars.* New York: Penguin, 2001.

Riggs, Brett. "The Christie Cabin Site: Historical and Archaeological Evidence of the Life and Times of a Cherokee *Métis* Household." In *May We All Remember Well: A Journal of the History and Culture of Western North Carolina,* edited by Robert S. Brunk, 1:228–48. Asheville, NC: Robert S. Brunk Auction Services, 1997.

Robertson, Lindsay G. *Conquest by Law: How the Discovery of America Dispossessed the Indigenous Peoples of Their Lands.* New York: Oxford University Press, 2005.

Rodgers, Daniel T. "Republicanism: The Career of a Concept." *Journal of American History* 79 (June 1992): 11–38.

Rosen, Deborah. *American Indians and State Law: Sovereignty, Race, and Citizenship, 1790–1880.* Lincoln: University of Nebraska Press, 2007.

Satz, Ronald N. *American Indian Policy in the Jacksonian Era.* Lincoln: University of Nebraska Press, 1975.

———. "The Cherokee Trail of Tears: A Sesquicentennial Perspective." *GHQ* 73 (Fall 1989): 431–66.

Saunt, Claudio. *A New Order of Things: Property, Power, and the Transformation of the Creek Indians.* New York: Cambridge University Press, 1999.

Shadburn, Don L. *Unhallowed Intrusion: A History of Cherokee Families in Forsyth County, Georgia.* Saline, MI: McNaughton and Gunn, 1993.

Sheehan, Bernard W. *Seeds of Extinction: Jeffersonian Philanthropy and the American Indian.* Chapel Hill: University of North Carolina Press, 1973.

Smith, Daniel Blake. *An American Betrayal: Cherokee Patriots and the Trail of Tears.* New York: Henry Holt, 2011.

Smith, Gordon Burns. *History of the Georgia Militia, 1783–1861.* 4 vols. Milledgeville, GA: Boyd, 2000.

Smithers, Gregory. *The Cherokee Diaspora: An Indigenous History of Migration, Resettlement, and Identity.* New Haven, CT: Yale University Press, 2015.

———. *Native Southerners: Indigenous History from Origins to Removal.* Norman: University of Oklahoma Press, 2019.

Smith-Rosenberg, Carroll. *This Violent Empire: The Birth of American National Identity.* Chapel Hill: University of North Carolina Press, 2010.

Snyder, Christina. *Slavery in Indian Country: The Changing Face of Captivity in Early America.* Cambridge: Harvard University Press, 2010.

Stremlau, Rose. *Sustaining the Cherokee Family: Kinship and Allotment of an Indigenous Nation.* Chapel Hill: University of North Carolina Press, 2011.

Takaki, Ronald T. *Iron Cages: Race and Culture in Nineteenth-Century America.* New York: Knopf, 1979.

Thornton, Russell. "The Demography of the Trail of Tears Period: A New Estimate of Cherokee Population Losses." In *Cherokee Removal: Before and After*, edited by William L. Anderson, 83–93. Athens: University of Georgia Press, 1991.

Turner, Frederick Jackson. "The Significance of the Frontier in American History." In *Rereading Frederick Jackson Turner*, edited by John Mack Faragher, 31–60. New York: Henry Holt, 1994.

Valliere, Kenneth L. "Benjamin Currey, Tennessean among the Cherokees: A Study of the Removal Policy of Andrew Jackson, Part II." *Tennessee Historical Quarterly* 41 (Fall 1982): 257–77.

Vandeveler, Paul. *Savages & Scoundrels: The Untold Story of America's Road to Empire through Indian Territory*. New Haven, CT: Yale University Press, 2009.

Vipperman, Carl J. "'Forcibly If We Must': The Georgia Case for Cherokee Removal, 1802–1832." *Journal of Cherokee Studies* (Spring 1978): 103–10.

Watson, Harry L. *Liberty and Power: The Politics of Jacksonian America* New York: Hill and Wang, 1990.

Weiman, David F. "Peopling the Land by Lottery? The Market in Public Lands and the Regional Differentiation of Territory on the Georgia Frontier." *Journal of Economic History* 51 (December 1991): 835–60.

West, Elliott. *Contested Plains: Indians, Goldseekers, and the Rush to Colorado*. Lawrence: University Press of Kansas, 1998.

White, Richard. *The Middle Ground: Indians, Empires, and Republics in the Great Lakes Region, 1650–1815*. New York: Cambridge University Press, 1991.

Wilentz, Sean. *The Rise of American Democracy: From Jefferson to Lincoln*. New York: Norton, 2005.

Williams, David. "The Cherokee Gold Lottery & Georgia's Gubernatorial Campaign of 1831." *Journal of Cherokee Studies* 15 (1990): 51–58.

———. "Gambling away the Inheritance: The Cherokee Nation and Georgia's Gold and Land Lotteries of 1832–33." *GHQ* 73 (Fall 1989): 519–39.

———. *The Georgia Gold Rush: Twenty-Niners, Cherokees, and Gold Fever*. Columbia: University of South Carolina Press, 1993.

———. "Georgia's Forgotten Miners: African-Americans and the Georgia Gold Rush." *GHQ* 75 (Spring 1991): 76–89.

Wilms, Douglas C. "Cherokee Land Use in Georgia before Removal," In *Cherokee Removal: Before and After*, edited by William L. Anderson, 1–28. Athens: University of Georgia Press, 1991.

Wolfe, Patrick. "Settler Colonialism and the Elimination of the Native." *Journal of Genocide Research* 8 (December 2006): 387–409.

Young, Jeffrey Robert. *Domesticating Slavery: The Master Class in Georgia and South Carolina, 1670–1837*. Chapel Hill: University of North Carolina Press, 1999.

Young, Mary E. "The Cherokee Nation: Mirror of the Republic." *American Quarterly* 33 (Winter 1981): 502–24.

———. "Conflict Resolution on the Indian Frontier." *Journal of the Early Republic* 16 (Spring 1996): 1–19.

———. "The Dark and Bloody but Endlessly Inventive Middle Ground of Indian Frontier Historiography." *Journal of the Early Republic* 13 (Summer 1993): 193–205.

———. "The Exercise of Sovereignty in Cherokee Georgia." *Journal of the Early Republic* 10 (Spring 1990): 43–63.

———. "Indian Removal and Land Allotment: The Civilized Tribes and Jacksonian Justice." *American Historical Review* 64 (October 1958): 31–45.

———. "Racism in Red and Black: Indians and Other Free People of Color in Georgia Law, Politics, and Removal Policy." *GHQ* 73 (Fall 1989): 492–518.

———. *Redskins, Ruffleshirts, and Rednecks: Indian Allotment in Alabama and Mississippi, 1830–1860.* Norman: University of Oklahoma Press, 1961.

Young, Jr., Otis E. "The Southern Gold Rush, 1828–1836." *JSH* 48 (August 1982): 373–92.

Index

Page references in italics indicate a figure.

Adams, John Quincy, 4, 23–24
Alabama: Cherokee border, 41, 54–55; Cherokee land in, 29, 156; Creek Indians and, 152, 154; federal troops from, 76; Pony Club in, 52, 68–69. *See also* Treaty of Indian Springs
American Board of Commissioners for Foreign Missions, 26, 109
Athens Southern Banner, 159
Augusta Chronicle, 53, 81

Baldwin, Abraham, 14
Berrien, John, 74
Bishop, William N., 134–38, 140, 142–49, 196n28. *See also* Highland Battalion

Calhoun, John C., 24, 26, 181n4, 183n27
Camp Gilmer, 92–93, 97, 109, 117
Cannon, Newton, 147
Carroll County: arrests by Cherokees, 62–63; census of, 56; Cherokees and whites, 55–56, 71; gold rush in, 73–74, 76–77; influence of location, 56–57, 71; land distribution and lottery, 38, 173; military in, 75–76, 153; Superior Court cases, 46, 61; violence in, 51–52, 55, 57–59, 62–65, 68–71, 175. *See also* Creek Strip; Pony Club
Cass, Lewis, 124
Cherokee Constitution of 1827, 4–5, 32–36, 69, 105, 180n5

Cherokee County, *118*, 120, 138, 140
Cherokee Lighthorse Patrol, 27–28, 32, 122, 175
Cherokee National Council: complaints of intrusion, 74, 81; concessions for removal, 191n36; criminalized by supremacy law, 86, 96, 106; extension law, 90; Guard effort to arrest, 105; purchase of land, 55; sovereignty, 27–28, 57. *See also* Treaty of New Echota
Cherokee Nations: Arkansas emigration, 101; Cassville jailbreak, 143; constitution of, 4, 28, 31–34, 175; definition of, 9; effrontery of, 140; federal help with gold miners, 81; federal land concessions, 17, 29, 32; federal recognition, 4; Georgia Guard and, 102–7; Georgia law and, 46–47, 132–33; land stewardship and culture, 16, 33, 175; legal white residents, 82–84; Morse's plan for civilizing, 26; multiracials, 6–7, 30, 34–36, 107–8, 134, 193n29; tolls and tollbooth operators, 31, 86, 105–6; Treaty Party and National Party, 143–44, 146; violence and fear of violence to, 136, 142–43, 152–53; white fear of, 151–52. *See also* sovereignty, Cherokee Nations

Cherokee Nations, borders of: constitution formalization of, 33; cooperation with whites and, 8, 180n11; reliance on federal military, 73; roadways through Cherokee land, 31; white Georgians, 5; white Georgians and, 8. *See also* Trade and Intercourse Act of 1802; Wofford, William and Wofford Settlement

Cherokee Nation v. Georgia, 90, 103

Cherokee Phoenix: census of bicultural individuals, 40; on the extension law, 86; on Georgia Guard, 103, 125–26, 129, 197n46; printing press stolen, 144; thievery report, 63; violence report, 49, 74, 99

Cherokee Protection Law, 134

Cherokee Removal: disposition of Cherokees, 172; federal policy of, 2; Georgia legal tactics and violence, 171; Georgia's role, 23, 95; Oklahoma, 172; postponement efforts, 163; treatment of Cherokees, 166–69; violence, fear of, 165; violence in, 157–59, 177–78, 200n41; violence prevention, 150–51, 155–56, 169; voluntary removal, 89, 121–24, 126, 128, 134. *See also* Indian Removal Act

Cherokees: Atawluny, 41; Baumgarter, Margaret, 45; Beanstick, Joseph, 63; Blackwood, George, 42; Boudinot, Elias, 50, 56, 86, 105, 119, 143, 187n14; Charlatehe, 42; Christy, Lacy, 41–42; Chuwoyee, 57, 61, 187n14; Four Killer, 41; Helms, Peggy, 41; Hicks, Elijah, 129; Hicks, William, 131; Langley, Goose, 41; Lee, Jim, 62; Lee, Johnson, 62; McNair, David, 106; Peacheater, 41; Raper, Jesse, 126; Rattlesnake, 42; Rice, Rachel, 126; Ridge, John, 52, 75, 143, 152; Robin, 125; Rodgers, Robert and Betsey, 45; Sanders, George, 53; Saunders, George, 69–70; Scott, Sam, 62; Silk, Bill, 46; Soft Shell Turtle, 46; Tahlegalooraytee, 41; Teesaskee, 125; Took, George, 130; Tucker, Thompson, 51; Vance, Hetty, 40, 43–45, 126; Vann, Joseph, 125, 142–43; Vann, Richard, 52; Vickery, Henry, 44; Walker, Thigh, 43; Ware, Elizabeth, 44, 126; Wassassee, 42; Watie, Stand, 143, 197n46; Willman, Aaron, 168; York, Thomas, 62–63; Young Bird, 41. *See also* Ross, John

Cherokee society: cooperation with whites and, 188n42; culture of, 180n5, 180n11; disruptions to, 30; ethic of harmony, 29–32, 34; *gadugi*, spirit of cooperation, 28, 41, 47; grazing practices, 185n36; intermarriage with whites, 6, 34, 40, 180n8; matrilineal tradition, 6, 29–31, 34, 180n8; slavery and, 31, 34

Cherokee Treaty of 1819, 17, 20, 27, 89, 191n36

Clark, John, 16–17, 23, 93

Clarkites, 16, 23–24, 66, 93, 100, 112, 116, 122, 133

Clayton, Augustin Smith, 20, 70, 85, 103

Compact of 1802, 3, 14, 24, 35–36, 183n32

Cooper, Samuel, 162

courts, Cherokee, 32

Crawford, William H., 16

Creek Indians, McIntosh, William, 4, 15, 23

Creeks Indians and lands, 4, 20, 23–24, 38, 52–53, 55, 68. *See also* Second Creek War; Treaty of Indian Springs

Creek Strip, 52–59, 73, 75, 77, 186n6, 187n14. *See also* Pony Club

Dahl, Adam, 10
Dekalb County, 54, 77, 130

Eaton, John H., 73, 76, 89
Edmonson, James, 145–46
election, presidential, 24–25, 183n35
elections, gubernatorial: Cherokee acculturation, 134; Gilmer and Clark, 92–93; Gilmer and Lumpkin, 112, 114–17, 133, 193n40; Gilmer and Schley, 150, 157–59; Lumpkin, 137–38; Ponyites at, 64; Troup and Clark, 23; white man's chance in, 3, 171
Ellisor, John T., 152
Evarts, Jeremiah, 74
expansion, European and American, 9, 15, 181n12, 182n8
extension law: backcountry whites and, 38; *Cherokee Nation v. Georgia*, 90; Cherokee sovereignty and, 59; Cherokees seek injunction against, 74; classified as free persons of color, 56; constitutionality of, 147; effect on Cherokee Nation, 37, 41, 46–47, 84–85; federal troops after, 86, 88; forcing Cherokees out, 44; Georgia claims

suzerainty, 76; *Georgia v. Tassels*, 185n26; legislative claim to sovereignty, 74; militia in Carroll County, 78; passage of, 7; state courts and, 60, 93, 132, 180n9

Featherstonhaugh, George, 37–38
federal agents: Currey, Benjamin F., 89, 123–26, 137, 141, 144, 146–47; Davis, William M., 124; Hawkins, Benjamin, 11–12, 16; Meigs, Return J., 11; Montgomery, Hugh, 35, 38, 43, 53–54, 57, 73, 81–83, 102; Williams, J. G., 43
federal government: borders unclear, 12; Hawkins line, 12; Morse's plan for Cherokees, 26; roadways through Cherokee land, 31
federal soldiers: Bynum, John Gray, 164; Calhoun, William, 165; Fowler, Lieutenant, 62–63; Jesup, Thomas, 160; Lindsay, William, 157, 163; Macomb, Alexander, 80, 162; Trenor, Lieutenant, 78–79; Wager, Philip, 77–80, 83–84, 88, 91
Forsyth, John, 140

Gallatin, Albert, 14
Georgia: map (1833), *10*; new counties creation, 20–21, 182n22; state citizenship for multiracials, 134; state constitutional convention, 135–36; state law compilation, 20; unequal legal racial treatment, 18–19; Yazoo fraudulent land sale, 13–14. *See also* sovereignty, Georgia
Georgia Athenian, 99
Georgia Brigade, 160–61, 169
Georgia courts: Cherokees in, 37, 41, 45–47, 112, 116; extension law in, 60, 93; Georgia Guard and, 108; militia in, 81; Pony Club in, 60–61, 64–65; superior courts, 21, 106, 128, 144–45, 106l10
Georgia Guard, 149; backcountry whites and, 104, 110, 174; Cherokees and, 95, 104–7; destabilization of region, 100; duty to bring order to region, 101–2; evictions of Cherokees and intruders, 103, 119–20; local citizens views of, 99–101; northern missionaries and, 108–12; paramilitary unit, 7, 90; payment question, 59–160; politicized grievances, 176; protecting gold mines and region, 92, 101, 104–5, 112; recruitment, 96–97; revived by Lumpkin, 142; supremacy law enforcement, 96, 108–9; Tennessee militia and, 124–25, 154; violence of, 97–99, 111–12, 174, 177. *See also* Georgia Brigade; Georgia Rangers
Georgia Guard, governor and: arrest of missionaries, 108–9; Cherokee protection promise, 106, 110, 162; county militia aid, 100; destabilization of Cherokees, 122; force reduction, 93; in forts to control Indians, 164; Guard creation, 91, 174; lack of violence, 169; mine trespass report, 104; partisanship and, 177; payment question, 150, 160–61; rental property authority, 101
Georgia Guard personnel: Brooks, Jacob R., 62, 103, 107, 109, 187n23; Coffee, John, 70, 117, 119, 124–29, 194n49; Foster, Ira R., 160; Henderson, Sergeant, 98; Townsend, Jesse, 45; Williamson, William W., 121–22, 126, 129–30, 141, 147. *See also* Nelson, Charles H.; Sanford, John W. A.
Georgia Journal, 47, 99, 186n46
Georgia legislature, 23–24, 85–86, 134. *See also* extension law; supremacy law
Georgia Rangers, 143–48, 154–56, 197n46
Gilmer, George Rockingham: Cherokee Removal violence, 151, 162–63; Congressional support for Cherokees, 108; disputed territory and, 4, 15, 96, 117; fear of violence, 2, 21, 62, 163; federal troops request, 72–73, 75–76; federal troops withdrawal, 84–85, 87–89; gold diggers expulsion, 74–75, 78, 81; gold mine ownership, 93, 158, 176, 193n40; Guard role with Cherokee leaders, 107; Indian court testimony proposal, 112, 116, 194n45; intruders into Cherokee lands, 5; militia strategy, 79, 190n16; multiracial Cherokees and, 7, 35–36; northern missionaries and, 111; orderliness, 6, 72, 94, 174; policy switch, 90; political proposals, 112, 115; Pony Club and, 64–66; portrait, *95*; rental properties, 82; state and federal problem, 76, 79; state ownership proposal, 112–14; states' rights, 7, 190n16; terms as governor, 1; Troup faction, 95, 117, 133; white complaints

218 / INDEX

Gilmer, George Rockingham (*continued*): of unequal treatment, 83–84. *See also* elections, gubernatorial; Nelson, Charles H.
Gilmer faction. *See* Troupites
gold miners: Castleberry, Mark, 98; Ligon, Robert, 98–100
Gold Rush and gold mines: Cherokee response, 74; "Great Intrusion," 49; lawlessness of, 47–50, 73–74; miners expelled, 77–78; public ownership controversy, 112–15; resistance to Guard, 101; trespassers, 2, 5; violent encounter with Guard, 97–99. *See also* Georgia Guard; Leather's Ford

Hall County, 20, 70, 78–79, 81, 99. *See also* Leather's Ford
Hamilton, Thomas, 38–39
Highland Battalion, 154–57
Hunter, Archibald R. T., 82

Indian Removal Act, 7, 88, 90, 108, 175, 191n34
Intercourse Acts: Cherokee enforcement, 62, 74; crime near border, 43; economic relations, 7; enforcement of, 53; federal enforcement withdrawn, 89; Georgia sovereignty and, 89, 104; land purchase requirements, 55; militia arrested by federal troops, 78; punishment of, 12; and supremacy law, 87; surveyors arrested, 106
intercourse law (1790), 73

Jackson, Andrew: Congressional support for Cherokees, 108, 121; Currey to supervise Indian emigration, 123; federal and state cooperation, 76; federal troops removal, 83, 85, 87–91; Georgia Guard replacement, 92; Georgia response to election, 36; Georgia sovereignty and, 89–90; Indian border defense, 72–73; Indian removal and, 10, 88–90, 175, 191n34; Indian removal policy, 2, 7; multiracial Cherokees and, 7; Schley's plan, 151; Second Creek War and, 152; states' rights, 91; warning of violence, 127; white male equality, 3, 22. *See also* elections, presidential

Jackson, James, 13
Jackson, J. W., 85
Jefferson, Thomas, 11–12, 14, 24, 88, 181n4
Johnson v. M'Intosh, 15

land distribution: American Revolutionary war veterans and, 179n1; doctrine of discovery, 15–16; federal role, 4; goal of replacing Cherokees, 8, 18–19; lotteries, 3, 16–18, 101–2, 117–20, 131–33, 142, 174–76; purchase from Indians, 12–13; rentals, 101–2; speculation and, 13, 18; Yazoo sale, 13–14, 16. *See also* Creek Strip; Treaty of Indian Springs; Wofford, William and Wofford Settlement
Leather's Ford, 97–99, 101, 104
Lincoln, Levi, 14
Lindsay's Mounted Militia, 157
lottery act. *See* land distribution
Lumpkin, Wilson, 196n28; Cherokee Protection Law, 134; enrolling agent, 162; fear of violence, 130; federal troops and, 89; Georgia Guard and, 117, 120–22, 124, 127, 129; Georgia Rangers and, 142–44, 147–48; Indian removal and, 18, 131, 136–37; lottery winners, 127; orderliness and violence, 19, 176; portrait, *139*; presidential election of 1828, 24; Ross's arrest, 125; Slicks and, 70; state militia, 140–41; supremacy law, 117; "white" party, 135, 138; whites encouraged to Cherokee territory, 119. *See also* elections, gubernatorial; political parties

Macon Telegraph, 39–40, 60, 64–66, 111, 158
Madison, James, 14
Manifest Destiny. *See* expansion, European and American
Marshall, John, 15, 74, 90, 119, 121, 151
McCormick, Richard, 17
military, federal: behavior during removal, 167–68; Cherokee removal, 164; governor's request, 72–73; infantry to expel intruders, 77–83, 176; lack of preparedness, 164; Scott's orders on removal, 163–64; troops removal, 87–89, 94; troops to Cherokee Nation, 76, 151, 156, 162
militia, Alabama, 156–57
militia, Georgia, 140–41, 188n31; behavior during removal, 167–68; border

protection, 21–22; Cherokee removal, 165; county volunteer militia, 140–41; federalized troops, 153, 155–57, 162; in Hall County, 78–79; Indian removal and, 153; intruders into Cherokee lands, 190n16. *See also* Bishop, William N.; Highland Battalion; Lindsay's Mounted Militia

militia, Georgia, personnel: Bishop, Absalom, 153–55; Boggess, Giles, 62–65; Culbreath, F. M., 166–67; Derrick, Captain, 166, 168; Floyd, Charles R., 165–68, 170; Hardin, Colonel, 78–79; Jones, John A., 66; Lloyd, Thomas, 53; Strickland, Henry P., 164–65; Tredwell, Lewis W., 168; Wales, Samuel A., 52–53, 186n6; Watkins, Benjamin, 168

militia, Tennessee, 124–25, 154–55, 162

Milledge, John, 14

Milledgeville Federal Union, 104, 115–16

Milledgeville Southron, 35

missionaries: Butler, Elizar, 108; Gambold, John, 27, 47; O'Bryant, Duncan, 105; Schmidt, Johann Renatus, 26; Wells, Minister, 109; Worcester, Samuel, 108–9, 112, 119, 176

Moravian missionaries, 26–27

Morse, Jedidiah, 26

Murray County, 132–33, 135–38, 140, 144–49, 153–55, 161, 163

Nelson, Charles H.: abuse of northen missionaries, 110; abuse of northern missionaries, 109, 111; embarrassing difficulties, 97, 100; embarrassing dificulties, 98; Georgia Guard and, 150, 157–60; gold miners expelled, 93; gold region intruders and, 101; Guard second-in-command, 96; Highland Battalion and, 153–54; letter to Gilmer, 94, 191n3; militia payment, 161; named a colonel of Guard, 94; named enforcement agent, 141; toll gate arrest, 105; warns of Cherokee violence, 158

nullification, 4, 7, 116, 135, 174

nullifiers. *See* political parties

Office of Indian Affairs, 11, 89, 123

orderliness: Cherokee eradication and, 18–19; disorderly settlers, 38, 44, 77, 101–2; Georgia Guard and, 100; lawful settlers and, 6, 9, 11–12, 15, 37; settlers' expectations, 21–22, 170. *See also* Pony Club; Slicks and Regulators

Ostler, Jeffrey, 10

Payne, John Howard, 146–47

Perdue, Theda, 33

Philpot, Reuben, 61, 187n22

political parties: Democratic Party, 116, 133, 161, 172; Democratic-Republicans, 13; "Indian party," 135–37; Second Party System, 17, 116, 133; State Rights Party (Nullifiers), 22, 117, 133, 135–38, 143, 145, 147, 157–59, 171–72, 198n15; Union Party, 133–34, 136–37, 144–45, 148, 157–59, 161, 171; Whig Party, 116, 127, 133, 147, 172

Political Reform Act of 1817, 32

Pony Club: Alabama territory, 68; Carroll County control, 55, 57, 59–62, 65–66; Cherokee and white cooperation against, 67; Creek Strip and, 75; defense of, 70; Georgia Guard and, 103; identities of, 66; lawlessness of, 174; militia cooperation, 64; origins of, 51–52, 54–55; posse's revenge kidnappings, 63–64; state encouragement, 56; voting incident, 65; white horse thieves, 8, 51, 71, 102, 140, 175, 187n18. *See also* Bishop, William N.; Slicks and Regulators

Pony Club associates: Burke, Calaway, 61, 66, 68–69; Butler, Elizar, 109, 112; Fambrough, Allen G., 21, 58–61, 64–66, 69–70, 76; Leathers family, 54, 60, 187n18; Philpot, Richard, 60

property theft and destruction by, 40–44, 46–47, 50–51, 185n33

racial issues: mixed-race, 30, 40, 107; power issue, 8; "pure" Cherokees and multiracial, 6–7; slavery and, 31, 43, 180n5; white superiority, 18–19, 172

Reed, Julie, 28

Regulators. *See* Slicks and Regulators

Ross, John: Cherokee Removal violence, 150–51, 158; complaints of intrusion, 53, 73; demand for sovereignty, 28, 57; portrait, *58*; Principal Chief of the Cherokees, 1; rejection of war, 152, 169; resistance to accommodation, 123–24; Scott's plan for expulsion, 2; supremacy law, 86, 119, 125; Supreme Court case,

Ross, John (continued): 74, 90; treaty negotiations, 146; Van Buren negotiation, 162–63

Sanford, John W. A.: contact with Cherokees, 104, 106; expanded scope of authority, 128; fear of three-pronged war, 152; federal policy role, 147; Georgia Guard commander, 93, 96; gold mines intruders, 105; Guard recruitment, 97; Guard's reputation, 100–101; harassment of ministers, 108–10; Leathers Ford and Guard, 97–100; patrol strategy, 104; renting lots in border counties, 101–2; view of Cherokee elites, 107–8

Schley, William, 144, 146–48, 151–55, 157–59, 169

Scott, Winfield, 2, 162–65, 167–69, 177

Second Creek War, 152–54

Second Seminole War, 152, 160

Slicks and Regulators: in Alabama, 68; backcountry ferment of, 188n39; Burke murder, 68–69; Cherokee law, 69–70, 188n41; Cherokee sovereignty, 180n11; extralegal justice, 67, 69–70; North Carolina namesake, 67; raids targeting Pony Club, 69, 175; slicking definition, 67–68; vigilantism of, 8, 51, 67–68, 70–72, 175; whites and Cherokees, 51, 72

sovereignty, Cherokee Nations, 4–5, 7, 22, 24–25, 27–28, 31–33, 73. *See also* Worcester v. Georgia

sovereignty, Georgia: Carroll County minerals, 74–75; Cherokee land and, 2, 4–5; extension law, 7, 37; gold miners effect, 5; improvement rationale, 15; mixed-race Cherokees and, 19, 36; orderliness, 6, 25, 133, 180n7; Pony Club and, 8; states' rights and, 4

states' rights: claim to sovereignty, 85–86; gold diggers expulsion, 75; interposition, 21–22, 183n27; land cessions and, 4, 174, 183n32; political issue, 23, 133; slavery and, 4. *See also* Treaty of Indian Springs

Stricklen, Oliver, 45

supremacy law: backcountry criminals, 117; declared null and void, 119; effect on Cherokee Nation, 132; Georgia Guard enforcement, 96, 101, 108; Guard treatment of whites and Cherokees, 107; merchant license requirement, 103; missionaries arrest, 109; National Council criminalized, 86; orderliness, 87; state sovereignty, 94

Supreme Court, 15, 72, 74, 90, 92, 119, 176

Tattnall, Josiah, 11
Telfair, Edward, 21
Thornton, Russell, 169
Trade and Intercourse Act of 1802, 12, 14, 181n2. *See also* Intercourse Acts
Treaty of Cherokee Agency, 17, 20
Treaty of Hopewell, 32
Treaty of Indian Springs, 4, 23, 52, 68
Treaty of New Echota, 149, 151–52, 155, 157, 177, 185n33, 197n51
Treaty of Washington, 4, 17, 52–53
Troup, George M., 4, 16, 23, 52
Troupites: charged with elitism, 114; Clarkites and, 16, 112; Jackson, support for, 24; protection for whites, 93; Union Party against, 135; Whig Party and, 116. *See also* Gilmer, George Rockingham

Ultras, 23, 25, 174
U.S. Claims Commission, 40, 51, 185n33

Van Buren, Martin, 1, 161–63
Vattel, Emer de, 15
vigilantism, 139. *See also* Slicks and Regulators
voting rights, 3, 22, 135–36, 172

Webster, Daniel, 74
Weiman, David F., 173
white Georgia: definition of, 9; disorderly settlers, 37–40; fear of Cherokee violence, 136–39, 141, 151–52, 163; goal of replacing Cherokees, 35–36; intruders into Cherokee lands, 36–37; marriage to Cherokees, 45–46; unequal treatment by federal military, 83–84, 176; view of Georgia Guard, 100. *See also* supremacy law
white Georgians: Adams, Francis, 68–69; Boswell, Ramson P., 60; Bowman, Lawson, 129–30; Brewster, John, 140; Brown, F. A., 106; Cobb, Howell, 138; Craddock, John A., 62; Curtis, Henry, 62–66; Davis, Jonathan, 60; Dukes,

David, 131–32, 195n21; Felton, Grief, 46; Freeman, George, 82; Goodman, B. L., 83; Goodwin, John, 66, 69; Greene, Alston H., 54; Harnage, Ambrose, 82; Harnage, Jacob, 46; Harper, Thomas A., 148; Herrod, Buck, 42; Holcomb, John, 41; Holder, Joshua, 142; Holt, Hines, Jr., 99; Merrill, Benjamin, 65; Mitchell, Robert, 99; Mosely, William, 43; Reaves, John, 126; Riley, Spencer, 142–43, 146, 197n43; Rogers, John, 82; Scudder, Jacob, 91–92; Stansell, Jesse, 69–70; Stark, 42; Trott, J. J., 109; Upton, James, 69; Walker, Hest, 41; Wheeler, John F., 82; Young, William, 62

"white man's chance": Cherokee Removal for, 84; economic success, 171; election of 1831 and, 3; election of 1833, 133; election of 1837, 159; Gilmer's proposals and, 93, 116; lotteries and, 173–74; Lumpkin's protection for, 138; military force and violence, 170; orderliness, 120; racial issues, 6; violence and disorder for, 7–8, 10, 91, 149, 177; voting rights and, 172; white citizens and government, 115; zero-sum game, 4

white on white violence: Bosworth, Philip, 61, 187n22; Philpot, Old, 58, 66, 69

white violence and crime, 5, 8, 27–28. *See also* Cherokee Lighthorse Patrol

Wilde, Richard Henry, 35–36

Wilentz, Sean, 23

Williams, Peter J., 83

Wirt, William, 74, 90

Wofford, William and Wofford Settlement, 11–13, 17, 24–25, 181n4

Wolfe, Patrick, 9

women, treatment and legal rights, 44–46, 131–32

Wool, John E., 154–56

Worcester v. Georgia, 72, 90, 151

Wright, Crawford, 69

Yazoo fraudulent land sale, 13, 16

York, Thomas, 62–64, 66, 168

Young, Mary, 169

Early American Places

On Slavery's Border: Missouri's Small Slaveholding Households, 1815–1865
by Diane Mutti Burke

Sounds American: National Identity and the Music Cultures of the Lower Mississippi River Valley, 1800–1860
by Ann Ostendorf

The Year of the Lash: Free People of Color in Cuba and the Nineteenth-Century Atlantic World
by Michele Reid-Vazquez

Ordinary Lives in the Early Caribbean: Religion, Colonial Competition, and the Politics of Profit
by Kirsten Block

Creolization and Contraband: Curaçao in the Early Modern Atlantic World
by Linda M. Rupert

An Empire of Small Places: Mapping the Southeastern Anglo-Indian Trade, 1732–1795
by Robert Paulett

Everyday Life in the Early English Caribbean: Irish, Africas, and the Construction of Difference
by Jenny Shaw

Natchez Country: Indians, Colonists, and the Landscapes of Race in French Louisiana
by George Edward Milne

Slavery, Childhood, and Abolition in Jamaica, 1788–1838
by Colleen A. Vasconcellos

Privateers of the Americas: Spanish American Privateering from the United States in the Early Republic
by David Head

Charleston and the Emergence of Middle-Class Culture in the Revolutionary Era
by Jennifer L. Goloboy

Anglo-Native Virginia: Trade, Conversion, and Indian Slavery in the Old Dominion, 1646–1722
by Kristalyn Marie Shefveland

Slavery on the Periphery: The Kansas-Missouri Border in the Antebellum and Civil War Eras
by Kristen Epps

In the Shadow of Dred Scott: St. Louis Freedom Suits and the Legal Culture of Slavery in Antebellum America
by Kelly M. Kennington

Brothers and Friends: Kinship in Early America
by Natalie R. Inman

George Washington's Washington: Visions for the National Capital in the Early American Republic
by Adam Costanzo

Borderless Empire: Dutch Guiana in the Atlantic World, 1750–1800
by Brian Hoonhout

Complexion of Empire in Natchez: Race and Slavery in the Mississippi Borderlands
by Christian Pinnen

Toward Cherokee Removal: Land, Violence, and the White Man's Chance
by Adam J. Pratt

A Weary Land: Slavery on the Ground in Arkansas
by Kelly Houston Jones

Generations of Freedom: Gender, Movement, and Violence in Natchez, 1779–1865
by Nik Ribianszky

www.ingramcontent.com/pod-product-compliance
Lightning Source LLC
Chambersburg PA
CBHW011756220426
43672CB00018B/2977